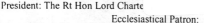

THE

CHURCH PULPIT

YEAR BOOK

2000

*Sermons for Sundays, Saints' Days,
and Special Occasions
Year B*

edited by Dr J Critchlow,
shortlisted for The Times Preacher of the Year
Award, 1997 and 1999

CANTERBURY
PRESS
Norwich

Copyright © Canterbury Press Norwich 1999

Published in 1999 by Canterbury Press Norwich,
a wholly owned imprint of
Hymns Ancient and Modern Limited,
St Mary's Works, St Mary's Plain, Norwich,
Norfolk, NR3 3BH

ISBN 1-85311-324-7

Typeset by Rowland Phototypesetting Limited,
Bury St Edmunds, Suffolk
Printed in Great Britain by
St Edmundsbury Press Limited, Bury St Edmunds, Suffolk

Editor's Preface

Following an editor of the calibre of Francis Stephens was a daunting prospect, until I realized that everything God calls us to do is impossible! I am deeply indebted to many friends and colleagues for their valued input, for an issue which in many ways continues the well-proven format of previous years, albeit with variations which in future issues will hopefully grow and diversify.

The present issue includes for the first time a selection of hymns to supplement each sermon; in general, these can be found in *Sing His Glory – Hymns for the New Lectionary, Years A, B and C* (also available from the Canterbury Press); but where hymns from other books have been chosen, the relevant sources are listed.

With a 'circuit' of more than forty churches, I generally preach at four, sometimes five, services each Sunday, and also at a number of mid-week services, to congregations ranging from evangelical to anglo-catholic: yet another 'impossible' challenge, made possible only by the grace of God. I am also involved with mission and Bible College founding, in Russia and China, my 'Aldersgate' occurring in November 1973, when I was delivered from a major hotel-fire in St Petersburg.

As space permits, in subsequent issues of the Year Book, I am hoping to include an 'Articles' section, and also to enlarge the section on Saints' Days and Festivals, together with sermons for other special occasions.

My sincere thanks go to the Revd Francis Stephens, the Revd Gordon Craven and the Revd Robert Cooper, for their generous help, material and encouragement; and to Mrs Christine Smith of the Canterbury Press and Miss Lesley Walmsley for their unfailingly kind and stimulating help and expertise. Any discrepancies herein are all my own.

J.C.

CONTENTS

The readings are taken from *Calendar, Lectionary and Collects* and are for Year B – the year of Mark – in the three-year cycle of the Revised Common Lectionary, unless otherwise stated.

vii

SERMONS FOR SAINTS' DAYS and SPECIAL OCCASIONS

First Sunday of Advent   28 November 1999
Principal Service   **Keep Awake!**   Isa. 64:1–9;
Ps. 80:1–7, 17–19; 1 Cor. 1:3–9; Mark 13:24–37

*'Therefore, keep awake for you do not know when the master of the house
will come, in the evening, or at midnight, or at cockcrow, or at dawn.'*
Mark 13:35

Alert and ready
Physical awareness can operate only in our waking hours; but
Jesus is here talking of spiritual alertness. There is a portion of
pure life in us, which never sleeps: it is here that the Holy Spirit
has been divinely implanted from the moment we accepted Christ
as our Saviour and Lord. And here, in the centre of our soul,
should be a constant readiness for God, to hear and respond to
his word. The body may sleep: the soul does not need to sleep,
though we can negate its ever-readiness by apathy, neglect or
worldly pressures.

Revelation
Mark 13 has become known as the 'Markan Apocalypse' (*apokal-
upsis*, revelation, literally 'uncovering'), dealing as it does with the
End-time and its attendant happenings. In v. 1 it is a disciple's
remark on the magnificence of the temple, that has initiated Jesus'
predictions. The illustration is apt: every Jew was only too well
aware that, grand as it was, the Jerusalem temple was not permanent. Solomon's – the first temple – had lasted from *c.*955 BC until
the Babylonians destroyed it *c.*587 BC. The second had gone up
under Zerubbabel in 516; re-built by Herod, it had barely reached
completion in Jesus' day, yet was to be destroyed by the Romans
under Titus in AD 70. And it is this destruction, among other
catastrophes, to which Jesus alludes in these verses – as well as
to happenings at the End-time. Wars, famines, earthquakes and
false Christs: all will take place before Jesus will come again in
glory.

'When he comes, who will make him welcome?'
The Bible is rich in instances of people being surprised by God:
Abraham was promised a son in his old age; David was anointed
king when tending his sheep; Ezekiel was ordered to preach life

1

into a valley of skeletons; Hosea, to marry a harlot; Mary, to believe for a miraculous conception ... And in the Markan Apocalypse Jesus is telling us that not only the End-time but also the years preceding it will be full of surprises: hard work for us to keep alert, but well worth the effort of living in the realization that God may even come before our most cherished plans come to fruition.

Watchman, what of the night?
Notice that Jesus cites the various 'watches' of the night: evening, midnight, cockcrow and dawn. These are times observed by the few, while the many are asleep. So God will surprise us when most of the world will sleep on and miss his coming. It has always been that way. We may look at two or three gathered together on a Sunday morning or evening – and five hundred thousand packed into a worship convention somewhere in Africa – and thank God that he deals with individuals, not statistics. 'What I say to you, I say to all: keep awake.'

Suggested Hymns
Sleepers wake! the watchcry pealeth; The advent of our King; Sometimes a light surprises; How lovely on the mountains

First Sunday of Advent *Second Service* Your King is Coming Ps. 25; Isa. 1:1–20; Matt. 21:1–13
' "Who is this?" the crowds were saying. "This is the prophet Jesus from Nazareth in Galilee." ' Matthew 21:10, 11

Sing 'Hosanna'
The chance to sing 'Hosanna' had all the generosity and mercy of which God is capable. From Bethany to Jerusalem is nearly two miles, and the pace would be slow, as the ever-growing procession negotiated the slope of the Mount of Olives, crossed the Kidron, and climbed to the wall of Old Jerusalem. God was giving plenty of people plenty of time to acknowledge Jesus. That day, the city indeed rang with cheers and singing; but there was an awful dearth of 'Hosannas' for the rest of what we now call 'Holy Week'. If the Palm Sunday cheerers were not the actual scoffers at Calvary,

they chose not to persevere with their allegiance. They believed 'only for a while', as did the folk in Jesus' parable of the sower (Luke 8:13).

Loyalty to the King

How many today keep those Palm Sunday crowds company, by believing for a while? The good resolutions of New Year's Day rarely last through to the end of January. Advent preparations may be smothered in the busyness of our modern Christmas. The interests and preoccupations, the prejudices and internecine struggles of the religious hierarchy appeared, for much of Holy Week, to predominate, and to sway the mind of a Jerusalem in religious ferment. And today it is dangerously easy for Christians to be side-tracked from giving one hundred per cent attention to Jesus and the message he is giving, the purposes he is unfolding for us – by struggles on both the secular and religious fronts.

Checking our footwear

As we begin the Advent preparation for the coming of our King at Christmas, we need to be careful in whose shoes we stand. There are the people who cut down branches and made a carpet of greenery for Jesus' donkey to walk on; the people who shouted 'Hosanna' and then faded out of the commitment picture. There are the people like Nicodemus and Joseph of Arimathaea, who had kept a low profile until drawn into the open by the tragedy of Calvary. There was Judas, who perhaps loved Jesus in his own strange way, but who wanted quick and dramatic results to keep his allegiance on the boil. There were the disciples – loyal and courageous while on their home ground, but pathetically feeble in the alien territory of the high priest's house, or near Pilate's judgement hall. And there were the women – Mary, Magdalene, Salome – keeping vigil at the cross, helping to prepare the body for burial, going to the tomb – and being first to hear of the resurrection.

As we hear this story from Matthew 21, and the events of Holy Week are superimposed on Advent, where do *we* stand?

The gaze of God

As we prepare to meet the Baby in the manger, we prepare to meet the gaze of God. The veiled deity will shine out to us, through innocent child-eyes; but it will be an innocence that probes and pierces. In the probing and piercing, the eyes of Jesus will make contact, in the very centre of our souls, with the Holy Spirit who lives in us. Our perception of this gaze of God will vary according to how straight and uncomplicated is the way between us and our Maker. We shall sing, probably several times this Advent:

> *Prepare we in our hearts a home*
> *where such a mighty Guest may come.*
>
> C. Coffin, tr. J. Chandler et al.

And on Christmas Day will come the test. As we greet the new-born Jesus, his gaze will reveal to us how thorough has been our Advent preparation. Will our 'Hosannas' stand the test of time?

The spiritual countdown
We are well versed in the secular countdown to Christmas: cards, presents, invitations, food . . . But how do we rate on the spiritual front? The person we have meant to forgive . . . the work we had promised God we would do . . . the verse in that lesson, the other Sunday, that spoke to us . . . the religious programme we had meant to watch, or listen to, or share . . . the 'quiet time' we had promised ourselves, or another . . . God allows us four precious weeks of Advent preparations: but we can squander them, if we so choose.

Suggested Hymns
On Jordan's bank the Baptist's cry; Make way, make way; Thou didst leave thy throne; Sing to God new songs of worship

Second Sunday of Advent   5 December
Principal Service   **The Coming One**   Isa. 40:1–11; Ps. 85:1–2, 8–13; 2 Pet. 3:8–15a; Mark 1:1–8

'He proclaimed, "The one who is more powerful than I is coming after me; I am not worthy to stoop down and untie the thong of his sandals." '
Mark 1:7

4

Who is this man?

Out from Jerusalem they trekked: priests, Levites, and the crowds who had heard of the latest attraction – a rough man of the desert, scantily clothed, on a frugal diet, yet with a fine grasp of the ancient scriptures and a powerful command of the preacher's art. He was also unselfish: all his message pointed to someone greater, someone who promised to be even more attractive than John himself.

Who is the Messiah?

They were looking for a *priestly* Messiah, these priests and Levites from Jerusalem who came to hear John: a Messiah who would take over the temple, and from the holy of holies lead Jewry in worship as in the golden days of centuries past. They were looking also for a *kingly* Messiah, who would send the hated Roman army of occupation packing, and restore the Davidic monarchy to Jerusalem. And they were looking for a *glorious* Messiah, who would usher in a new age, a new relationship with Jehovah. And John told these lookers: 'Among you stands one whom you do not know' (John 1:26). But they had become so used to looking, they still had not found their Messiah, when they had crucified him and he had risen.

Improving 'Jesus-sight'

Sometimes we, too, fail to recognize Jesus – in an act of kindness, a move towards peace, the settling of a disagreement, uplifting worship, music, talent: 'Where two or three are gathered in my name, I am there among them,' Jesus has promised (Matthew 18:20). John's preaching was powerful, but it looked to the *coming* Jesus: today, we have him present, in our midst. Yet, as John constantly pointed his listeners away from himself to Christ, this unselfishness is not less vital now. Perhaps we can consider the quality of our 'Jesus-sight': is it binocular, telescopic, spectacular, short-sighted – or have we, at times, double vision, with attention to Jesus diluted by lesser concerns? John the Baptist could not be deflected from this purpose, as he preached in the Jordan Valley: his was a witness of commitment rather than preferment. Born to an aged couple – as had been Isaac centuries before – like Isaac, John was willing to be sacrificed, if such was God's will.

Beyond the point of no return

True commitment takes us beyond the point of no return. Oswald Chambers, one-time principal of the London Bible College, called this sort of dedication a 'reckless abandon' to God: a commitment so radical, we cannot pull out of it. Yet so few are willing to risk 'all for Jesus'. God may be in the risk business up to the hilt, having entrusted us with the gospel; but so often we like the odds to be stacked more evenly. The call to a deeper commitment may come at any time, by any one, in any place – and it is often triggered in the unlikeliest way. Two men were walking one day in the grounds of a large country house near Dublin. As the conversation faltered, one turned to his companion and remarked: 'The world has yet to see what God can do with a man who is totally committed to him.' Mulling over these words later that night, his friend decided: 'Well, by God's grace, I'll be that man.'

His name was Dwight Lyman Moody – and the people he was going to point to God were to be numbered in their tens of thousands.

Jesus is coming

He will meet us at Christmas, in a few short weeks; he will come again, when his gospel has been preached in every country on this earth (Mark 13:10); but it is the fact that he is here now that can encourage us to take the extra step, beyond the point of no return. It was encouragement of this ilk that led the rough man of the desert to the Jordan Valley, to challenge the leading religious thinkers of his day. John was Jesus' cousin: we are his brothers and sisters.

Suggested Hymns

Hark! a thrilling voice is sounding; How firm a foundation; O come, O come, Emmanuel; When Jesus came to Jordan

Second Sunday of Advent *Second Service*
Are You the One? Ps. 40; 1 Kings 22:1–28; Matt. 11:2–11

'Are you the one who is to come, or are we to wait for another?' Matthew 11:3

Away from the storm
Generally we excel in crises; we rise to the occasion magnificently, practising with panache all we have preached on overcoming difficulties, and meeting opposition with courage. But let us have a period of stagnation, of isolation, when our life's vessel is becalmed: then, in the solitude and deprivation it is easier to give way to doubts – self-doubt and doubt of others. As John was left with his own company – it is thought, in Herod's gloomy fortress-prison of Machaerus – thoughts which had not troubled him in the dramatic days of preaching in the Jordan Valley, crept into his mind and grew until he gave way to sending this message to Jesus.

How dangerous are doubts?
Charles Haddon Spurgeon – he of the great sermons – once said: 'Doubting, like toothache, is more distracting than dangerous. I never heard of its proving fatal to anybody yet.' Certainly Jesus did not seem to be worried about John's doubts: 'Among those born of women no one has arisen greater than John the Baptist.' And when Thomas doubted the resurrection, Jesus kept him waiting only one week before comprehensively cancelling his doubt (John 20:24–29). We are not automatons, expected to accept all data without question or hesitation. St Paul told his friends at Thessalonica: 'Do not despise the words of the prophets, but test everything' (1 Thessalonians 5:20, 21). John, prison-bound, needed reassurance. Jesus sent back the messengers with ample, giving John no cause for guilt or contrition. Sometimes we can be too hard on ourselves, over-scrupulous in what we think God expects of us. He is not in the business of making plaster saints, but of refining us into the people he knows we can become – and that may be very different from our perception of ourselves.

John's mission
John had been the forerunner. Once Jesus arrived and presented himself for baptism, John's mission was accomplished. Herod may order his decapitation, but he could not un-do the work that had been fulfilled. Probably John considered prison as a waste of time – just as someone who has led an active ministry may fret if illness necessitates a time of inactivity and apparent uselessness. We love to be busy, and equate activity with amassing Brownie points. God works to a different schedule. Jesus in the gospels was never

in a hurry, even when his friend Lazarus had died (John 11:6). Often the more we hurry, the less time we find we have: so we hurry and worry all the more. There is a saying in Russian Ortho-doxy: 'Do not worry about whether you will have time to do this or that: if you live, you will have time for it – if you die, you won't need to do it.' In our neat and tidy schedules, we should probably have liked to see John regally assumed into heaven, even while the dove hovered over the baptized Jesus (Matthew 3:16). No one, not even John, saw the point of languishing in prison. Only God knew why the Baptist's end had to be so brutal.

What is needful?
A person who has led a healthy, active life collapses, and lies in a coma for two months before dying; and we ask: 'Why the burden of eight unnecessary weeks?' A prospective mother goes the full term, but her baby is still-born. What have the nine fraught months achieved? We read the Bible, and see that every life which has counted for God has been filled with difficulties, hardships and struggles. Yet when their modern counterparts suffer these 'thorns in the flesh', we still ask: 'Is it necessary?' St Paul simply tells us: 'Fool! What you sow does not come to life unless it dies' (1 Corinthians 15:36). If we want to live, really to *live*, then it is needful for us to die – a little every day.

If we wonder at God's dealings with us, he will not mind if, like John, we ask him for re-assurance.

Suggested Hymns
Christ when for us you were baptized; The Lord will come and not be slow; When he was baptized in Jordan; Come, thou long-expected Jesus

Third Sunday of Advent 12 December
Principal Service **Give us an Answer** Isa. 61:1–4, 8–11; Ps. 126; 1 Thess. 5:16–24; John 1:6–8, 19–28
'Then said they to him, "Who are you? Let us have an answer for those who sent us. What do you say about yourself?"' John 1:22

What do you say?
These priests and Levites had come down from Jerusalem, to hear what John had to say. They knew he was well versed in the scriptures; they knew he preached with power, with conviction, with integrity, with boldness. But they did not know who he was. And John had nothing to hide. He did not mind telling them. Those who had sent them would get an answer, if not the one they wanted. 'Let us have an answer.' Knowing as we do what lay ahead, this demand has an ominous ring – one, perhaps, which we do not wish to linger over, in these days so close to Christmas. Yet the Christmas story is worth celebrating only because it cost so much.

The price of Christmas
Jesus emptied himself of glory, to take on not the National Debt, but the World Debt, of sin and suffering and shame. It is so unbelievable, it either has to be true – or nothing in this world makes sense any more. Whether we are ready for it, or not, the Christ of the manger will meet us again this Christmas. He will look out from the infant-veiling of deity, and his innocent child-eyes will pierce us to our souls. And the Child who engages us is not just a child: he is also the Victim of Calvary, the Victor of the empty tomb, the Christ in glory.

God is love
His gaze pierces and probes; but because he is love, there is mercy with the piercing and the probing. Because he is love, and we meet the Crucified as well as the Child, we can rejoice more – *much* more – than even the angels who gave the good news to the shepherds, for we have

> *a song which even angels*
> *can never, never sing;*
> *they know not Christ as Saviour,*
> *but worship him as King.*

> *Albert Midlane*

The priests and Levites in the Jordan Valley that day were looking for a Saviour. They were still looking, after they had crucified him and rejected the love he had brought. This Christmas, he will bring love again, but millions of people will crucify him again – with their apathy, their bigotry, their selfishness and pride, if not with nails and spear. Love came down at Christmas, along a way that man has never travelled. Love cared enough to make the effort.

God's magnificent unfairness
God is so magnificently unfair, that even though we have done nothing to deserve his love, he still loves us. The Christ-Child came to a world that could not appreciate what true love was. Today's world still has a very skewed perception of true love. A carpenter's son, who may have been expected to live a reasonably long life and die a reasonably obscure death, instead had his fore-runner at the centre of religious hierarchical attention, and was himself destined to shoot from obscurity to prominence in three short years. He would die an ignominious, vicarious death. But he would not stay dead.

Our Advent response
The priests and Levites requested a response. What do *we* ask of John this Advent? – we, who know (or profess to know) to whom John was pointing? Do we need John to guide us to Jesus this Christmas? Do we value the Baptist with the worth God gave him? As in the case of Mary and Joseph, God could have effected the salvation of the world without human involvement. We may take time to wonder how these people coped. How often did they feel they were dreaming? How often did they wish they were dreaming? Each one looked on the face of God, and lived. Let *us* have an answer for Jesus, when Advent leads us to Christmas.

Suggested Hymns
Be thou my vision; Love divine, all loves excelling; Lo, in the wilderness a voice; The people that in darkness sat

Third Sunday of Advent   *Second Service*
Mission Accomplished   Ps. 68:1–20; Mal. 3:1–4; 4; Matt. 14:1–12
'And he said to his servants, "This is John the Baptist; he has been raised from the dead."' Matthew 14:2

Why John *redivivus*?

Have you ever wondered about these words of Herod? The resurrection of Jesus had been part of the sacred prophecies for centuries, ever since David's day, though many had rejected it as too preposterous (the Sadducees, for instance). Nevertheless, there it stood as part and parcel of the scriptures. In Herod's day, it was still unfulfilled, still a possibility. Not so the resurrection of John: no one had prophesied that he would rise from the dead. So, where did Herod get this notion from? And why was it thought worthy of record in three out of the four gospels? Perhaps Herod was confused between John and Jesus: he was, after all, not purely Jewish, being the son of the Idumaean Herod ('The Great') and the Samaritan Malthace. Perhaps he was also confusing the issue with what he had been told of Elijah, who many people saw as reincarnated in John. Whatever his line of reasoning, however many and misguided his counsellors, Herod the Tetrarch's mistake shows how obfuscated was the life and witness – and death – of John, to people who did not understand the Baptist's authority, nor the greater authority of Jesus.

The role of John

It can be easy even for Christians to reduce John to practically a nonentity, and to concentrate on the role of Jesus. Of course, as our Saviour, Redeemer, Life, Truth and Way, Jesus should be predominant; but if we accept that all holy scripture was written for our learning, then we are obliged to work on such knowledge as we have of John: to work on learning how he fitted in to the incarnation period of Jesus, how he was used by God, and how God's authority over him made possible the saving work of Jesus. By studying how God worked in the cousin of Jesus, we can be helped into understanding how God's authority can work in our lives.

A raw deal?

Born the son of a priest, trained in the law of the Lord, drawn to a life of asceticism, later breaking off family ties, John emerged from the desert to cross swords verbally with aristocratic Sadducees, proud Pharisees, lawyers, soldiers and anyone else who would listen. For one brief shining moment he experienced glory, as he baptized Jesus in the Jordan. His work was done. The glory faded. Jesus began his mission. His disciples had a comparatively free and easy life-style, attending weddings and suppers, mixing with rich and poor, Jew and Samaritan. John and his dwindling coterie still preserved ascetic principles of little food and clothing, and regular fasts. Then came prison, and death.

John's legacy

Yet John's work could not be erased. Even Herod suggested he could return from the dead. And it is surely no coincidence, that the verses many believe are the oldest in the gospels (from 'Q', the postulated source behind Matthew and Luke), give us 98 per cent of what we know about John. The authority of John was twofold: he was to prepare the way for Jesus, and to baptize Jesus. It is a mark of the mystery of this authority, that God's chosen man was so unorthodox in the world's eyes, and his life so tragic. It was religious incongruity, spiritual foolishness, and divine wisdom, that the silent tongue of John, the posthumous authority of the Baptist, could call forth such words from Herod. John *redivivus*?

John's worth

The force of Herod's words was all the greater, considering how John had died. The tetrarch was assuming the resurrection of a decapitated body: a gruesome point, yet further evidence of John's worth and the power of his authority. John's life illustrates for Christians of all time, the supreme and unassailable authority of God – against which every temporal authority needs to be set in perspective. It teaches us that when we are tempted to think that God's authority has been misplaced – when we fail to see the wisdom in his purposes – the life, work, humanity and questionings of John need to be placed alongside our own lives, work, humanity and questionings ... to teach us that we do not need to understand, but simply to have faith that God *is* working out his purposes, and doing us the honour of involving us.

Suggested Hymns

Sing we the praises of the great forerunner; Thy kingdom come, O God; Soldiers of Christ, arise; Hail to the Lord's anointed

Fourth Sunday of Advent 19 December
Principal Service **Divine Implant** 2 Sam. 7:1–11, 16;
Ps. 89:1–4, 19–26; Rom. 16:25–27; Luke 1:26–38

*'The angel said to her, "The Holy Spirit will come upon you, and the
power of the Most High will overshadow you; therefore the child to be
born will be holy; he will be called Son of God."'* Luke 1:35

More than a child
That which is to be divinely implanted in Mary's womb may
emerge looking, sounding and acting like a child: but he will not
be just a child. We, with our New Testaments to hand, know what
is still a mystery to Mary on the day of annunciation. We know
Jesus will eat and sleep like a normal person; he will get tired, he
will weep, he will get angry – and he will suffer. But he will not
accept sickness, disease or lasting death.

The Christmas Jesus
At Christmas it can be easy to humanize, even to de-sanctify Jesus.
He is small, weak and helpless – a baby in his mother's arms. We
can cope with that. He makes little demand on us and, in the
bustle of a modern Christmas, how deeply do we think about
something as obvious as a little baby? Yet, if Christmas is really
to make an impact on our spiritual life, really to bring us further
on our way to God, it is only in the realization that it cost God
an unimaginable amount, in sheer love. Jesus came down a road
that man had never travelled – has never yet travelled; down from
a height so far beyond our comprehension that we do not come
within a trillion miles of it.

God and man
The holy thing that was implanted in Mary was God and man.
From conception to Calvary, Jesus was never just the one without
the other.

> *God of the substance of the Father,*
> *begotten before the worlds;*
> *and Man, of the substance of his Mother,*
> *born in the world.*

Perfect God, and perfect Man,
of a reasonable soul and human flesh subsisting.

Quicunque Vult

We can relate to his humanity, because we share it now. We can relate to his divinity, because we shall share it in his glorious kingdom. God does not do things by halves. Other babies growing up in Judaea (at least, those who were not to be indiscriminately slaughtered on the orders of Herod) may have had more luxury at birth, a more affluent childhood, a more highly paid profession, and a less harrowing death; but while they are forgotten, Jesus is no longer dead.

The tingle-factor?

When we have lost the capacity to be moved by it all; when we no longer thrill to the story of Christmas – we have no part to play in the Christmas celebrations. It takes a mere human to celebrate Christmas without wonder, awe and reverence: and by God's mercy, grace and love, we Christians are no longer merely human – for we have, somewhere in our make-up, a divine implant, even as Mary had. Our implant, the 'holy thing' which is in us, is the Holy Spirit. As St Paul tells us, our bodies are the Spirit's temple (1 Corinthians 6:19).

Working the Spirit

We can give the impression, by our independent attitudes, that the Spirit is virtually an appendix: present, but ineffectual – in fact, surplus to requirements. How much this is at variance with what the Bible tells us about God and his workings! The Almighty is omniscient, omnipresent and omnipotent. The Saviour is constantly interceding for us. Is the Holy Spirit the only part of the Godhead who does not work? If we realized more often that our indwelling Spirit has an energy that can light the world, would we not put him to work? In prayer we can involve him in intercession, intention and thanksgiving. He is a friend to be converted and reasoned with. We cannot overwork our dynamic implantation: our minds will stand the strain of trying, and so will his stamina. The alternative is not being recognized as a Christian. We have no longer enough time to risk such a mistake being made.

14

Tell out, my soul, the greatness of the Lord; The angel Gabriel from heaven came; For Mary, Mother of our Lord; Ye who own the faith of Jesus

Fourth Sunday of Advent *Second Service*
Magnificat Ps. 113 (131); Zech. 2:10–13; Luke 1:39–55

'Blessed is she who believed that there would be a fulfilment of what was spoken to her by the Lord.' Luke 1:45

Strong faith
Elizabeth, Mary, Abraham, Hannah ... all had been promised a son by God, and had believed for it: Hannah for a year, Abraham for twenty-five years, Elizabeth and Mary for nine months. Their belief came with the promise, before the fulfilment. This is not prevarication: it is sound biblical truth. Jesus told us: 'Whatever you ask for in prayer, believe that you have received it, and it will be yours' (Mark 11:24). In the natural, there was no way any of these conceptions could take place. Let us wonder at the faith that could accept what as yet could not be seen. Is there any word of God in our lives for which we are believing, in faith?

A rejoicing spirit
'My spirit rejoices,' sang Mary. And well it might, with the Saviour of the world in prospect. What gives *you* cause to rejoice in spirit? Or are you so weighed down with the cares and pleasures of this life that you have forgotten how to be joyful? God is a patient Father, but at times he must think he has made a world of abnormally serious, sober saints. Mary was elated: she had 'gone with haste' to Elizabeth. And then she sang her Magnificat. The Russians say: 'To sing is to pray twice.' Can we not pray more?

Jesus could sing
On the night of the Last Supper, before going out into the gloom of Gethsemane and Judas' betrayal, Jesus led his disciples in the singing of a hymn (Matthew 26:30; Mark 14:26). Who does not tremble in awe at the Saviour's courage in singing, knowing all

that was to come? Does God make you laugh? Does he make you want to dance? Long ago, David danced before the Lord, to celebrate the return of the ark to Jerusalem. He 'danced with all his might', and Michal his wife 'despised him in her heart' (2 Samuel 6:14, 16). It was such unbecoming behaviour for a king! Michal would find many fellow critics, were she to come back to earth today. But God rebuked her, where it really hurt: 'Michal . . . had no child to the day of her death' (2 Samuel 6:23).

Patience

Has God given you a word that takes your breath away? Remember Mary, believing and trusting for the impossible, and hang on to the vision. Perhaps the promise is so great, so incredible, that after a while 'reason' sets in, and you feel you must let God's word go. It is time then to clutch it ever more tightly. God has never yet reneged on a promise. Sometimes it seems as though he has forgotten; but God's memory never fails. Quite possibly, until the baby began to grow in her womb, Mary had times of questioning. What, for instance, were her thoughts when the Roman census was arranged for the time when her baby was due?

Judaea in turmoil

Mary had probably not had much to sing about until now. Joseph would be busy with his tools; she would be alone for much of the time. She would be constantly aware of the Jewish tension against the Roman army of occupation. God, in his wisdom, had chosen a time for the coming of his Son when Judaea was in a turmoil of unrest. But this was Mary's hour, and the progress of a divinely-implanted baby, once begun, was set to continue.

Domine, fiat voluntas tua

Mary's *fiat* was the brave act which began her miraculous conception. Not knowing of the angel's visit to Joseph (Matthew 1:18–25), only she knew how she was going to cope with a pregnancy out of wedlock. We are so familiar with the Christmas story that the problems which Mary must have had are often largely overlooked. God still undertakes to do the impossible; and he still looks to us to move the mountains.

Suggested Hymns
Mary immaculate, Star of the morning; Maiden, yet a Mother (both
from the *Celebration Hymnal*); Shall we not love thee, Mother dear?;
Lo, he comes with clouds descending

Christmas Eve   Friday 24 December   Fear Not
2 Sam. 7:1–5, 8–11, 16; Ps. 89:2, 21–27; Acts 13:16–26;
Luke 1:67–79

*'. . . we, being rescued from the hands of our enemies, might serve him
without fear'. Luke 1:74*

Do not be afraid
It is easy to underestimate fear, to see it as part and parcel of
every-day life, a necessary adjunct which keeps the adrenalin
flowing. But the Bible tells us that fear is a sin, and those who
give way to it head the list of the damned who will end 'in the
lake that burns with fire and sulphur, which is the second death'
(Revelation 21:8). The gospels are strewn with Jesus' commands
'Fear not', and we hear the same from the angels, as they come
to tell the shepherds of Jesus' birth (Luke 2:10). We are permitted
to fear only God (1 Peter 2:17). Yet at Christmas, fear does not
normally predominate: the baby in the manger is small, weak and
helpless; we are not likely to fear – and perhaps we come close,
in the Christmas joy, to experiencing the love that really does
annihilate fear.

Fear or faith?
When Jesus stilled the storm on Galilee, he was scathing about
the disciples' fear: 'Why are you afraid? Have you still no faith?'
(Mark 4:40). Has he cause to say the same to us today? Are we
fearful of what our computers may do in a week's time? It is
usually the mystery, the unknown, that elicits fear; but if we would
only really accept that God knows, can we not trust him to see us
through?

The army of occupation

Zechariah had no perplexing keyboard to operate, but he knew what it was to live under the Roman army of occupation. This was not the best of times to tell Jewry to live without fear. The Romans hated the oriental people, with their religious feasts and fasts and fashions; daily the Jews were subjected to laws they could not understand, and restrictions which were alien to their culture. Each riot and insurrection was met with heavy-handed brutality; and who could wonder that the Jews longed to be 'rescued from the hands of their enemies'? John's task was twofold: 'to prepare the way of the Lord, and to give knowledge of salvation to his people' – a knowledge that would free them from fear.

Freedom of choice

With the offer of this same freedom from fear, God continues to give us freedom of choice. We can choose to fear, and we can choose not to fear. One would think that only a moron would opt for living in fear – yet apparently the world is full of morons. God does not take away the things that cause us to fear, but he gives us the power not to yield to fear – if only we are willing to use it. To a land under enemy rule, with a misguided ecclesiastical hierarchy, a self-seeking puppet king and frequent insurrections, Jesus was to say: 'Do not let your hearts be troubled' (John 14:1). This was the 'mighty saviour', the Lord whose way had been prepared by John the Baptist. Yet who would take note of the prophecy of old Zechariah?

What is Jesus to you?

As we consider Zechariah's words, do they describe our Jesus? We meet him at Christmas in the manger, this infant who was the 'mighty saviour' of the old man's song. He grew to be the Man of Galilee, the Victim of the cross, Victor of the tomb, and Christ ascended. What is he to us, today? Brother, friend, Redeemer, Lord? Do we meet him only in the manger – or do we meet him in the homeless, the refugee, the depressed? The child asks for love. How much love have we to give? The answer surely is: as much as he has given us.

> *He giveth more grace, when the burdens grow greater;*
> *He addeth more strength, as the labours increase.*
> *To added affliction, he addeth his mercy,*

18

To multiplied trials, his multiplied peace.
When we have exhausted our store of endurance,
When faith seems to fail, ere the day is half done,
When we come to the end of our hoarded resources,
Our Father's full giving is only begun.
His love has no limit, his grace has no measure,
His power has no boundary known unto men,
For out of his infinite riches in Jesus
He giveth and giveth and giveth again.

Annie Flint

Suggested Hymns
Adoramus te, Domine; Purify my heart; I will sing the wondrous
story; When came in flesh the incarnate Word

Christmas Day   Saturday 25 December
At Midnight or Early Eucharist   **The Time Has
Come**   Isa. 62:6–12; Ps. 97; Titus 3:4–7; Luke 2:1–7
*'While they were there the time came for her to deliver her child.' Luke
2:6*

The appointed time
Koheleth (the preacher) had said 'there is a time to be born'
(Ecclesiastes 3:2), and the time for Jesus has come. Some, including
Mary and Joseph, may not have thought it the most appropriate
time: away from home, Bethlehem crammed to the doors, bedding
down in a stable, among strangers, with animals as silent witnesses. Is this how Jesus finds our welcome today – with the place
at sixes and sevens, and peripheral matters threatening to crowd
out the little child?

More than a baby
Yes, a child can be swamped quite easily; but Jesus meets us as
more than a child. Mary had known him intimately for nine
months, but we have our gospels to hand. The Jesus who meets

us today is the Jesus of the miracles and teaching: the Last Supper and Gethsemane; Calvary and Easter morning. We can come to him and see his helplessness and innocence; but we can only come because this Jesus has lifted the baggage of our sins from our shoulders. We can come, as the prayer says,

with courage, gaiety and a quiet mind.

When the tinsel has come down, and the tree and its decorations have had their fleeting glory, the only gift of Christmas which is worth having, will still be with us – for he promised: 'Remember, I am with you always' (Matthew 28:20). Jesus has passed through time, while we are still in it – even as Mary was in it, on the night she knew her baby was being delivered. The time of Advent has been leading us up to this morning; tomorrow, the baby will be a baby no longer: he will be standing in the courtroom of heaven, to welcome Stephen, the first Christian martyr (Acts 7:56). Shall we, too, be able to make the transition, from worshipping the child to adoring the glorious Christ? If Christmas is to mean anything, we must – like the shepherds, like the magi – come to the baby, but then go out enriched and re-vitalized, to share what we have experienced.

The holy family
As we come to Mary and Joseph, and the child in the manger, can we hold up to God the families we know: struggling, perhaps, to stay together, to make ends meet; coping with illness or grief; sharing their joys and their anxieties? Soon our holy family will set out on the 250-mile journey into Egypt, to escape Herod's massacre of the Bethlehem children. Perhaps Mary and the child rode on a donkey; perhaps Joseph walked all the way. Families today have no monopoly on hardship.

Silent night
But the trek into Egypt is still to come. Today, the bustle that is Bethlehem is beyond the stable walls. And even though we may need to travel – to worship, to visit family or friends – there is a strange, serene quietness on many roads and in the city centres, as on this day of days families draw together, the business world is hushed, and bells peal out in gladness. Many families are celebrating Christmas without knowing what it is about. How do we

begin to tell them? St Peter tells us, 'always be ready to make your defence to anyone who demands from you an account of the hope that is in you' (1 Peter 3:15). The time for sharing our Christmas joy is here: it has reached the end of its nine months' preparation. Mary was ready, even though external circumstances may not have been the most opportune. Are we ready? If, in this worship, we can focus on even one aspect – one 'best' reason for being here today – and then take it out to share with someone else, the Christmas joy will grow.

Opportunity knocks
'My time has not yet come,' said Jesus, to his disciples, some time before his passion, 'but your time is always here' (John 7:6). Let us claim this promise today, and start by making the most of our Christmas time.

Suggested Hymns
While shepherd watched; Silent night; O little town of Bethlehem; It came upon the midnight clear

Christmas Day   *In the day: Principal Service*
Glory to God   Isa. 62:6–12; Ps. 97; Titus 3:4–7; Luke 2:8–20
'And suddenly there was with the angel a multitude of the heavenly host.' Luke 2:13

God does not do things by halves
The angels appeared in force: *plethos* means 'a great number'. We do not know whether they actually joined the first angel on the ground, or hovered above the shepherds: the former seems more probable from the text. In any case, they greatly outnumbered the shepherds. God was at pains to impress upon these men of the hills that a most important event had occurred. Could they – would they – believe it?

So amazing!

There is an expression current in certain circles: 'Such-and-such is so amazing, it's untrue!' Is this a contradiction in terms? Or can truth be so unbelievable? Where is the borderline to be drawn between truth and fantasy? How rigid are we in drawing a borderline? Do we insist on strict parameters for what we believe, and when, and how, and why? A lot of questions – but take time to look at everything Jesus did and said, in his three-year ministry. Practically all of it was 'so amazing', most people thought it was untrue. One angel would have been enough, surely, to have caught the shepherds' attention. But God sent an abundance of reinforcements. He has not changed in two millennia. He cannot change, for munificence is part and parcel of his nature. As the prophet Malachi wrote: 'Bring the full tithe into the storehouse, and thus put me to the test, says the Lord of hosts; see if I will not open the windows of heaven for you and pour down for you an overflowing blessing' (Malachi 3:10). Mary and Joseph, with the child, may have been in the lowliest of delivery rooms; yet the Saviour's birth had its full quota of glory, out there in the shepherds' fields.

Godly focus

Sometimes, within the parameters of our worldly wisdom and understanding, we look in the wrong place for God. Sometimes he comes to meet us without our looking – and because we are unprepared, we fail to read his signposts. At least the shepherds realized who had sent the angelic message – it was 'the Lord' (v. 15). If we can recognize God in a situation, we are well on the way to responding in line with God's will. God alone knows what would have happened, had the shepherds not heeded the angels; but when they went and 'made known what had been told them', they were doing something so out of line with their calling as shepherds, that some people would go to see for themselves; others would laugh, and yet others would take their news to whisper it in high ecclesiastical circles – in the Bethlehem synagogues and the Jerusalem temple – where it would receive a very mixed response . . .

Peace on earth

Peace was at a premium in Judaea, with the Romans occupying the country. Yet those whom God favours are told they will have peace. Only when God rules in the heart do we have the capacity to recognize and make peace with him. To spread peace on earth, we need first to know the peace of heaven. To hear God's voice, our hearts this Christmas need to be open to him and to what he brings.

Christ's ambassadors
The shepherds were the earliest Christian ambassadors, though they would not have described themselves in those terms. They were faithful in spreading the wonderful news, no matter how people received it. We are not called to save anyone: we are called to spread the good news of the gospel. God will see to the work of salvation – in every heart we have told, or in some, or in none. Perhaps, if the Church in general recognized with greater clarity the work she has been called to do, and trusted God to perform his part, there would be an increase in glory. We are partners with God, by his grace, and we have the advantage even over the angels, for we know Jesus Christ as Saviour.

Suggested Hymns
O come, all ye faithful; Christians awake; Hark! the herald angels sing; Virgin-born, we bow before thee

Christmas Day *Second Service*
Broken Bread and Poured-out Wine
Ps. 8; Isa. 65:17–25; Phil. 2:5–11

'Though he was in the form of God, [he] did not regard equality with God as something to be exploited, but emptied himself . . .' Philippians 2: 6, 7

Getting alongside
'Getting alongside' the homeless, and sleeping in a cardboard box on the street for a night, is a dramatic, if transient, gesture. Jesus came alongside us for over thirty years, the effects of which have never worn off. We cannot determine the dimensions of glory which he left, nor adequately appreciate the love that cared enough to make the effort. Love 'got alongside' the very poorest in society, giving us an example that is timeless: 'You always have the poor

with you' (John 12:8). While the earth remains, we shall be never short of the opportunity to minister to the poor. Shorn of glory, naked as an earthly child, he emerged from Mary's womb. Despised and rejected, naked he was to hang on a cross and receive burial in a borrowed grave. But then came the time for a reversal – a return to what had been since the world began.

Let go, and let God

Only when we release back to God the gifts, status and opportunities which are his, do we open the door for him to move in and use those talents for the benefit of others. The broken bread and poured-out wine, symbolizing all that Jesus gave, do not look very much. As he hung on the cross between two thieves, there was nothing very remarkable in yet another crucifixion – except that what Jesus did, he did for the sake of the whole world. The weight on his shoulders brought him down to the ground, for it was the world's sin; he died guilty of theft, adultery, murder and every other possible sin. Broken bread and poured-out wine. He let go glory, power and high position, for God to fill the world from his emptiness. There is no logic in it, no commonsense at all. It is God at his most magnificently unfair. The test is: can we, also, let go what we prize so highly, and let God use our emptiness to fill another's life?

Not as we think

It takes courage to step out in faith and to allow God to use us as he will – not as we think we should be used. We sometimes spend so much time in looking ahead to what we believe God may be planning for us, that we fail to see what he is presently doing with our lives. Quietly, unobtrusively, he is working out his purpose. He may allow us to see the results – or he may call us home before we can see them. One may sow, another may reap. We cannot set a time limit on the workings of a God who sees 'one day like a thousand years, and a thousand years like one day' (2 Peter 3:8). We, like Jesus, have the form of God (Genesis 1:27), and are under a similar obligation not to exploit this, but to let God use us as broken bread and poured-out wine.

The Christmas sacrifice

In the wonder of the virgin birth, the drama of the manger, the glory in the shepherds' fields, and the mystery of the magi, there is not too much emphasis on the sacrifice it cost, to exchange glory for poverty. To have a sacrifice recognized and appreciated goes a long way towards mitigating the cost involved. Jesus had no such compensation, for the world rejected him. Only 'for the sake of the joy that was set before him' (Hebrews 12:2), was his sacrifice made durable. It is this same joy that meets us at Christmas, as the child in the manger looks out with eyes that have met the challenge of the world's sin and enmity, and have shown that love is stronger still.

Suggested Hymns
Child in the manger; O little one sweet, O little one mild; The first Nowell; What child is this?

First Sunday of Christmas 26 December
Principal Service **The First Christian Missionaries**
Isa. 61:10–62:3; Ps. 148; Gal. 4:4–7; Luke 2:15–21
'When they saw this, they made known what had been told them about this child; and all who heard it were amazed at what the shepherds told them.' Luke 2:17, 18

On business for God
This missionary work of the shepherds is often overlooked: we are more used to seeing them portrayed either in the fields looking skywards in amazement, or as kneeling in wonder before the child in the manger. Yet Luke implies that they did not return directly to their sheep, but went round telling folk the good news; and they surely would not have had far to go. Bethlehem was packed to its corners for the census. The shepherds were beginning something which was to become the hallmark of a Christian: they were sharing the good news of Jesus with others. St Paul was to tell the Christians in Rome: 'Everyone who calls on the name of the Lord shall be saved. But how are they to call on one in whom they have not believed? And how are they to believe in one of whom they have never heard? And how are they to hear without someone to proclaim him? And how are they to proclaim him unless they are sent?' (Romans 10:13–15). Everyone who has been entrusted with

the gospel has a commission to share it with anyone who will hear.

The response
Some whom the shepherds met would take no notice. Some would laugh. Some would think they were drunk. The response was not the shepherds' problem. They were fulfilling their mission. The people they told could take it – or leave it. That has been the case ever since. Today as in first-century Bethlehem, the worldly-wise will get by quite happily without Jesus: stepping out in sheer faith is too difficult for those who put all their reliance on what the world has to offer, or what their commonsense tells them. Perhaps the shepherds felt aggrieved when people laughed at their news. Perhaps they returned to show Jesus to a few who did believe them. Perhaps they had great difficulty in actually describing the angels, to folk whose minds were filled with other matters. The more we meditate on how life was transformed for the shepherds that night, the more amazing it all is. I wonder whether the shepherds were bold enough to go to the nearest synagogue and tell the priest? And, if so, what was the priest's reaction?

A piece of news
Today we may receive strange news, from the most unlikely quarter. The normal reaction is: 'Whatever does (s)he know about such things?' People said just the same about Jesus: 'Jesus went up into the temple, and began to teach. The Jews were astonished at it, saying, "How does this man have such learning, when he has never been taught?" Then Jesus answered them, "My teaching is not mine, but his who sent me"' (John 7:15, 16). If we are willing, like the shepherds, to let God take us over; if we give him the chance to use us as his instruments, then we can expect that most people will not understand us. In fact, they will probably ridicule us, give us the cold shoulder, or try to 're-educate' us. They did all that to Jesus. Why, as his present-day ambassadors, should we expect to be treated any differently?

Where does Christmas take us?
Do we celebrate Christmas and emerge afterwards just as we were before? We cannot, if we have been to the manger, and have looked into the face of Christ. The love that left a glory of unimaginable splendour to visit our world for a season, has touched us, at some

26

point, this Christmas. If we can take time to recollect what that point was, he will, in his mercy, show us why he came so close. <u>For at Christmas God comes to everyone who is prepared, willing and waiting to receive him.</u>

Suggested Hymns
Angels from the realms of glory; In the bleak midwinter; Love came down at Christmas; Once in royal David's city

First Sunday of Christmas   *Second Service*
Did You Not Know?   Ps. 132; Isa. 35:1–10;
Col. 1:9–20 or Luke 2:41–52
' "Child, why have you treated us like this? Look, your father and I have been searching for you in great anxiety." ' Luke 2:48

Casting all your care
Mary was only human. Any caring mother would have said the same. And if Joseph was not the natural father, no one but the two of them knew it. This outburst from Mary prompted a very mature rebuke from the twelve-year-old; but hers was not a mortal sin. We, too, forget from time to time that we are not bearing the whole world's troubles. Does God mind when we get angry with him? Yes, surely he does – but he understands, because some years ago the woman he valued above all others did exactly the same. Mary, like us, was on a learning curve, as far as offloading her worries on to God went. Or, maybe, she had unburdened herself in prayer – and then, as we so often do, had taken the weight back on to her own shoulders.

A little knowledge . . .
. . . can be so dangerous: the knowledge that we have told God what is bothering us, gives some measure of relief. Taking back the care quickly annuls it. Knowing to make a 'no-return deposit' is one of the hardest lessons to learn. The Dutch evangelist Corrie ten Boom used to illustrate God's forgetfulness vividly: when we take our sins to him, repent of them, and ask forgiveness, he drops them into the deep sea of his love, and puts up a sign: 'No Fishing'.

27

It is all of a piece with the Psalmist's understanding: 'As far as the east is from the west, so far he removes our transgressions from us.' But even so, at times we manage to take them back. It is as if Jesus is saying again: 'Did you not know?' Did we not know our Father's love and concern had removed those sins, had unburdened us of our cares? Here, we are beyond the realm of logic and commonsense. We are deep inside the loving unfairness of God. And because we are in uncharted territory, we draw back – just as Mary had drawn back from leaving her care with God.

In the Father's house
Who knows what had stirred in Jesus' heart, as he assimilated the atmosphere of the temple – its magnificent architecture and furnishings, the gorgeously-apparelled priests, the smoking sacrifices and measured chants of worship? Attracted by high theological debate, he had drawn closer and closer to the doctors, until he was questioning as well as listening. Did he find their theology was awry? Was that why 'all who heard him were amazed' (v. 57)? Twenty or so years later, he was to be constantly at variance with the next generation of doctors. Perhaps some of those would remember the stripling who had debated so astutely in the temple. Today, many of our churches have an 'unbalanced' *modus operandi*, with the priest expounding the scriptures virtually unchallenged. Perhaps we should widen the scope of theological debate either within the context of worship, or alongside it. Jesus was at pains in the gospels to show the right use of his Father's house. At times we may stand in danger of creating a 'market-place' image (John 2:16); rarely do we encourage comprehensive theological deliberation, as was current in Jesus' day. 'Did you not know ... ?' There is so much in the pages between Genesis and Revelation that we do not know. Perhaps we should become much more serious about redressing the balance. Knowledge of God and his dealings will outlive all else. 'Heaven and earth will pass away, but my words will not pass away,' Jesus has promised (Mark 13:31).

Suggested Hymns
The heavenly child in stature grows; Jesus, hope of every nation; To us a child of royal birth; Of the Father's love begotten

Second Sunday of Christmas   2 January 2000
Principal Service   **Grace and Truth**   Jer. 31:7–14;
Ps. 147:12–20; Eph. 1:3–14; John 1:1–9, 10–18

*'From his fulness we have all received, grace upon grace. The law indeed
was given through Moses, grace and truth came through Jesus Christ.'
John 1:16, 17*

Divine amalgam

John has already told us that Jesus was 'full of grace and truth'
(v. 14). Now he underlines the message. God's word is a divine
amalgam of these two precious qualities. How do we define
'grace'? It is the loving disposition of God, given freely to those
who (usually) have done nothing to deserve it. It is a blessing
from God, especially the blessing brought about by Jesus which
saves us from our sins. We use this word 'grace' so frequently, its
significance may have become blurred: 'the grace of our Lord Jesus
Christ', is the self-denial, abundant love, vicarious suffering and
deep concern which prompted the Son of God to make the effort
of leaving his glory for a time to come among us and to effect our
redemption. Paul often uses the greeting: 'Grace be to you!', which
can also be rendered: 'May joy and gladness be yours!' Not an
ephemeral happiness, but the deeper joy of God. 'By grace you
have been saved through faith, and this is not your own doing; it
is the gift of God' (Ephesians 2:8). It is the grace of God working
in us, which not only brings us to a realization of our salvation,
but also persuades us – undeserving though we are – to accept
the love and the freedom from sin that God is holding out to us.
Grace, then, is the course of our salvation: a gift from God.

What is truth?

Literally, the other half of Christ's make-up is this mysterious
quality, 'truth'. Philosophers in ancient Greece tangled with its
definition, and decided it was the whole reality of God's universe,
and the inter-relating of what we know of existence with that
reality. We can be grateful that the New Testament deals with
truth more simply. Jesus told his disciples: 'You will know the
truth, and the truth will make you free' (John 8:32), since they
would learn to worship God 'in spirit and in truth' (John 4:23, 24).
And the 'Spirit of Truth' was the Comforter, whom Jesus promised

to send to his disciples after his ascension. But people in general would not receive the Spirit of Truth, because they neither saw nor knew him as Jesus had taught his disciples to know him. When the Spirit came, promised Jesus, 'he will guide you into all the truth . . . he will declare to you the things that are to come' (John 16:13).

Relating to the truth
It is much easier to relate to Jesus in the manger; Jesus on Galilee; Jesus on the cross; even Jesus ascending to his Father – than to Jesus as a spiritual amalgam of grace and truth. Yet John, writing the fourth gospel, intends us to try. Jesus told Pilate: 'Everyone who belongs to the truth listens to my voice' (John 18:37). And – whether in desperation, despair, anger or scorn – Pilate cries: 'What is truth?' And Truth stood before him, bruised, bleeding and full of dignity.

What *is* truth?
Sometimes it helps to look at the opposite; and, since the opposite of truth is falsehood, it comes as no surprise to find St John's definition of the devil as 'a liar, and the father of lies' (John 8:44). But Jesus tells us that *we* shall know the truth, and it is this truth that will make us free. Yet often, it seems, lies and intrigue predominate, while grace and truth are at a premium. Our world understands lies, but it has a problem with those who step out in faith and give God the chance to use them as he will. The world does not understand a Christian brimful of grace and truth. There is still a Pilate waiting to meet us at every turn. We battle constantly against the current of the world's river, bearers of a grace and a truth which are diametrically opposed to much of what the world accepts. Yet the world needs our truth as never before; for from the depths of our Spirit of Truth we can give it, with the abundance of God's grace, life-giving 'love, joy, peace, patience, kindness, generosity, faithfulness, gentleness and self-control' (Galatians 5:22, 23).

Suggested Hymns
Angel-voices, ever singing; God is working his purpose out; Child in the manger; A great and mighty wonder

Second Sunday of Christmas *Second Service*
As a Family Ps. 135; Isa. 46:3–13; Rom. 12:1–8;
Matt. 2:13–23

' "Get up, take the child and his mother, and flee into Egypt . . . Get up, take the child and his mother, and go to the land of Israel." ' Matthew 2:13, 20

Family life
God had been at pains to provide his Son with earthly parents who supported and cherished each other. An angel had forewarned Mary about her divine implantation; and Joseph, in turn, had received angelic assurance about the unusual conception. Now, together, Mary and Joseph were to safeguard the precious child by taking him to Egypt, out of the danger posed by Herod's insecurity and suspicion. Time and again in the Bible we hear of God's especial care for the 'widows and fatherless'. Biologically, Joseph was not essential for the conception and delivery of Jesus; but God provided for the support of Mary and the child; and Joseph proved himself worthy of involvement in God's plans. Some time after Jesus was twelve, and before he began his ministry, it would seem that Joseph died; but Jesus, in his extreme agony, gave his mother a companion (John 19:27). In the pattern of parenthood and family life that God safeguarded for the child Jesus, we see the pattern for all Christian families. The Mosaic law had allowed divorce, but Jesus was to teach that this was less than what God required (Mark 10:2–8). Today's world, with its high rate of marriage breakdown, an ever-increasing number of marriage counsellors, and many children born out of marriage, or aborted, has moved a long way from the Christian ideal. Are we to continue along this road, or to make a greater effort to return to Jesus' marriage guidelines?

Joseph's obedience
In a town of even Nazareth's humble proportions, Joseph would normally have expected to spend his entire working life in full employment. His was not a travelling trade – which would make the long journeys to and from Egypt all the more harrowing. But at least his carpentry skills would serve him well, in any place. God had not chosen a priest, dependent on a synagogue or temple

for his livelihood, for the earthly father of his Son. 'Get up and go.' Is God saying something like this to us? If so, are we taking him seriously? Virtually everyone whose life has counted for Christ, has been prompted to do the unusual. Others – many others – have probably experienced similar prompting, but have ignored it as wishful thinking, foolishness or wildly impossible. God is a master of the impossible: if we ever doubted it, or doubt that we could do what he is asking we should, let us remember the Nazareth carpenter, trudging with his family 250 miles into the alien land of Egypt. Or the tent-maker from Tarsus, preaching to a variety of congregations from Ephesus to Thessalonica, Cyprus to Athens, Corinth to Rome.

The Magi
They had come, these foreign *literati*, with gifts for one King, and news for another. The news they brought incited the temporal king to seek the Other's life. So it has often been since: innocence and goodness move the devil to do his worst. One hears of a peace treaty being signed somewhere – and immediately an attempt is made to undermine the peace. A nation has a joyful event to celebrate – and before the festivity has dropped into history, the devil gets to work and a tragedy of some kind hits the headlines. It was only to be expected that the birth of the world's Saviour would infuriate Satan. Yet, as Christians, we are in duty bound to move mountains, as Joseph did. If we sit back and do nothing, only the devil is content.

Suggested Hymns
Father God, I wonder; Jesus, good above all other; Lord, the light of your love; O worship the King

Feast of the Epiphany   Thursday 6 January
Christ's Revealing   Isa. 60:1–6; Ps. 72: 1–15;
Eph. 3:1–12; Matt. 2:1–12
'On entering the house, they saw the child with Mary his mother; and they knelt down and paid him homage.' Matthew 2:11

Journey's end

The magi had presumably come a great distance. We do not know how many times they had stopped to ask after 'the child who has been born king of the Jews' – but with Herod the warning bells definitely sounded. Christ reveals himself to different people in different ways, but each time his revealing calls for a positive response of effort: a plus of determination on the part of his followers. The simple shepherds had been given a simple path to follow to the manger; the magi had had to cope with a more complex journey. Who were they, these mysterious magi, who walk into our New Testament at the start of Matthew's second chapter, and journey out again, twelve verses later? They were not leading lights of the powerful Roman world, nor were they sophisticated Greeks. We are indebted to literate Church Fathers, like Tertullian, for most of the meagre details available: their country of origin was probably Persia (Iran); their religion, a form of Zoroastrianism; their names, Caspar, Melchior and Balthazar; their relics, now preserved in Cologne.

Kingly gifts

That they were kings is inferred from passing references in Isaiah and Revelation. The gifts they brought were certainly costly, and related to messianic expectations: gold for a king, frankincense for a priest, and myrrh for a sacrifice.

What star is this?

Astronomical portents were not rare in classical literature: a star guided Aeneas to the place where the Eternal City would be founded (Virgil, *Aeneid* ii.694). Another star foretold the birth of Augustus (Suetonius, *Augustus*, 94). Cicero mentions Alogi from Asia seeing a very bright star on the auspicious night when not only did the great temple of Ephesus burn, but also Alexander the Great was born (Cicero, *De Div.* 247). Stars of rare size and brightness were also mentioned by Pliny (*Nat. Hist.* 30:6) and Seneca (*Epistles* 58); and in the *Midrashim* writings of the Jews. When the magi reached Jerusalem, they seem either to have lost sight of their star, or it actually halted over Herod's palace. In asking directions, they may have come very close to jeopardizing the entire mission.

Heavy weather

We can ponder, in this Epiphany season, do *we* make heavy weather of the way to Jesus? Do we lose our spiritual concentration? Do we, at times, appeal to secular sources for direction? Herod ruled in Jerusalem as a puppet king under Roman overlordship, from 40 to 4 BC. He was cruel, rapacious, vindictive – and an opportunist. While the Jewish religious leaders did not make the effort to go to Bethlehem and see for themselves, Herod acted. The star was not needed for the last stage to Bethlehem; but its re-appearance gave the magi fresh heart, and an assurance of success in their search. The heavenly light stopped over the place where Jesus was. Whatever science says about this stationary star is irrelevant: according to Jewish belief, the birth of Christ was to be a secret. As St John tells us: 'When the Messiah comes, no one will know where he is from' (John 7:27). So his birth had to be divinely revealed.

All sorts and conditions

Only God knows why the first visitors to the child Jesus were simple Jewish shepherds – or why the next of whom we have record were pagan, regal philosophers. Perhaps the magi were comparatively young, with many years ahead of them in which to spread the good news. In any case, their standing would encourage an impressive dissemination of the news, once they returned home. Let us thank God, this Epiphany-tide, for the wideness of his mercy in opening his kingdom to Gentiles as well as Jews. Let us thank him for his first coming – in company today with the Orthodox Church, for whom this is Christmas – as we continue to prepare for his second coming.

Suggested Hymns

As with gladness men of old; Brightest and best; O, worship the Lord in the beauty of holiness; Songs of thankfulness and praise

First Sunday of Epiphany (*The Baptism of Christ*)   9 January   *Principal Service*
The Baptism of Christ   Gen. 1:1–5; Ps. 29; Acts 19:1–7; Mark 1:4–11

'In those days Jesus came from Nazareth of Galilee and was baptized by John in the Jordan ... And the Spirit immediately drove him out into the wilderness.' Mark 1:9, 12

Heavens opened, and the dove descends

At the Jordan river, God broke into the natural world with super-natural intervention, altering the equilibrium of nature; and those to whom he revealed his Spirit accepted that revelation by an act of faith. The crowds listening to John would have a pretty vague notion of the identity and function of the Holy Spirit. But John, in the best way he knew, was preparing them for a better baptism in store. The power of the Holy Spirit, thirty years or so earlier, had brought into operation the miraculous conception of Jesus; now, it confirmed Jesus, publicly, as 'the Beloved'. Jordan had seen some amazing happenings, but none more amazing than that. John had faithfully done his work in preparing the way for Jesus. Taking no credit for himself, he had consistently and unselfishly opened the path for Jesus to start his more important, far-reaching ministry.

Anti-climax?

But then, what happened? There was no great inaugural conven-tion, no immediate, large-scale Spirit-baptism. Instead, with unparalleled literary economy and impact, St Mark tells us: 'The Spirit immediately drove him out into the wilderness.' The verb is different from the Matthaean and Lukan parallels: Mark means that Jesus was 'cast out', 'sent out' into the wilderness. After the heavenly voice has thundered out its message, Mark's understand-ing is that the Holy Spirit took over Jesus' will and impelled him out into the next phase of God's purpose. After the drama of the baptism, God had planned for Jesus no immediate launch into an exciting, vibrant public ministry – but, instead, a time of privation and preparation, in the inhospitable Judaean wilderness.

Nothing new under the sun

The circumstances may have been unique, but the pattern was well established; for the Bible is rich in instances where a divine interruption of natural laws is followed by a period of physical and spiritual testing. Think of Jacob's vision at Beth-el, of the ladder reaching from heaven to earth – a vision followed by greater recognition of God's power and presence, and then years of service among Laban's flocks for Rachel. Think of Moses' vision at the burning bush, followed by the testing trauma of plagues preceding the exodus. Think of the call of Samuel, in the hushed temple court one night: a heavenly voice followed by quiet, faithful service in the temple under the priest Eli, before one of the greatest prophetic ministries. Think of Paul's 'Damascus Road experience', followed by a dark time of blindness, then a period of 'retreat' with the disciples, before his launch into what was to be the greatest ministry yet seen.

From ecstasy to exercise

There are times in our lives when God seems very near: times when we feel at one with our Maker, when earthly worries take second place. In fact, we may even become unaware of our surroundings and ourselves. When we come down to earth, we are elated; often we are convinced we can accomplish anything – and we promise ourselves we will always be like this. But God does not deal thus with us, until we have finished the course. While we are still on the way, always, after the glory, comes the duty, the exercise of ministry. Yet, as God was in the ecstasy, he is also in the mundane. He comes back with us from the prayer and communion, to the 'trivial round', where the world is waiting to see whether we have the stamina to fight its temptations – or whether we are going to let God's grace slip away. A wonderful revelation came that day in the Jordan Valley, when God's voice thundered over Jesus. But to those whose souls were still asleep; to those whose minds were clouded with worldly matters, that revelation was merely thunder.

Suggested Hymns

Breathe on me, breath of God; Spirit divine, attend our prayers; O love, how deep, how broad, how high; Spirit of the living God, fall afresh on me

First Sunday of Epiphany *Second Service*
The Holy Spirit Ps. 46; Isa. 42:1–9; Eph. 2:1–10;
Matt. 3:13–17

'And when Jesus had been baptized, just as he came up from the water, suddenly the heavens were opened to him, and he saw the Spirit of God descending like a dove and alighting on him.' Matthew 3:16

Holy Spirit, Holy Ghost
In some versions of the New Testament, the Spirit is called 'Holy Ghost': just one more name for the Third Person of the Trinity, and one which is found only in the New Testament, where the Greek supercedes the Aramaic and Hebrew. The first occurrence is in Matthew's Gospel, where God tells Joseph not to shy away from taking Mary as his wife, because that which was conceived in her was of the Holy Ghost/Spirit. Incidentally, the Greek implies that the source or cause from which Jesus emanated was the Spirit – an implication which divided the Eastern and Western Churches in the fourth century, and over which theologians can still get excited today. This was the Spirit which alighted on Jesus at his baptism: the same Spirit which indwells each one of us. Therefore, we should know him so well.

The Spirit's functions
He is to be invoked at every baptism carried out by Jesus' disciples (Matthew 28:19). He is given freely by God to those who ask (Luke 11:13). He is God's Spirit, given to everyone for a duration – not of seventy years, but 120 years, from the days of Noah (Genesis 6:3). He is the Spirit of adoption, by whom we are empowered to call God 'Father' (Romans 8:15). He is the Spirit of Christ, by whom we stand as Christ's brothers and sisters before God (Romans 8:9); the Spirit of counsel, giving us wisdom to know the will of God (Isaiah 11:2); the Spirit of glory, standing between us and evil (1 Peter 4:14). He was with God at creation (Genesis 1:2), full of goodness (Psalm 143:10); the Spirit of grace, given to David in abundance, and – by grace – to David's heirs and assigns, whom we are, through Jesus (Zechariah 12:10). He is the Spirit of holiness (Romans 1:4), promise (Ephesians 1:13), truth (John 14:19), wisdom (Ephesians 1:17), power, love and self-discipline (2 Timothy 1:7). One could continue, and it would be a sermon to end all sermons

37

if it exhausted the names and functions of the Holy Spirit. What a mighty powerhouse we have within us! And – in general – how we undervalue and under-use it!

The wisdom of God
The Spirit is wise to all God's will, and is empowered to make us wise, to bring us to a knowledge of our God, aptly suited for that purpose by his unique proximity. As Tennyson wrote:

> *Speak to him thou, for he hears;*
> *Spirit with spirit can meet;*
> *Closer is he than breathing –*
> *Nearer than hands and feet.*

The Higher Pantheism, 1847

No thing and no one is closer to us than the Holy Spirit. We may not aspire to know intimately the God of 'mighty thundercloud and flame'; but who cannot long to learn more of the divine dynamo within us, who for all his power speaks in that 'still, small voice of calm'?

The gentle dove
God was concerned to underline the importance of Jesus' baptism, so the crowds were given a visible, memorable sight of a dove descending from a height where no earthly dove flew, to alight on Jesus. In John's Gospel, we hear that John the Baptist had been told to expect the dove: 'And John testified, "I saw the Spirit descending from heaven like a dove, and it remained on him. I myself did not know him, but the one who sent me to baptize with water said to me, He on whom you see the Spirit descend and remain is the one who baptizes with the Holy Spirit"' (John 1:32, 33). Age does not weary, nor do the years condemn, the power of the Spirit. He can move in our lives with the gentleness of a dove; or he can inspire us to turn the world inside-out and right-way up for God. But he is a Gentleman. He will only act if we pray him to act.

Suggested Hymns
Crown him with many crowns; Name of all majesty; O worship the King; Thou whose almighty Word

Second Sunday of Epiphany 16 January
Principal Service **The Call of God** 1 Sam. 3:1–10;
Ps. 139:1–6, 13–18; Rev. 5:1–10; John 1:43–51

*'Nathanael said to him, "Can anything good come out of Nazareth?"
Philip said to him, "Come and see."' John 1:46*

Misunderstanding

When we consider the reluctance – even the brusqueness – of
many people, on hearing the call of God, we may be forgiven for
thinking it is a wonder some of them turn out as well as they do:
in fact, when we read the Bible, it is often amazing how many
people misunderstand, when God comes close to them. Yet, in his
goodness and mercy, he understands, he forgives, and he showers
them with blessings, because he has called them into his purpose.
When God has made up his mind about something or someone,
there is not a lot we can do about it. When Philip wanted Nathanael
to come to Jesus, Nathanael's response was blunt to the point of
rudeness. Nazareth, it is true, had a poor reputation; but Nathanael
was allowing for no exceptions. Yet Jesus did not ostracize him
for his rudeness. Instead, he shared with him a revelation of
coming glory. Jesus' dealings with his disciples is a lesson in
patience and understanding. He does not pounce on every hasty
word, though on one occasion he was quick to reprimand Peter
for disrespect (Matthew 16:22, 23). Knowing our humanity so well
– for he has shared it – he makes allowances: for Nathanael's
rudeness, for Thomas' doubting, for the impetuous outbursts of
James and John ... The list continues, and you and I are on it
somewhere, too.

God's ideal

We are often our own sternest critics, fearful of approaching God
until we are 'perfect' – forgetting that, as everything in the natural
world grows from a small beginning, it is the same with the spiritual life. We cannot run to God before we have learned to walk
to him. We cannot move mountains until we have grasped the
essentials for moving molehills. As has been said: heaven is not
reached in a single bound. We need to be tolerant to a degree,
even when we do not understand ourselves. God is a judge, and

will call us to account one day; but he is also a loving and merciful Father who knows his children as no one else knows us.

Open to God

Nathanael was not open to considering that there could be exceptions to the poor reputation of Nazareth. If we develop a similar over-critical nature, we are in danger of missing God's signs, and giving ourselves an awful lot more trouble in spiritual navigation. Criticism is infectious: we get back what we give, and it can stifle not only our spiritual progression, but also that of someone else. Being open to God is to look for the best in others; to be amenable to change – not for change's sake, but as an opportunity for growth. It means seeking God's will, even in areas of our lives where normally we would not expect him. It means allowing God the freedom to use us as he wants, and not necessarily always as we think he should. It means holding our possessions for him, and being willing to part with them at any time. Nathanael was not a bad character: in fact, Jesus praised him for his lack of deceit. But he also lacked generosity of spirit, and it was a serious flaw in his character. As the rich man was told just one thing stood between him and salvation (Mark 10:21), so Nathanael was brought to realize that his critical outlook needed attention. Perhaps there is only one aspect of our nature that is inhibiting our way to God. Let us take it to the Lord in prayer. It will not be beyond his capabilities.

Suggested Hymns

Be still and know that I am God; I cannot tell why he whom angels worship; Just as I am; The race that long in darkness

Second Sunday of Epiphany   *Second Service*
Amazing Jesus   Ps. 96; Isa. 60:9–22; Heb. 6:17–7:10; Matt. 8:5–13

'When Jesus heard him, he was amazed and said to those who followed him, "Truly I tell you, in no one in Israel have I found such faith." '
Matthew 8:10

The gift of faith

Faith is not our birthright, neither can it be bought or sold, nor can it be given away. But once received from God, it can be manifested, shared and increased. It can also be lost – and there is the *caveat*. A little faith can go a long way: Jesus tells us faith as small as a mustard seed can move mountains (Matthew 17:20).

So, what *is* faith? It is believing in God, affirming and confessing the belief, and putting what we believe into action. In his hymn 'Give me the faith which can remove and sink the mountain to a plain', Charles Wesley wrote:

> *My talents, gifts and graces, Lord,*
> *Into thy blessed hands receive;*
> *And let me live to preach thy word,*
> *And let me to thy glory live;*
> *My every sacred moment spend*
> *In publishing the sinners' Friend.*

Wesley's crisis

When John Wesley's faith was at such a critical point, and he even wondered if he had lost it, he met Peter Böhler, a Moravian. The Wesley brothers had been introduced to the Moravians on their journey to America, and had been impressed with their simplicity and dedication. John opened his heart to Böhler, and was advised: 'On no account neglect God's gift of preaching: preach faith, *until* you have it; then preach it *because* you have it.' Shortly after this, Wesley had what was later called his 'second conversion', at Aldersgate, and went from strength to strength in his ministry.

Faith in word and action

The centurion in our reading showed his faith in word and action; he came to Jesus, rather than waiting for Jesus to come to him. And his faith-filled words called forth such praise from Jesus, as would make the listening Jews uncomfortable – even though, as St Luke tells us in his account of the episode, the Jews had recommended the man to Jesus: 'He is worthy of having you do this for him, for he loved our people, and it is he who built our synagogue for us' (Luke 7:4, 5). He was one of the few foreigners whom the Jews had accepted. Even so, their magnanimity was severely tested when Jesus praised the centurion's faith above their own. Were the Jews not custodians of the scriptures? Did they not – by virtue of the ancient prophecies and revelations – have a monopoly on the grace of God? Definitely not! Jesus implies. This Gentile has out-believed you! Their faith was in their temple, ritual, inherited scriptures and patronage. The centurion, on the other hand, not only had faith: he gave proof of his faith by asking Jesus for a miracle, and believing it was done before he knew it had been.

Abrahamic faith

This was all of a piece with St Paul's understanding of Abraham's faith: because he believed in a God 'who . . . calls into existence the things that do not exist. Hoping against hope, [Abraham] believed' (Romans 8:17, 18). That was faith: mountain-moving faith. And one of the lessons we learn, from Abraham and from the centurion, is that each of us comes to faith on our own. Others may tell us of God, may lead us towards him, may give us wonderful encouragement, support and affirmation; but no one becomes a Christian by proxy: when we get serious about it, faith is some-thing between us and God. The centurion had come to faith by belief, by trust, by commitment. He was open to God. His 'proof of faith' was seen and heard in his belief that Jesus could heal at a distance – by 'remote control'. When we pray, we are to believe that our prayer has not only been heard, but has been acted upon. Jesus said: 'Whatever you ask for in prayer, *believe that you have received it*, and it will be yours' (Mark 11:24). The proof of our faith means that we can pray and trust God to do what is necessary – putting as much faith in God's power to answer, as in our need to ask.

Suggested Hymns

Give me oil in my lamp; Father, I place into your hands; Jesus Christ is waiting; Ye servants of the Lord

Third Sunday of Epiphany   23 January
Principal Service   My hour is not yet come
Gen. 14:17–20; Ps. 128; Rev. 19:6–10; John 2:1–11

'And Jesus said to her, "Woman, what concern is that to you and to me? My hour has not yet come".' John 2:4

God's time

It takes us a lifetime to discover the difference between God's time and ours. John, in his Gospel, has two references which point up this difference: our text for today, where it is Jesus' mother who elicits his reply: 'My hour has not yet come'; and the approach of the Festival of Booths (Tabernacles), when his brothers advise him to go to Judaea, and he replies: 'My time has not yet come, but your time is always here' (John 7:6).

St Peter tells us: 'Do not ignore this one fact, that with the Lord one day is like a thousand years, and a thousand years are like one day' (2 Peter 3:8). While the earth remains, day follows night (Genesis 8:22), and the seasons maintain their pattern; but the history of chronology shows us that no human timekeeping has ever fathomed the timing of nature: every so often, we need our leap years, our allowances for the odd second – as was seen, for example, at the end of 1998. Opinions are still divided as to the precise year of Jesus' birth; and many have been the alternative theories since the King James Bible 'fixed' the start of Genesis at 4004 BC!

Minding Jesus' business

The two Johannine instances of Jesus saying 'My time has not yet come,' occur when members of his family tried to tell him what to do: first Mary, then his brothers. Each time, Jesus eventually did what they suggested, after initially refusing. In fact, in today's reading, Mary pointedly ignores his refusal, and calmly instructs the servants to do whatever Jesus orders, leaving him apparently no choice in the matter. Had Jesus already shown her he could solve the problem of no wine? We can only guess at the confidence which prompted her command; but it should also give us courage to approach Jesus with similar assurance. As the author of Hebrews bids: 'Let us approach with a true heart in full assurance of faith' (Hebrews 10:22). God requires respect, but not grovelling: boldness, but not familiarity. 'Come now, let us argue it out, says the Lord' (Isaiah 1:18). God treats us like sons and daughters, not as babies who never grow up.

Ordering our case

Our time, as Jesus told his brothers, is always here. Whenever we need to plead our cause, God will listen. We are not to wait for an 'appropriate' time, which could be one day, or never. God is

never short of time to hear and respond. Our lives are so circum-
scribed by time that we cannot fathom this. We are not required
to. God will see that we have all the time we need: his time is not
our business. The timing of God was a cause of perplexity to the
first-century Jews, when Jesus was describing his relationship in
time to Abraham: '"Your ancestor Abraham rejoiced that he
would see my day; he saw it and was glad." Then the Jews said
to him, "You are not yet fifty years old, and have you seen Abraham?" Jesus said to them, "Very truly, I tell you, before Abraham
was, I am".' (John 8:56–58). One of the questions raised by this,
is: What is/was the 'day' of Jesus? Before Abraham was born, or
while he lived, or after he died? We have reached the limit of
language here, where the concept of 'day' merges into historical
(and pre-historical) time. In digging into this mystery, we surely
get a glimpse of the permanence and indestructibility of the Power
that not only rules the universe, but which can also be concerned
about so trivial a matter as wine at a marriage breakfast.

Suggested Hymns
A Man there lived in Galilee; I, the Lord of sea and sky; Lord,
enthroned in heavenly splendour; Stand up, stand up for Jesus

Third Sunday of Epiphany   *Second Service*
The Ministry of Jesus   Ps. 33; Jer. 3:21–4:2; Titus 2:1–8,
11–14; Matt. 4:12–23
*'Jesus went throughout Galilee, teaching in their synagogues and pro-
claiming the good news of the kingdom and curing every disease and
every sickness among the people.' Matthew 4:23*

For God, nothing is impossible
In this verse, which encapsulates the ministry of Jesus, nothing
is beyond his power to heal. Whatever sickness or disease was
presented to him, he could effect a cure. Today we have a health
programme and learning greater than ever before – yet the best
of our medical skill falls short of curing every sickness and disease.
There are faith healers, homoeopathic remedies, 'natural' cures
backing up conventional medicine; yet have we missed the point

as far as 'healing ministry' in its primary sense is suggested by this text? Do we rely on proof rather than on sheer, naked faith? Perhaps the fear that 'it may not work' prevents us from going the whole way. Of course, healing was only a part of Jesus' ministry: alongside it went the teaching and preaching. One could say that these aspects were directed towards the spiritual health and well-being of the listeners, while the healing cared for their physical needs. But Jesus does not differentiate between the two: his was 'holistic medicine', aiming for the complete ministry to people, bringing the whole person – body, mind and spirit – into a right relationship with God: a relationship intended as the norm by their Maker. Jesus saw the healing of a cripple as freeing that person for fruitful service and ministry. According to him, it was not God's will for sickness and disease to render a person unfit or incomplete for service.

'Sickness is sent to try us'

We often hear this, as a prelude to an exhortation to be patient and learn from invalidity or sickness. This is not the message that comes from the ministry of Jesus. He said that a house divided against itself 'will not be able to stand' (Mark 3:25). Therefore, if it was God who sent the sickness and disease, what was Jesus doing healing people from them? That would, indeed, have been 'a house divided against itself'. Take, for instance, the healing of the man with the withered hand: when the crowds carped about Jesus working on the Sabbath, 'he looked around at them with anger, being grieved at their hardness of heart' (Mark 3:5). When Jesus healed the man born blind (the only instance in the Gospels where he healed congenital disease, disease for which there was no human reason) and the people asked him: 'Who sinned, this man or his parents?' Jesus replied that the affliction was, rather, the opportunity for God's power to be revealed (John 9:3). That, again, does not square with God being the inflicter of the disease. God is good. There is no darkness in him. While he may allow us, through our rashness or through the act of another, to suffer sickness and disease, he is not responsible for it. Nowhere in the Gospels do we find Jesus breaking a leg, or falling prey to paralysis or leprosy. How could he heal people from infirmities from which he himself was suffering?

He bore our afflictions
As he hung on the cross, Jesus took upon himself every sin and affliction of the world. He hung guilty of murder, adultery and everything evil that can happen to man: but he did not hold those evils; he took them out of the world, through hell, and annulled their sting and longevity for ever, in his own pure body. After death and resurrection, he carries the scars, to prove that their wounds have for ever lost the power they once had. Therefore, we can have boldness to believe in faith his words: 'These signs will accompany those who believe: by using my name they will cast out demons; they will speak in new tongues; they will pick up snakes in their hands; and if they drink any deadly thing, it will not hurt them; they will lay their hands on the sick, and they will recover' (Mark 16:17, 18).

May we resolve to use *all* the power God has given us, to his glory.

Suggested Hymns
Thine arm, O Lord, in days of old; From thee all skill and science flow; Immortal love, for ever full; For the healing of the nations

Fourth Sunday of Epiphany   30 January
Principal Service   **A Busy Ministry**   Deut. 18:15–20; Ps. 111; Rev. 12:1–5a; Mark 1:21–28

'They were all amazed, and they kept on asking one another, "What is this? A new teaching – with authority! He commands even the unclean spirits, and they obey him." At once his fame began to spread throughout the surrounding region of Galilee.' Mark 1:27, 28

A 'plus of determination'
This phrase, coined by modern psychologists, aptly describes the ministry of Jesus. He was concerned to make full use of the time to fulfil the will of God, to preach, teach and heal – and to find time to pray. The Sabbath described in today's gospel reading and continuing beyond v. 28, is a lesson in making the most of all the opportunities for service. First, Jesus preaches, then he heals the man with the unclean spirit, then he restores Peter's mother-in-

law; after this, he heals everyone who comes seeking a cure; then he prays – and following this he extends his preaching, teaching and healing ministry through town after town after town. This Sabbath in Capernaum was the start of a concerted attack on the physical sickness and spiritual poverty of Galilee and Judaea.

Little sleep, much work
While Jesus, according to the gospels, was never rushed, never in a hurry, never wasting time, he worked steadily on through the days God allowed him on earth; and we hear of him either praying through the night, or rising very early to pray. It is a model for his followers, to seek a quiet place, and to commune with God – alone. But after the solitariness, the ministry continues with the disciples (Mark 1:36).

God's authority
It seems to have been the combination of preaching and healing which commanded immediate attention and respect from the people at Capernaum. Most people love their bodies, and the doctor who effects a cure is sure of approval. If he can also improve life on the spiritual front, he is assured of even greater regard. Everyone who has been entrusted with the gospel has a duty to the whole person, to fit that person for the work God has prepared. Life today may seem to move much faster than in first-century Palestine – but it cannot out-pace God or his ministers invested with the Great Commission.

Realizing potential
In general, we realize neither our physical nor our spiritual potential. But God does, and requires of us nothing more – and nothing less – than we are capable of. We have the authority of the gospel of Jesus. Do we exercise it to the full? Dwelling within us, we have the dynamic Holy Spirit: but how often is the Spirit underworked? When the army of Aram threatened the smaller Israelite force, Elisha was confident of victory, for he saw the spiritual forces ranged alongside Israel (2 Kings 6:16). And St John reiterates this unconquerable back-up which is presently available to each of us: 'The one who is in you is greater than the one who is in the world' (1 John 4:4). We have the authority to preach and heal, as Jesus did – if only we will use it. We have the mandate to take the gospel into new territory, as Jesus took it – if only we will go;

never hurrying, never wasting time, but 'straining forward to what lies ahead' (Philippians 3:13).

Suggested Hymns
Christ is our cornerstone; O for a thousand tongues to sing; Son of God, eternal Saviour; Thy Kingdom come, O God

Fourth Sunday of Epiphany   *Second Service*
Seeing Eyes, Hearing Ears   Ps. 34; 1 Sam. 3:1–20; 1 Cor. 14:12–20; Matt. 13:10–17
'But blessed are your eyes for they see, and your ears for they hear.'
Matthew 13:16

Many are called
While God's invitation is given to all, most will reject it – through ignorance, pride, laziness or fear, it will be allowed to pass them by. Koheleth (the Preacher) once said: 'There is nothing new under the sun' (Ecclesiastes 1:9); and throughout the Bible this is a recurring phenomenon. The Third Millennium is likely to see it continuing: God's message will, in all probability, be given to more people than ever before – and more people than ever before will let it pass. We can seek answers to this problem; but when we search through the Gospel accounts of Jesus' ministry, the answers we find are often hard to accept. In three out of the four accounts, we find the disciples being told to press on to the next towns – to take the gospel to new communities – if their message is rejected (Matthew 10:14; Mark 6:11; Luke 9:5): 'Shake the dust of that place off your feet.' Where is tolerance here? Was this stringency meant only for the earliest disciples, in a ministry that was to see Jesus operating 'in the flesh' for a brief, three-year period? If we believe that, we must seriously consider re-writing much of the New Testament. It is not the preacher's obligation to *force* anyone into accepting the gospel. That is God's business: *'C'est Son métier,'* as Henri Heine once remarked. While there is life and breath, God allows time for acceptance: he alone decides the 'cut-off' period.

Taking to the road

We may do well to ask how mobile the gospel is, in our particular community, and how much need there is to increase its scope. Are we – as individuals or as a parish – fulfilling our missionary calling? In the early 1990s a young man took some Bibles to a series of remote villages in south-west China. In the first village he came to, people left their work in the fields, to see the new arrival. They sat round in a tight circle to listen as, through an interpreter, the young preacher told them of Jesus. At first, they listened politely, then with real interest. At the end, an old man came up in tears. 'Tell us, how long have you in the West known about this Jesus?' 'Nearly two thousand years.' 'Then *why* has it taken you so long to come and tell us?'

Though there will be more who will reject our preaching than who will accept it, we are still obliged to take the gospel to as many people as we can, in all the ways we can, with all the time we have. And we need not spend too much time in analysing why the message is rejected. Those who do not accept it will find one reason or another, without our help.

The germinating seed

There is always the hope, to keep alive our fervour and commitment, that seed once sown may germinate at a later date. James Montgomery's hymn spells it out:

> *Sow in the morn thy seed,*
> *At eve hold not thy hand;*
> *To doubt and fear give thou no heed,*
> *Broadcast it o'er the land . . .*
>
> *Thou know'st not which may thrive,*
> *The late or early sown;*
> *Grace keeps the precious germs alive,*
> *When and wherever strown.*

When God allows us to see the fruits of our labours, it is good; when he allows us to reap the harvest from seed sown by others, that too is good; but let us also remember that we are obliged, in turn, to keep on sowing for the next generation of reapers.

Father of heaven, whose love profound; Join all the glorious names; There is a Redeemer; Firmly I believe and truly

Candlemas (*The Purification of the Virgin; The Presentation of Christ in the temple*)
Wednesday 2 February   Nunc Dimittis
Mal. 3:1–5; Ps. 24:1–10; Heb. 2:14–8; Luke 2:22–40

'"Master, now you are dismissing your servant in peace, according to your word; for my eyes have seen your salvation."' Luke 2:29, 30

Jesus became poor
Forty days after his birth, the young Jesus was taken to the temple by his parents, to be offered to the Lord – formally presented at the central focus of his nation's religion. An offering of a dove for a sin-offering was obligatory. If funds permitted, a female yearling lamb must also be offered. If a family was poor, then the gift was two doves. Mary and Joseph showed their poverty by the doves they brought. Six weeks before, they had settled for a stable as overnight accommodation-cum-maternity-ward. Now their poverty is underlined, a poverty which later prompted St Paul to write: 'You know the generous act of our Lord Jesus Christ, that though he was rich, yet for your sakes he became poor, so that by his poverty you might become rich' (2 Corinthians 8:9). Familiarity with the gospel should not blunt our appreciation of the cost to Christ of becoming poor for our sake.

Theotokos – Mother of God
The humility belongs to Mary, too: she, who was to be called 'Mother of God', had been confined since Jesus' birth, denied the joy of visiting synagogue or temple with other women. Now she had come several miles to Jerusalem, had waited at the temple gate for the priest, with her two doves, had redeemed Jesus with the statutory five shekels, had seen him blessed, received him back – all in accordance with Jewish law regarding a first-born son. No

special treatment, even for the Son and the Mother of God ...
until an old man approaches, takes the child in his arms, and says
these amazing words of the *Nunc Dimittis*.

Old meets new

The celebration of Candlemas is very ancient. Certainly from at
least as early as the sixth century, people held church processions
with lighted candles; and the day came to be known in the Latin,
Catholic West as 'Candlemas, the Purification of Our Lady'; and in
the Orthodox East as 'The Presentation of the Lord'. The Anglican
Church, ever good at striking a balance, has taken on board both
titles – and, in fact, both are taken from the opening verse of
today's gospel reading: 'When the time came for their purification
... they brought him to Jerusalem to present him to the Lord'
(Luke 2:22). Today, in many churches, candles will be blessed,
often in two bundles – one of long, thick, decorated candles for
use in the church until next Candlemas; and the second of smaller
candles, lit and held during today's services by the worshippers
– all to symbolize the 'light for revelation to the Gentiles'. For
the great significance of Candlemas is in the meeting of the old
dispensation and the new: of Simeon and Jesus. The baby in the
old man's arms will be the watershed between animals being
offered on behalf of sinful people, and Jesus vicariously suffering
on the cross: so simple, so humble, so uncomplicated – just a child
in an old man's arms, and yet so hard for us to understand, and
to accept. As Sir Frederick Faber once wrote:

> If our love were but more simple,
> We should take him at his word.

The true light

We have our lighted candles to illustrate the breakthrough, freedom, simplicity and light which the coming of Jesus brought into
the world. As Simeon spoke, did Mary recall her song to Elizabeth?
'He has helped ... in remembrance of his mercy, according to the
promise he made ... to Abraham and to his descendants for ever'
(Luke 1:54, 55). And who, in the temple that day, did not know
that God had said to Abraham: 'in you, *all* the families of the earth
shall be blessed' (Genesis 12:3)? As the light of our candles can
alter a darkened church or home, so the light of Jesus can change
a world in dark despair. But unless we keep the Candlemas light

burning in our hearts and lives, its message will go out for us when our little candles are extinguished.

Suggested Hymns
I sing the Lord God's praises (*Celebration Hymnal*); Maiden, yet a mother! (*Westminster Hymnal*); Sing of Mary; Ye who own the faith of Jesus

Fifth Sunday of Epiphany (Proper 1)
6 February   *Principal Service*   **Seeking for Jesus**
Isa. 40:21–31; Ps. 147:1–11, 20; 1 Cor. 9:16–23;
Mark 1:29–39
'In the morning, while it was still very dark, he got up and went out to a desert place, and there he prayed. And Simon and his companions hunted for him. When they found him, they said to him, "Everyone is searching for you."'   Mark 1:35–37

Knowing how to seek
'When you search for me, you will find me; if you seek me with all your heart' (Jeremiah 29:13). Knowing how to seek is all-important. The people who were looking for Jesus in today's gospel reading were not the ardent seekers of Jeremiah's prophecy, but those wanting to hear more of Jesus' authoritative preaching, and to see more of his healing miracles – which were laudable reasons, but not 'heartfelt' in the true sense of the word. So Jesus told his disciples to move on with him to the next towns along their missionary route. The Markan seekers can be seen today: they go to church because a particular preacher has been rostered; or because a particular service happens at a time that will accommodate their secular schedule for the day; or because someone has leaked the information that the service is going to be 'different' ... while the heartfelt seeker goes to hear God's word (which is greater than the preacher); to partake of the sacraments (which are greater than the celebrant); and predominantly to worship God (who is greater than any service format). Seeking to know about

Jesus is invariably secondary to seeking truly to know him. Even the Devil knows about Jesus.

Concentrating spiritual energy

Generally our energy is concentrated most on the things we like the best. So it should be with Jesus. If we are to seek him whole-heartedly, it means giving him our time and talents, and showing him we care. The question should be not: have we merely done our duty – by him, by others, by ourselves – but: have we satisfied Jesus? Have we gone the second mile, beyond the call of duty? In the gospel reading when Jesus, after a long day, had gone out very early to pray alone, he was exceeding the call of duty: stated times of prayer began later in the day, when the first gleams of light were seen in the east by the priests on duty in the temple. Simon and the others went hunting for him, disturbing his prayer time because of the demanding crowds; and his refusal to accede to their request was an implied rebuke.

God never sleeps

We can never disturb God at slumber; and Jesus, re-united with his Father, is likewise now always interceding, always with us – as Hubert Richards has written:

> *His believers, when they've met,*
> *know he's there with them,*
> *and yet he's with God –*
> *what makes us think that's somewhere else?*

Yet we can still disturb God by selfish requests, unnecessary worries, time-wasting monologues – when we could instead be sharing his gospel with someone else, or when he has indicated a certain path of duty for us. There are times when he does want us to 'come away to a deserted place all by ourselves and rest awhile' (Mark 6:31); but we need also to be alert to other times, when he tells us to 'get up, let us be going' (Matthew 26:46). The more we seek for Jesus with all our energy of will, the more clearly shall we hear his voice, whether it comes as thunder, with cataclysmic force, or as the still, small voice which the world and its demands can so easily drown.

A stranger once did bless the earth; Praise ye the Lord, 'tis good to raise; Seek ye first the kingdom of God; We have a gospel to proclaim

Fifth Sunday of Epiphany   *Second Service*
Catching People   Ps. 5; Num. 13:1–2, 27–33;
Phil. 2:12–28; Luke 5:1–11

'Then Jesus said to Simon, "Do not be afraid; from now on you will be catching people." When they had brought their boats to shore, they left everything and followed him.' Luke 5:10, 11

Aggressive discipling
This is Jesus at his aggressive best: the Greek verb rendered 'catching' does not mean a meek and mild 'detain', or even 'engage in polite conversation'. It translates 'actively seek out, track down and secure – by force of arms and argument'. Such aggressiveness may come as a surprise to some; but this was not the only occasion when Jesus showed himself anything but 'meek and mild': 'You are hypocrites!' he thundered at Pharisees, lawyers and Sadducees. 'Tell that fox Herod what I am doing!' he ordered Herod's courtiers. 'Don't you dare make my Father's house a den of thieves!' he shouted to the profiteers in the temple court, as he took a whip, overturned their *bureaux de change*, and let their doves fly free. 'Get behind me, Satan!' he could say, even to his closest friend, Simon Peter. 'Go into the highways and hedges, and *compel* people to come to my feast,' he told a congregation listening to his parables. And this tough talking survived his resurrection: in the evening of that first Easter Day, when he overtook the two disciples on the road to Emmaus, he listened to their tale of woe, and then he let fly: 'O *fools*, and slow to believe all that the prophets said would happen!'

Do likewise
Why should we not, also, be aggressive in our work for God? 'Do not be afraid; from now on you will be catching people.' Jesus is not merely being aggressive to Peter and the others, but also to

us – for, later, when he told his disciples to go into all the world and preach the gospel to everyone, he knew full well eleven men could not evangelize the world. 'Do not be afraid' – we are not to fear the enormity of the undertaking; we are not to sit down and let the challenge get the better of us. We are not worthy of the commission; we are not worthy even to be called Christians. But by virtue of Jesus' blood shed for us, *his* worthiness is infused into us by his Holy Spirit – and by divine love we become worthy, in God's eyes. As Zechariah says: it is 'not by might, nor by power, but by my Spirit, says the Lord of hosts' (Zechariah 4:6).

Doing the impossible
When we have accepted the enormous truth, that everything God calls us to do is impossible, we are well on the way to giving him the initiative, and all the glory. Did the eleven disciples, shattered at the departure of Jesus, terrified by the enormity of the command to preach the gospel world-wide, sit down and cogitate how it all could happen? No! St Luke tells us: 'they returned to Jerusalem with great joy; and they were continually in the temple blessing God' (Luke 24:53). A praising heart counteracts self-pity, worry and nerves. It becomes the secret of staying in the will of God. When a challenge comes, praise God. If worry launches an attack, praise God. Sing, pray, worship, bless, intercede: the disciples found it worked, and God is no respecter of persons; whoever gets serious with God, will find it works, too – for whatever God calls us to do, he gives us the strength, the opportunity and the means to do it.

God's purposes
Simon Peter and the others rose to the challenge; and we, in our generation, with all the advances and opportunities God has given us, must also rise – for the purpose of God, the catching of people, is an ongoing process. There are still many, many fish to be caught in Peter's net.

Suggested Hymns
O Jesus, I have promised; Follow Christ and serve the world as he did; In fancy I stood by the shore one day; Will you come and follow me

Sixth Sunday of Epiphany (Proper 2)
13 February *Principal Service* God's Choice
2 Ki. 5:1–14; Ps. 30; 1 Cor. 9:24–27; Mark 1:40–45

'A leper came to him begging him, and kneeling he said to him, "If you choose, you can make me clean."' Mark 1:40

The Lord can always do it
There are times when we ask God to act, but in such a despairing, half-hearted way, we give the impression that our request is greater than God's power. We can never out-think God: the tremendous truth of this should persuade us to put as much faith in his power to act, as in our need to ask. The leper in our gospel reading was not half-hearted: he had full confidence that Jesus could heal him. The only question was: did he want to heal him? We may come to Jesus with boldness, 'in full measure of faith' (Hebrews 10:22), but the bottom line is: we are not (yet) perfect; we are sinners, dependent on the grace of Jesus. And the choice always lies with Jesus, not with us. The leper had no choice about being leprous.

God's decisions
We do not know why God chooses to heal some people, and not others. No one knows fully what is in someone else's spiritual, physical and mental make-up. It may be that others may be blessed somehow by a person's incapacity or disability. Some would suggest that prayers for healing – even the sufferer's own faith – have been lacking in some vital particular; but this, as well as undermining confidence, seems too simplistic. Jesus never taught that any prayer goes unanswered. Therefore, if we pray for healing – of ourselves or others – and no healing takes place, we are not to believe God has not answered, still less, that he has not heard. Though no healing may have been manifested, because we have prayed we can believe that we have received it, and we can praise God for it, *before* it is manifested. 'Whatever you ask for' in prayer, believe that you have received it, and it will be yours' (Mark 11:24).

Paul's 'thorn'
'To keep me from becoming too elated, a thorn was given to me in the flesh, a messenger of Satan, to torment me, to keep me from

being too elated' (2 Corinthians 12:7). We do not know whether this thorn was an illness or disease, or a spiritual 'pain in the neck': but at any rate it emanated from Satan. Paul prayed and prayed for God to take it away, but God told him: 'My grace is sufficient for you, for power is made perfect in weakness' (v. 9). At times we, too, need to learn how to trust God more; and if he decides that our trust will increase as our physical strength lessens, we can be confident that one day the strategy will be explained.

Continue in prayer
It is not wrong to keep on praying for healing: nowhere in the Bible do we find justification for accepting sickness and disease as inflictions from God. Only a moron would settle for illness rather than health. So we need to keep our sights on wholeness of body, mind and spirit. We can serve God better when we are completely well – at the same time remembering that we may sometimes influence others for good in special ways *through* sickness and weakness. If God can bring good – to us and to others – out of Satan's 'messengers', he will do so, in more ways than we can imagine: and, as we look back to that time, we shall realize how ingenious were his workings. There are people whom we would not meet, were we healthy: if those people can be touched by our infirmity, who are we to feel regret? Health is good, and we should give it true value while we have it. If we use it for God, in all the ways we can, at all the times we can, to all the people we can, the Lord may well decide that we can keep it.

Suggested Hymns
Firmly I believe and truly; Jesu, the very thought of thee (Parts 1 and/or 2); O love, how deep, how broad, how high!; Praise to the holiest in the height

Sixth Sunday of Epiphany *Second Service*
God's Way of Daily Living   Ps. 6; Num. 20:2–13; Phil. 3:7–21; Luke 6:17–26
'Blessed are you who are poor . . . hungry . . . who weep . . . when people hate you . . .' Luke 6:20–22

Turning our wisdom upside-down

These verses come from Jesus' 'Sermon on the Plain', according to St Luke's Gospel; Matthew sites his version of it on a mountain. Whether or not the whole of this teaching was given in one great sermon, it forms the main part of the most uncompromising – if not strange – preaching of Jesus. We are so familiar with it, at times there is a danger of hearing it without fully taking it on board. It is Jesus at his most blunt, and in almost every verse it turns upside-down the ways and so-called wisdom of daily life.

'Blessed are you who are poor.' Do we not rather look for a bank balance in credit, for what we like to call a 'comfortable income'? 'Blessed are you who are hungry now.' Are we ever hungry, on three or four meals a day? 'Blessed are you who weep now.' If we cry, or see someone else crying, doesn't it mean something is wrong? 'Blessed are you when people hate you.' If we are ever in that position, we're usually pretty unhappy about it; we rarely 'leap for joy', as Jesus says we should. Could we really imagine ourselves in a warm glow of spiritual peace and joy, while our bodies were screaming out for health and nourishment, our eyes were blinded with tears, and even close friends were playing us false?

Practising what we preach

Scholars, doctors and the like have been working on the texts behind these verses for nearly two thousand years; yet the words which can be so easily memorized, so quickly read, are still proving difficult to live out in daily Christian life – impossible to live out in the lives of non-believers. We make a little progress, and slip back a little way, time and again. And so it has always been, on the personal, local and national fronts. From the earliest times until now, the legal system (whether holy or secular) has issued a set of laws; time passes, and the laws are modified to suit people, places and circumstances. The system becomes so diluted and unworkable, that a reform is undertaken. A new set of laws is promulgated – or the old set re-issued – and the process of adaptation and modification begins all over again. In the Old Testament we see this pattern very clearly. The laws of Moses were an attempt to return to the first laws of God. Morals and standards had slipped so far that, in time, King Josiah presided over a great reform. This, in turn, was diluted, until King Zedekiah masterminded another reform. By the time of Jesus, the temple authorities were working on such a mishmash of laws as to make Jesus' teaching in the Great Sermon imperative. Yet, less than a century later, we find human nature hiccupping over their stern morality; and a little work called the *Didache*, or *Teaching of the Twelve Apostles*, was written for use in the Church of the early second century, which (very honestly) says, *inter alia*, 'Be perfect, *if possible*; if not, do the best you can' (cf. Matthew 5:48).

Trying our best
We all fall short of perfection; but that is a poor reason for not continuing to pursue it. Jesus has issued no modification of his teaching in the Great Sermon. He still points us to his highest ideals. He is still telling us to aim for perfection. Like the early disciples, are we not still doing the best we can?

Suggested Hymns
A charge to keep I have; Blest are the pure in heart; Not for our sins alone; O for a heart to praise my God

Septuagesima (Proper 3)   20 February
Principal Service   **Nothing Like This**   Isa. 43:18–25; Ps. 41; 2 Cor. 1:18–22; Mark 2:1–12

'And he stood up and immediately took the mat and went out before all of them, so that they were all amazed and glorified God, saying, "We have never seen anything like this!"' Mark 2:12

Strange happenings in Capernaum
There had been nothing like it: the crowds, the new, authoritative preaching; four determined men breaking up a roof; a paralytic healed not only physically but spiritually. It all left a drama in the air, that here was a very special Man. Prior to this, Jesus had been healing every case of sickness and disease brought to him. The crowds had coped with that; but when this miracle doctor claimed authority over a man's spiritual condition, they were out of their depth: 'Why does this fellow speak in this way? It is blasphemy! Who can forgive sins but God alone?' (v. 7).

The burden of sin

Adam's legacy had dominated Jewish history from its inception. A sin committed by someone in the family was taken to heart by all the members; and retribution by the aggrieved party could be exacted on the whole family. It was to correct this stringent law that the Deuteronomic precept: 'An eye [only] for an eye, and a tooth [only] for a tooth,' was promulgated. Once a year, on the Day of Atonement (*Yom Kippur*), a goat was sacrificed, and another (the scapegoat) was driven into the wilderness, for the people's corporate sin. Now, Jesus was linking freedom of sin with freedom of illness and physical affliction. It was a novel concept. Who could accept it? We do not know if Jesus' amazing words were prompted by the magnitude of faith shown by the paralytic's friends, who thought no measure too extreme to get their burden to Jesus. As portions of the roof fell on the crowd assembled below, these brave men would almost certainly bear the brunt of protests and outrage. That they persevered, made an immediate impact on Jesus.

Sins made known

Whether the paralytic's sins were known or not to the assembled crowd – whether they were great sins or small – Jesus made his sinful condition public. Our sins are not obliterated by ignoring them, or keeping quiet about them; only by being open about them to God – or even, as in this case, accepting that God reserves the right to do what we dare not – are we to be relieved of them. There are those who support the theory that sickness and disease is a result of sin: 'a healthy mind means a healthy body'. This can be very hurtful to those suffering great physical pain through apparently no fault of their own; but, equally, others may well realize that a fault on their part has led to physical problems. Be this as it may, this episode teaches us the value of friends; the paralytic was blessed in the resourceful quartet who spared no effort to get their friend to Jesus. Can we, too, not build a ministry of intercession and help, bringing those whom we hold dear to the Source of healing – physical, spiritual, mental? The four friends did not give up at the first obstacle: how often do we pray for a sick friend, and then acquiesce when the way to help seems barred?

Accepting forgiveness

God's power is as strong as it ever was to forgive sins – even
though the sins of today may seem greater than those of time past.
We cannot out-sin God's forgiveness. But we can leave repentance
and confession too late. Like the men attacking the Capernaum
roof, we need to waste no time in taking our problems to God.
He is always on reception duty.

Suggested Hymns
A debtor to mercy alone; 'Lift up your hearts!' We lift them, Lord,
to thee; This, this is the God we adore; Through the night of doubt
and sorrow

Septuagesima   *Second Service*   Do As You
Would Be Done By   Ps. 10; Num. 22:21–23:12;
Phil. 4:10–20; Luke 6:27–38
'Do to others as you would have them do to you.' Luke 6:31

The whole law

There were two rival rabbinical schools in Jerusalem: one headed
by the hardline, austere Rabbi Shammai, the other by the gentle,
much loved Rabbi Hillel. One day, a young aspirant presented
himself before Hillel, with the challenge: 'You'll make a proselyte
out of me, if you can tell me the whole law while I stand on one
leg!' Hillel regarded him steadily, then quietly replied: 'Do not do
to others what you would not do to yourself. That is the whole
law. The rest is commentary. Go and learn' (TB *Shabbat*, 31a).

When we love those who give us cause to hate, we are emulating
our Father, who loves us with equally little justification. The realization of God's unconditional love is one of the hardest gifts to
accept. How can we cross the high threshold of our pride, into
the very heart of God? Well, we make a start by crossing the
high threshold of pride, unforgiveness and animosity which so
frequently divides us from our neighbour. St John clearly says:
'Those who do not love a brother or sister whom they have seen,
cannot love God whom they have not seen' (1 John 4:20). A law
enforcement officer may temporarily disarm a criminal of his

weapon, but there is only love that can make a deeper impression on the physical and spiritual fronts.

Love without compromise
Love that accepts everything our neighbour does, is capitulation. God asks us to give up nothing that will harm us; but he also requires that we do not lower our Christian standards. If we know that a person is 'without' the law of Christ, we are not to accommodate to it, but rather to show where we stand on the matter – by precept, example, and Christian living. Jesus said: 'No one comes to the Father except through me' (John 14:6). How does this square with the understanding of the millions of believers of other faiths who may acknowledge God, but not Jesus? We need to seek respect for them, while not compromising our own faith; and we cannot do this in our own weakness, but in the spiritual stamina of God.

Christianity is built on a foundation of love – vicarious sacrifice – akin to nothing else; and, as Christians empowered by the Holy Spirit of Love, we are equipped as no other believers to reach out to others with this unique creed. There is nothing of the stoical about Christ's love: it is vulnerable and tender – yet stronger than anything that can come against it.

Emptying yourselves, yet replenished
Loving our enemies, doing good, and lending without looking for recompense (v. 35), seems a recipe for running our spiritual batteries dry; yet the divine balances work so differently from the natural scales, that in giving out we receive more than we ever had before.

> Be still, my soul; thy Jesus can repay,
> From his own fulness, all he takes away.

Katharina von Schlegel, tr. Jane Laurie Borthwick

Whether it is our time, our talents, or ourselves, God's principle works magnificently. As Malachi said: 'Bring the full tithe into the storehouse, so that there may be food in my house; and thus put me to the test, says the Lord of hosts; see if I will not open the windows of heaven for you, and pour down for you an overflowing blessing' (Malachi 3:10). This is not a fair exchange. It is God at his magnificently unfair best.

Suggested Hymns
God of mercy, God of grace; City of God, how broad and far; Lord of our life, and God of our salvation; Ye that know the Lord is gracious

Second Sunday before Lent (*Sexagesima*)
27 February   *Principal Service*
He Came to His Own   Prov. 8:1, 22–31;
Ps. 104:24–35; Col. 1:15–20; John 1:1–14
'He came to what was his own, and his own people did not accept him.'
John 1:11

A light for us
Jesus came, as Simeon had said when he held the child in his arms that day in the temple, as 'a light to the Gentiles'. He did not come only for the Jews (his 'own' people); he came into the world that he had made, and the people there did not accept him. When the angel appeared to the shepherds, on the first Christmas night, he said he was bringing 'good news of great joy for all people' (Luke 2:10). Yet, since most of the Jews did not come to terms with the identity of Jesus, it was little wonder that Peter, some time after Christ's ascension, had such trouble in persuading his fellow disciples to believe that the Gentiles were to have equal rights as believers with Jews.

Slow to recognize
With hindsight, we may wonder why the Jews did not recognize Jesus for what he was – because the Devil and his entourage had no difficulty: 'As the sun was setting, all those who had any who were sick with various kinds of diseases brought them to him; and he laid his hands on each of them and cured them. Demons also came out of many, shouting, "You are the Son of God!" But he rebuked them, and would not allow them to speak, because

they knew that he was the Messiah' (Luke 4:40, 41). These verses show us something which is often overlooked in our reading of the gospels: the ongoing, intensive clashing of God's goodness with Satan's demonic forces. Because this war of wills is generally unseen, it can also be generally unrecognized. And it was the lack of recognition Jesus received that had impacted on John when he wrote the Prologue to his Gospel.

A weapon *par excellence*

It was a tragedy for the Jews, but it need not be so for us. However Satan tries to blind us to Jesus and his work, we have a weapon superior to anything in the Devil's armoury. We have the means not only of counter-balancing the power of evil, but of out-weighing it by a great margin. God has undertaken to supply his troops with all the power at his command: 'Do not neglect the gift that is in you' (1 Timothy 4:14) – 'And God is able to provide you with every blessing in abundance' (2 Corinthians 9:8) – 'The one who began a good work among you will bring it to completion by the day of Jesus Christ' (Philippians 1:6). These are cast-iron, 100 per cent proof promises, as strong as the day they were first made. Jesus in the wilderness was able to conquer Satan every time he opened his mouth and hit the Devil with a promise from God's word. And he told his disciples they would do ever greater things than he had done. Yet sometimes we carry on as though we believed God's power is not what it once was.

A light for all

'Ah, yes, Jesus healed the sick, raised the dead, stilled the storm, and fed the crowds . . .' and now? 'Ah, it doesn't happen like that now!' But in Africa, in parts of Asia, in Latin America, and in many of the poorest areas of Eastern Europe, people are experiencing great miracles, great power, great works of God. 'What has come into being in him was life, and the life was the light of all people' (John 1:4). And why not in Britain? There is no problem on earth too hard for God. His Holy Spirit is more than able to turn people inside-out and right-side-up for God – just as he is doing so powerfully in parts of Russia and China, who do not advertise to the rest of the world that they are Christian countries. If we believe Satan has lost none of his vindictiveness, we should at least give God the credit for maintaining his power too. Jesus still comes to his 'own' people – those who have taken up his challenge. He is also still being rejected by some of them who have allowed other things to come between them and the light. What can *we* do about this, with all the light of Christ at our command?

Suggested Hymns
Light's abode, celestial Salem; Give to our God immortal praise; O Lord of every shining constellation; The spacious firmament on high

Second Sunday before Lent   *Second Service*
Where is Your Faith?   Ps. 65; Gen. 2:4b–25;
Luke 8:22–35

'He said to them, "Where is your faith?" They were afraid and amazed and said to one another, "Who then is this, that he commands even the winds and the water, and they obey him?"' Luke 8:25

'We seemed like grasshoppers'
The stilling of the storm does not show the disciples in a very good light: in fact, Jesus' question implies that their faith had completely gone. They were acting like their ancestors, whom Moses had sent as spies into Canaan, who returned with wonderful tales of the bounty of the land – it even took two men to carry one bunch of grapes. But, they reported, in that land flowing with milk and honey, the people were giants – 'and to ourselves we seemed like grasshoppers' (Numbers 13:33). This may sound defeatist – even ridiculous – but it was enough to ground the whole invading army of Israel. So Israel wandered to and fro on the wrong side of the Promised Land, and waited until the timid generation had given way to one with more courage and faith. God had told the fearful ones to march in and take the land that he had promised them; they should have had faith that he would see them through. God was more than a match for the occupying giants.

Lack of faith
It is the same question, in today's gospel reading. Often we focus on the storm, but the storm is not the central part of the story. The key is faith – or, rather, lack of faith. Jesus had said, 'Let us

go across to the other side of the lake' (v. 22). That should have been good enough for the disciples. They should have had faith that Jesus' words would come to pass, whatever met them between this side and the other. If the Lord of the universe commands a course of action, we can surely believe in faith that nothing is capable of preventing that action. When the wind increased, even when the ship filled with water, the disciples should have hung on to the words of Jesus. Faith-filled words would have given rise to faith-filled actions, and faith would have seen them across. Instead, they took note of the weather, and faith left them – just as their ancestors had taken note of the opposition, without bringing God into the equation. After all, probably the Canaanites, though settled, were really not much bigger than the desert-wandering Israelites. God had been feeding his people, and surely he does not deal in iron rations. And the storm was probably not so very bad: if the ship had been absolutely full of water, Jesus would hardly still have been asleep.

Panic

The disciples shipped a quantity of water and, local fishermen though they were, they panicked. In effect, they were saying the storm was beyond their seamanship. Did they really believe Jesus would let them drown, or would drown himself? Sometimes we may believe God is pointing us in a certain direction, telling us to do something that seems too hard, or illogical, or even unnecessary. If the disciples had exercised their faith, that day on Galilee, there was no storm in God's command that could have prevented them getting Jesus to the opposite shore. There is the reverse of walking by faith. Some are very quick to meet trouble before it comes: to read a high pollen count, and anticipate hay fever; to see the temperature plummet, and think themselves into 'flu. This is calling into being something that is not, until it very soon is.

Speaking positive faith

If 'faith' works in this negative way, it surely works also in a positive way, a 'Jesus way'. Jesus said: 'If you will say to this mountain, be cast into the sea, and doubt not, it will be as you say' (Mark 11:23). Let us pray God to keep a watch on our lips, that we do not forfeit entry into our Promised Land by talking about grasshoppers – or receive a withering rebuke from Jesus when we talk of danger instead of trusting the word of God.

Dear Lord and Father of mankind; Hear us, O Lord, in heaven thy dwelling place; Man of Galilee, will you come and stand by me; Now come to me, all you who seek (*Celebration Hymnal*)

Sunday next before Lent (*Quinquagesima*)
5 March   *Principal Service*   **In the Glory**
2 Ki. 2:1–12; Ps. 50:1–6; 2 Cor. 4:3–6; Mark 9:2–9

'Then Peter said to Jesus, "Rabbi, it is good for us to be here; let us make three dwellings, one for you, one for Moses, and one for Elijah."'
Mark 9:5

In God's will

It is fair to say that Peter did not fully understand what was happening, up on the Mount of the Transfiguration; but his spirit told him things were all right. He and the others were plumb in the middle of God's will. There are times in our lives when 'Rabbi, it is good for us to be here' could not be further from our minds: when trouble, grief, doubts, illness hit us. But then there are the other times, when we can say it with conviction: when God seems close, we have good news. For a time, as Peter experienced, it seems like heaven on earth. And God, who has brought us through the bad time, has borne so patiently with our moans, is saying: 'You see, I love you! I love you so much, I have waited to give you this moment – at the very best time for you!' But, as in the Transfiguration, God loves us too much to keep us on the mountain of mystery and delight: the 'beautiful moment' is a time of revitalizing, enabling us to return to the daily round with new confidence and strength.

Delight in service

It can take a lot of effort to regain spiritual equilibrium, whether after ecstasy or tragedy. But we are well on the way if, with the Psalmist, we can meet God with the affirmation, 'I delight to do your will' (Psalm 40:8). It does not take us to heaven in a single bound – but it helps; for we can do God's work from a sense of duty (as, in fact, we do most of what we do), but to do his work for no other reason than that we love him, is the butter on the bread of duty. On the Mount of Transfiguration, the disciples were given an experience of love and cherishing far beyond the sense of duty: it was God at his most divinely generous. And not only did it encourage Peter and the others, but it also gave them, and us, a glimpse of the Life Hereafter.

Living continuum
It tells us that we do not leave our identity in the grave; we keep our names, our profiles, our looks and our purposes. Moses was there as the prime lawgiver of old, Elijah as the prophet whose mission had been predominantly fulfilled in the lives of John the Baptist and Jesus. We also keep our faculties: speech, language, sight, hearing – and, presumably, smell and taste. Jesus, after his resurrection, enjoyed food with his friends on more than one occasion. It is good to know that, while God may have created us from nothing, he did not create us for nothing. Whatever we do, think, say, write, pray – whatever we fill our lives with here for God, is a preparation for what we shall be called upon to do, hereafter. We do not know the details: even Peter and the disciples, after the Transfiguration, did not know. But, because of that experience, at least we know something of what we shall be. If God had not intended us to meditate on the Transfiguration, to use it as encouragement for what we can do in the way of preparation here and now, we can be sure he would not have shared the experience with us. Jesus could have gone up the mountain on his own, and the disciples need not have known a thing about it.

Take heart
Thank God, it happened as it did. Let us take the experience with us into this year 2000. Let us use it, to give us joy in our ministry, encouragement in our work, and fervour to do our utmost for God – praying, with the fourteenth-century mystic, Richard Rolle:

> *May you lead your life*
> *in light-heartedness;*
> *keep hopelessness far away;*
> *May gloom not remain with you;*
> *but may God's cheerfulness forever sing out merrily*
> *in your life.*

Christ is the world's true light; Christ, whose glory fills the skies;
'Tis good, Lord, to be here; In days of old on Sinai

Sunday Next Before Lent *Second Service*
Through Suffering to Glory   Ps. 2; 1 Ki. 19:1–16;
2 Pet. 1:16–21; Mark 9:2–13

'He said to them, "Elijah is indeed coming first to restore all things. How then is it written about the Son of Man, that he is to go through many sufferings and be treated with contempt?"' Mark 9:12

Wonder of wonders
Perhaps people had become so conditioned to the old prophecies that their fulfilment was still considered to be some time in the future. Such would account for the general unpreparedness with which Jesus and his work and message were met. The Jews had formulated their particular pattern for the Messiah, built up over the years from the scrolls and their accumulated commentaries and interpretations, to suit their expectations. He would be a priestly Messiah, after the order of Melchizedek, restoring the religious heart of the nation and presiding over its worship. He would be a kingly Messiah, of the lineage of David, who would oust the occupying Roman army, and restore the davidic monarchy in Jerusalem. And he would be a wonderfully glorious Messiah, ushering in a Golden Age to put Solomon's in the shade.

Christ incognito
And the Messiah duly came: the priestly Messiah who cleansed the temple, overthrew the moneychangers' tables, and let the sacrificial doves fly free. So, too, came the kingly Messiah, riding in triumph to Jerusalem astride a donkey, feted by the crowds. And, also, came the glorious Messiah, transfigured before disciples and ancient seers. But he went unrecognized, this Son of a carpenter, who talked of suffering and contempt. His message was too simple for sophistication to comprehend.

Ongoing suffering

Sergei Bulgakov, the Russian theologian, once remarked: 'As long as there is evil in the world, the Lamb is still being slain.' Jesus suffers still, while the scars remain from the wounds of Calvary. We cannot comprehend the divine love which laid itself open to such agony. That the realization of such suffering does not shame us out of sinning, is the most solemn wonder of all time: that it was foretold only adds to the poignancy. To the disciples, that a ministry barely begun should end prematurely in suffering, was perplexing enough; that Jesus should embargo their publicizing of the Transfiguration experience, 'until after the Son of Man had risen from the dead' (v. 9), was beyond belief. So it is to many today: we share the gospel with them; we tell them of what Jesus has done for us, what he means to us, what he can do in their lives, if they accept what he is wanting to give. And they walk away. Another nail is driven into the flesh of the Crucified. How much more can he take?

Showing we care that souls are not needlessly lost is difficult; it is less harrowing to surround ourselves by fellow believers. But how, then, will the others hear? Paul wrote: 'I make it my ambition to proclaim the good news, not where Christ has already been named, so that I do not build on someone else's foundation, but as it is written, "Those who have never been told of him shall see; and those who have never heard of him shall understand."' (Romans 15:20, 21). May God grant each of us compassion to share his love, courage to tell of his suffering, and faith to share his risen power.

Suggested Hymns
Oft in danger, oft in woe; Through the night of doubt and sorrow; In the Cross of Christ I glory; When I survey the wondrous Cross

Ash Wednesday   8 March   *Principal Service*
Anyone Without Sin?   Joel 2:1–2, 12–17 or Isa. 58:1–12; Ps. 51:1–17; 2 Cor. 5:20b–6:10; Matt. 6:1–6, 16–21 or John 8:1–11

'When they kept on questioning him, he straightened up and said to them, "Let anyone among you who is without sin be the first to throw a stone at her."' John 8:7

All have sinned

Paul plainly told the Christians in Rome: 'All have sinned and fall short of the glory of God' (Romans 3:23). While we are not to wallow in remorse, we are nevertheless to be mindful that no merit on our part, only the blood of Jesus, stands between us and eternal oblivion. Jesus' blood cleanses us from all sin: large, small, black or pale-grey: every sin in the book (1 John 1:7). There is a strange irony in the fact that it is often so difficult to accept the cleansing power of Jesus: far easier to magnify our sin until our judgement is awry. The woman in today's reading from John's Gospel had committed a sin which is no less frequent today; and, while the Jewish law prescribed stoning, we can assume it was not always carried out. In this case, she seems to have been the excuse for testing Jesus: would he condone the sin and lay himself open to a charge of law-breaking?; or would he condemn the woman and violate his own gospel of love and for-giveness?

The divine option

When all human options appear to be exhausted, God can still act. At a stroke, Jesus gave the woman a new start, and caused her accusers to convict themselves. There are some scholars who query these Johannine verses: certainly they are not found in some of the ancient texts; in others, they are in a different place. But originality need not concern us here; there are too many valuable lessons to be learned, including:

1. We cannot test God and get away with it.
2. God's love is willing to give a sinner another chance.
3. Critics can be their own worst enemies.

Putting God to the test

We all, at some time, try to bargain with God. We tell him what we will do, if he will act (or forbear to act) in such and such a way – and, if he takes us at our word, often we get into a pretty pickle, and the bargain backfires on us as it did on the scribes and Pharisees. 'My thoughts are not your thoughts, nor are your ways my ways, says the Lord' (Isaiah 55:8). He is our Father, and we can with confidence call him '*Abba*' – but he is also God. 'Do not put the Lord your God to the test' (Deuteronomy 6:16). Satan tried, when he taunted Jesus in the wilderness, and Jesus rounded on him with this Deuteronomic command (Matthew 4:7). If we do bargain with God, we are showing allegiance to Satan and not to him.

Another chance
We are not told that the woman taken in adultery was repentant, nor are we told what it was that Jesus wrote on the ground. It probably had a bearing on the woman's predicament, for nowhere else in the Gospels do we find Jesus doing anything aimlessly. Perhaps she did signify her contrition in some way. At any rate, Jesus cleverly removed her accusers, until she stood before him unmolested. A free woman? Not quite: for her sin remained known to God. It was left to the Mediator to come between God and the woman's adultery; and, while she did not compound the offence, she could go free. 'If we confess our sins, he who is faithful and just will forgive us our sins and cleanse us from all unright-eousness' (1 John 1:9).

Do not criticize
Criticism, carping, accusation – all are anathema to spiritual growth. All are contagious, in that we get back what we give. The scribes and Pharisees paid a heavy price for their action. They lost face. We are not asked to overlook sin; but can we not take a spiritual sight-test to improve our recognition of the good, rather than the bad, in others? Giving up criticism for the forty days of Lent could become a longer-lasting habit.

Suggested Hymns
Be thou my vision; Christian, seek not yet repose; Forty days and forty nights; Lord Jesus, think on me

Ash Wednesday   *Second Service*   Alive Again
Ps. 102; Isa. 1:10–18; Luke 15:11–32

' "*But we had to celebrate and rejoice, because this brother of yours was dead and has come to life, he was lost and has been found."* ' *Luke 15:32*

An uncomfortable parable

The Prodigal Son is among the best-known of Jesus' parables, but not the best loved, mainly because it impacts too deeply for comfort. According to the state of our souls when we read it, we see something of ourselves in either the greed, impatience and stupidity of the son who went off to seek the good life – or in the meanness and jealousy of the son who stayed at home, a martyr to duty and good behaviour. And, in the uncomfortableness, we let the climax of the story pass us by. For the climax is not the father's kiss and embrace, nor the gold ring, nor the fatted calf. It is not even the assurance to the elder son, that his inheritance is unaffected by all that has happened. The climax is: 'Your dead brother is alive; the lost is found.'

Over-stating the case?

It is an affirmation Jesus was, by implication, giving to every repentant sinner. Yet, isn't the language over-strong? 'This brother of yours was *dead*, and has come to life?' No, we find it explained in Ephesians 2:1, 'You were *dead* through the trespasses and sins in which you once lived.' Whether we are children, or Christians of many years' standing, there is a lot of mystery about our souls, and how they impose on our physical bodies. The soul is physically indestructible: it cannot die at our hands. But the Devil can destroy it, as Jesus warned: 'Do not fear those who kill the body but cannot kill the soul; rather fear him who can destroy both soul and body in hell' (Matthew 10:28). This soul inside each of us, strong enough to be untouched by physical death, burning or the grave, can be killed by sin: its death is accomplished by the supernatural power of evil. Its resuscitation is accomplished when God responds to the Christian's repentance and atonement, restoring the soul to at-one-ment with God. It is an at-one-ment which recognizes the goodness of God – who, though we owe him so much, demands only our love and repentance, to cancel all debts, all offences.

A surviving relationship

It is only by recognizing our soul's vulnerability to the power of sin, that we can more fully appreciate the sacrifice of Christ, and the reconciliation he has made possible between us and God. When the prodigal son left home he was, to all intents and purposes, dead. In spiritual terms, he was a walking skeleton. But, though spiritually dead, his kinship and status remained capable of revival

– his kinship with his heavenly Father; and, through God, with his earthly family. It is that same kinship which ties us to our fellow beings, whether dead in sin or alive in Christ.

'*This brother* of yours was dead.' The Greek syntax is emphatic: his kinship is undying. The sense of Jesus' words is: 'This man who has come to his senses, is still *your brother*. The Devil has had a fine time with him, taking his money, his house, his friends – but he is still *your brother*.' God never loses sight of his relationship with us, even though at times we may give a fair impression of having become estranged from him. It is an awesome privilege, to be responsible for something as vulnerable, and yet powerful, as a soul. Charles Wesley once wrote:

> *A charge to keep I have,*
> *A God to glorify . . .*
> *Thy servant, Lord, prepare*
> *A strict account to give . . .*
> *Help me to watch and pray,*
> *And on thyself rely,*
> *Assured, if I my trust betray,*
> *I shall forever die.*

Be consistent

It is very dangerous for us to be inconsistent, to blow hot and cold, where our dealings with God are concerned. At Calvary, Jesus looked not on our inconsistency, but on our spiritual potential to be consistent: on the spark of pure life (= soul) in each of us, capable of being saved. In today's parable, we are not told what the elder brother did, after his father's action had sunk home. It is left to us to decide what we should have done, had we been in a similar position.

Suggested Hymns

A charge to keep I have; Forgive our sins as we forgive; O love, how deep, how broad, how high; Rock of ages

First Sunday of Lent   12 March
Principal Service   **Divine Compulsion**   Gen. 9:8–17;
Ps. 25:1–10; 1 Pet. 3:18–22; Mark 1:9–15

'And a voice came from heaven, "You are my Son, the Beloved: with you I am well pleased." And the Spirit immediately drove him out into the wilderness.' Mark 1:11, 12

Into the wilderness

Here, probably more than at any other place in the gospels, we are made aware that Jesus is 'under orders'. God had sent him on a mercy mission, and he had a contract to fulfil. It was a contract so appalling, no one had ever been called upon to accept it before; and if Jesus completed it, no one would ever need to again. By the time he presented himself before John at the Jordan, the first thirty years had been accomplished, to God's satisfaction: 'With you I am well pleased.' And the next phase followed immediately: God drove him into wilderness solitude and temptation.

There are times when we experience spiritual and physical deprivation, and the world attacks us with one test after another. It is easy to believe that somehow we have offended or disappointed God. We search our conscience for a likely reason, and if one does not come to mind we are left feeling aggrieved against a God who capriciously has punished us without due cause. It may come as a shock, to have it spelled out so crudely; but if we do not actually explain it to the 'nth degree, this is how we act. God's driving of Jesus into the wilderness shows us that a time of hardship is not always a sign of divine disapproval: indeed, the scholar who once remarked that 'God only ploughs good earth for his best harvests,' may have a vital truth.

No running into temptation

While Mark's account has the harsh 'drove him', and Matthew's and Luke's the softer 'was led up' and 'was led into the wilderness', none of the accounts leaves open the possibility that Jesus went there of his own volition. He was no moron: he did not court privation or penance. God was the prime mover: it was the Father's will. We are not to seek rigour for rigour's sake – only to promote the gospel of Jesus, and the will of God. This was the two-pronged approach of Jesus to ministry that surfaces constantly in the gospel narratives. He had an aim, and he stuck to it. May we be ever as single-minded. Lent is a time for examining our lives to see whether we are carrying excess baggage. No one is fit to run the race of life encumbered with impedimenta alien to the example of Jesus. With the desert creatures for company, and ministered to by angels, Jesus had forty days to take stock of his life to date, and his ministry to come.

Alone with God
God may have driven him into the desert, but God had not deserted him. He was preparing his 'Beloved' to meet Satan's temptations, to pit his strength against the wiles of the Devil. In divine communion, God gave him just one weapon: his holy word. Jesus was to attack Satan with this weapon every time. Satan even quoted scripture back to him, but Jesus quickly told him: 'Do not tempt God.'

This warns us to be very cautious when dealing similarly with Satan, for the Devil can pass himself off as 'an angel of light'. He can quote scripture as often as it suits him, for he has been with God – before he fell from grace. Far better than we often give him credit for, Satan knows how to gift-wrap suggestions of death to resemble suggestions of life. And sometimes the glitz deceives us. Let us take into Lent this awesome picture of Jesus, the Beloved, being *inspired* to go into the wilderness, to do spiritual battle for *our* sins. No other man has had greater love than this.

Suggested Hymns
How firm a foundation; O, for a closer walk with God; Spirit divine, attend our prayers; Thy way, not mine, O Lord

First Sunday of Lent   *Second Service*
Tell that Fox   Ps. 119:17–32; Gen. 2:15–17; 3:1–17;
Rom. 5:12–19 or Luke 13:31–35
'He said to them, "Go and tell that fox for me, 'Listen, I am casting out demons and performing cures today and tomorrow, and on the third day I finish my work'."' Luke 13:22

A challenge

This was a direct challenge to Herod (Antipas). The Pharisees' warning to flee from Herod's wrath was an oblique threat, which Jesus immediately recognized. His thoughts would inevitably go back to a day, thirty or so years before, when another Herod (the Great) had tried to kill him, and Joseph had been ordered to take his family out of harm's way into Egypt. Jesus is not running from Antipas. He tells the Pharisees exactly where he is going: let Herod kill him in Jerusalem, if he wants to! Herod Antipas, tetrarch of Galilee and Peraea, was the son of Herod the Great and his third wife, the Samaritan Malthace. What he lacked of the questionable statesmanship of his father, he made up for in cunning, hence Jesus' contemptuous title, 'that fox'. It was Antipas who, incestuously marrying his niece Herodias, called forth the wrath of John the Baptist, which led eventually to John's beheading. We are not told that Jesus and Antipas met before the morning of Good Friday, when Pilate, at a loss to know what to do with Jesus, on hearing he came from Galilee sent him bound to Herod, who had come up to the city for Passover. Though not a full-blooded Jew, Herod observed the main feasts and customs when it suited him. On seeing Jesus, he was delighted, for he thought he would be treated to a miracle. Even though this was not forthcoming, Luke gives us a piece of news: 'That same day Herod and Pilate became friends with each other; before this they had been enemies' (Luke 23:12).

That fox

In Jesus' mind could have been the scheming craftiness of Herod, or perhaps the tetrarch's wickedness in ordering the beheading of his cousin John – or even the thought that Jerusalem and the Passion being now so close, Herod could do his worst and the outcome would not be affected. The Pharisees' willingness to be tale-bearers could be used to advantage, to show the fox that this man was not going to panic. How do we react to anyone whom we believe is trying to harm us? Do we take the fight into their territory, or do we calmly walk away from certain conflict, or do we continue with our own work, leaving them to retreat or advance?

Jerusalem's record

Jerusalem had lain like a tawny lion basking in the sun, for centuries of conflict. She had the blood of countless prophets on her hands, and she was soon to have more. Jesus has prayed to his Father, and in Gethsemane he will pray again; yet he knows for his mission to be successful, Jerusalem waits.

The future
The grim future was not hidden from Jesus, as it is from us; and this would surely compound his agony. We can review our own lives, and see what a blessing is the hidden future. Yet Jesus could weep over the city that was to see his crucifixion. Knowing the fickleness and volatility of the crowds who could hail him one day and call for his blood the next, he could still yearn for them as a hen mothers her chicks. The magnanimity of our Lord is astounding. Each of us falls short of his great-heartedness: how short, dare we acknowledge?

Suggested Hymns
Christian, dost thou see them; Lord of our life, and God of our salvation; O, the love of my Lord is the essence; Jesus, lover of my soul

Second Sunday of Lent 19 March
Principal Service **Sacrificial Living** Gen. 17:1–7, 15–16; Ps. 22:23–31; Rom. 4:13–25; Mark 8:31–38
'He called the crowd with his disciples, and said to them, "If any want to become my followers, let them deny themselves and take up their cross and follow me."' Mark 8:34

No smooth passage
Peter could not bear the thought that Jesus would suffer, be rejected and die. So appalled was he by these horrors, he seems not to have heard their sequel, 'and after three days rise again'. Trouble and worry have that effect: their power obliterates hope of recovery, and inhibits rational thinking. 'Get behind me, Satan!' was stern in the extreme, but did it only have the effect of worsening Peter's panic? We have become so conditioned to smoothing life's passage, deadening pain with drugs, alleviating grief with sedatives, choosing the easier of two options – that these words

of Jesus come like an icy douche. We are used to the idea of him suffering rejection and torture: for we know it ended in resurrection and life. But when it comes to applying the suffering to our own lives, it's a different matter. How deep does our commitment go? How much are we willing to suffer, for Jesus' sake? We can probably face ridicule and scorn better than physical damage. But if neither is meted out to us, is it because we are not totally committed to God's work? Does the example of those who are suffering make us feel guilty? These are hard questions, but they arise from our gospel reading for today.

Ashamed of Jesus?
Who has not sat down to a meal, and felt bad about no grace being said, yet has lacked the courage to be the one to say it? A little thing, maybe, but 'because you have been trustworthy in a very small thing, take charge of ten cities' (Luke 19:17). We face the greatest challenge of all time, every minute of the day, as ambassadors for Jesus, to show him to the world – for the world is forever watching us, and judging. Once we realize this privilege, of being Christ's hands and feet, his voice and compassion, it surely gives us the strength to meet one challenge at a time: to deny ourselves, take up the cross, and follow.

Who bears the cross?
Because Jesus loves us more than we can know, and because he knows that he accepted Simon's help in bearing his cross, we do not bear ours alone. Always, Jesus' strength is in front of ours, taking the greater load. Cannot anything be borne, in the realization of such support? Oswald Chambers once wrote: 'The saint realizes it is God who originates circumstances, consequently there is no whine, but a reckless abandon to Jesus ... Be reckless immediately, fling it all out on him. You do not know when his voice will come, but whenever the realization of God comes in the faintest way imaginable, recklessly abandon. It is only by abandon that you recognize him. You will only realize his voice more clearly by recklessness' (*My Utmost for His Highest*). We can safely leave the caution and wisdom to Jesus – and, from the relatively light end of the cross, abandon to him, asking no questions, giving our Lord credit for knowing the way he is leading us.

Art thou weary, art thou languid?; I, the Lord of sea and sky; Take up thy cross, the Saviour said; Will you come and follow me?

Second Sunday of Lent   *Second Service*
Assurance of Faith   Ps. 135; Gen. 12:1–9; Heb. 11:1–3, 8–16

'Now faith is the assurance of things hoped for, the conviction of things not seen ... By faith we understand that the worlds were prepared by the word of God, so that what is seen was made from things that are not visible.' Hebrews 11:1, 3

Approaching in faith
'Let us approach with a true heart in full assurance of faith' (Hebrews 10:22). The author of Hebrews is at pains to emphasize this message of faith. It is an elusive quality: we either have it, or we don't. If we have it, we must use it, or it vanishes. We cannot give it away, but Satan can deprive us of it. Faith cannot be seen or touched (though its effects can move mountains); but it is a firm assurance, a cast-iron conviction, of things that are invisible. And Abraham had it in such abundance, that it moved him to obey (v. 8), to stay (v. 9), to look forward (v. 10), and to receive power of pro-creation (v. 11), which according to natural laws was impossible at his age. At 75, he received God's promise of a son. Twenty-five years of faith later, Isaac was born. Faith overcame all natural hazards, because faith was the inner power that Abraham found was greater than anything the world and the natural order could muster.

Stronger by far
If we take faith on board, we shall experience the spiritual poise that characterized Jesus: the confidence that led him to lie down and sleep in a storm-tossed boat; the confidence that led him to walk through a bunch of rioting unbelievers who wanted to throw him over a cliff (Luke 4:28–30); the confidence that took him through the Passion – because he knew that his superior faith force was going to rip through hell and out the other side, leaving Satan's doors off their hinges. That is truly living the life of faith.

Meeting the opposition

It is living the life of faith when people speak against us, tell lies about us, take our name in vain; when we lose our job, get sick; when everything that can go wrong, does go wrong. Ever since Jesus powered his way through hell and left Satan wondering what had hit him, every tunnel we enter has a blessed opening the other end. With God's faith force on our side, we shall always come out of the darkness; like a cork in water, no matter how people press us down, we shall rise again to the surface . . . if only we have faith. The quarter century must have seemed a lifetime to Abraham; but every night he could go out and recall God's promise of a family that would rival the stars in number. God had changed his name to 'Abraham' ('Father of many nations'). No matter how many people sneered at an old man with no heir calling himself that, Abraham kept faith for the things he hoped for, convinced of those things he could not yet see.

God delivers

For ever, those who are on our side, are greater than the opposition. Jesus told us not to be afraid, not to let our faith slip – when we are ridiculed, persecuted or lied about, for his sake. We are not even to fear those who physically can kill us and still think they are doing God's service; we are to live by faith, not fear, even then. For, let's face it, most people stop short of murder.

Suggested Hymns

At the Name of Jesus; I'm not ashamed to own my Lord; Give me oil in my lamp; My spirit longs for thee

Third Sunday of Lent   26 March

Principal Service   **Seeing is Believing**   Ex. 20:1–17; Ps. 19; 1 Cor. 1:18–25; John 2:13–22

'After he was raised from the dead his disciples remembered that he had said this; and they believed the scripture and the word that Jesus had spoken.' John 2:22

Simply believing

We are called to do what the disciples apparently could not do: to believe without first seeing proof. It is almost incredible to think that more faith is required of us than of the men who were being charged with building the Church. They had Jesus in the flesh, Jesus on hand to help them when they failed (Mark 9:18), Jesus to extricate them from awkward situations (Matthew 17:27). On the other hand, we have the New Testament as well as the Old; and we have the Holy Spirit indwelling us. But our faith needs to be very strong, or we shall not go far. We simply have to believe that Jesus is, God is, our Holy Spirit is – even as we know we are. Sheer, naked faith – or, as a popular song has it, 'Dedication's what you need'.

Slow to understand

On any reading of the gospels, Jesus' disciples, time and again, come across as slow to understand what he was saying. Every time he alluded to the future – his passion, burial and resurrection – the disciples misunderstood. When there was a prophecy as back-up, they comprehended rather better (v. 17). But they did not realize that, even as he spoke, Jesus was writing a *new* scripture (covenant, testament). They, and their misunderstandings, were walking into history – just as we, and our witnessing for Jesus, are walking into a history that is two millennia closer to the Parousia.

My Father's house

It was fitting that Jesus' prediction of his passion should take place in the courts of the temple where held sway the ecclesiastical hierarchs who would howl for his blood. That his actions in evicting the entrepreneurs would fuel the priestly anger, did not concern him. Today, we need this confidence, to take the gospel into places where evil and malpractice are rife. Jesus' action showed the value of taking the fight into Satan's territory: that that territory also happened to be a temple dedicated (officially) to the worship of God, is particularly poignant. It also tells us to beware of compromising where our own places of worship are concerned. Are we, indeed, keeping them primarily for worship, and not accommodating to secular pressures of the times? Money, to some extent, is necessary for repairs and maintenance of buildings; but it becomes a millstone when seen as an end in itself. As the sacrificial doves flew free out of their cages and into the sky above the pinnacles of the temple, Jesus was showing that people need to be free of secular encumbrances, if they are indeed to worship God with all their heart, mind, strength and will. John is the only evangelist to place the cleansing of the temple near the beginning of Jesus' ministry. Of course, it is possible that the event was repeated. But if it was a 'one-off', there are arguments on both sides: if it happened at the start of his mission, it was a way of declaring his intentions; if near the end, it was the lighting of the fuse that led to his arrest and trial. In any case, Jesus was showing that, no matter how secular matters impose, there is a right and a wrong way to use the House of God. May this lesson guide us in our own parochial life.

Suggested Hymns
Be thou my vision; God be in my head; O, for a thousand tongues to sing; We love the place, O God

Third Sunday of Lent *Second Service*
Sheep among Wolves Pss 11, 12; Ex. 5:1–6:1;
Phil. 3:4b–14 or Matt. 10:16–22
' "See, I am sending you out like sheep into the midst of wolves, so be wise as serpents and innocent as doves." ' Matthew 10:16

Divine madness?
St Thérèse of Lisieux once said: 'Our Beloved was *mad* to come down on earth looking for sinners to make them his friends . . . What happiness that he became man so that we might love him. If he had not done so, we would not have dared.' Jesus – mad? Yes, it seems madness to send a flock of sheep among a pack of wolves. Who in his senses would do such a thing? But the so-called wisdom of the world – logic, sense, normality, convention – is turned upside-down by God, and one does not go far before it happens. Then a text strikes a chord in our conscience, and the feel-good factor evaporates. We may squirm inwardly, even close the Bible and busy ourselves with a less provocative occupation. Yet if God is operating in us, that madness we have read about

will not go away. If God has really got hold of us, we may lose some sleep that night.

Open and above-board
Nothing is trivial with God. We may decide a matter is unimportant, yet if it is part of his purpose God will not let us forget it. In Revelation we hear of the heavenly city with its polished floors of gleaming stones – onyx, chalcedony, sardius, topaz ... God does not cover that beauty with carpets: there are no rugs in heaven under which to sweep trivial matters; everything is open and above-board. When God sends us out among wolves, it is as much for the sake of the wolves as it is for us; they are to see, not visibly-defended warriors who will repel any attack, but vulnerable sheep who physically cannot defend themselves. Our Christian armour is under the surface, but primed and ready for any battle.

Steel under the scapular
In 1945, when the religious sisters came straggling back to their convents, in Poland, Hungary, Austria and the other freed countries, outwardly they were walking skeletons; it was said that the only way one could tell a sister was by the steel under her scapular – the unseen force of God which had brought her through starvation, torture and forced labour. And the sheep Jesus sends out among wolves must be wise as serpents and harmless as doves – vulnerable in appearance, but with hidden, indestructible steel under the scapular. It is a steel, a wisdom, which – because it is on God's business – fills 'every unforgiving minute with sixty seconds' worth of distance run,' treating triumph and disaster, success and suffering, with equanimity, attacking life with gusto, regarding nothing as unimportant.

Our full attention
Jesus was what the religious of earlier days called 'recollected': his mind was concentrated on God and his mission. He told his disciples: 'We must work the works of him who sent me while it is day; night is coming when no one can work' (John 9:4). Calmly and steadily, he kept on keeping on. If there is anything standing between us and what God is pointing us to do (and knows we can do), he will keep on reminding us of it, until he has our full attention; because it is then, when he knows he has us simply and

wholly, that we are ready to be sent out among the wolves – to heal and to minister to a community who, in the year 2000, needs the gospel ever as much as in the first century of the Christian age.

Suggested Hymns
Be still, for the presence of the Lord; Jesus, our hope, our heart's desire; Lord, I have made thy word my choice; My God, I love thee not because

Fourth Sunday of Lent (*Mothering Sunday*)
2 April   *Principal Service*   **A Mother's Love**
Ex. 2:1–10 or 1 Sam. 1:20–28; Ps. 34:11–20 or
Ps. 127:1–4; 2 Cor. 1:3–7 or Col. 3:12–17; Luke 2:33–35
or John 19:25–27

'When Jesus saw his mother and the disciple whom he loved standing beside her, he said to his mother, "Woman, here is your son."' John 19:26

A Son's care
Even in his extreme agony, Jesus thought about his mother, and gave her into the care of the disciple whom he loved. This young man, vindictively and tragically crucified in his mid-thirties, made time to provide for his mother. It was a sacred charge, and the disciple at once took on a son's responsibility. Mary had been quietly there over the years, supporting Jesus throughout his ministry, though at Cana she had virtually catapulted him into performing his first miracle. Now, she equally quietly goes on to the next stage of her own ministry. Certainly Jesus must have loved her dearly; and she was as loyal to him as only a mother can be.

Marian traditions
In Eastern Orthodoxy, there are many churches dedicated to the 'Dormition ("Falling Asleep") of the Virgin', since in Orthodox belief Mary died and was buried. In the Holy Land, pilgrims are taken to what is believed by some to be her tomb. By contrast, the

Western Catholic Church observes 15 August as Mary's Assumption, her bodily entrance into heaven. Sadly, in an over-zealous rejection of Catholic Marian belief during and after the Reformation, many Protestant churches neglected or virtually ignored Mary from Good Friday until Christmas. Happily, this situation is now altering. The hymnwriter, John Wyse, wrote in one of his most beautiful Marian hymns:

To live and not to love thee
Would fill my soul with shame.

God's choice

However much or little we understand about Mary, several things are certain: God chose her, above all women, to bear his Son. God's power is infinite; he could have chosen to save the world through Jesus without involving Mary. But he chose her. At a time when women did not have a high standing in society, he chose to give Mary that unique place in his plans. Mary was very special to Jesus. He was God: he did not need a mother; but he loved and cherished Mary. And the love was reciprocated: deserted at Calvary by so many of his disciples, Mary was still there; and it would take real courage for a woman to stay by the cross: how much more, when the victim was her son!

Ave, Maria!

If Mary was worthy of such love from Jesus, surely she is worthy of some from us. When we meet Jesus in Paradise, will Mary be far from him? Whenever death comes, it is *too soon* for so many of us; we think of a myriad of 'if onlys', and seek for reasons, scapegoats, justification and meaning. Mary and the beloved disciple, in the dreadful time between the crucifixion and Easter Sunday morning, must have discussed at length the tragic events that had led to Calvary. Then life brought hope again. We do not know, but perhaps we can reverently surmise, that, when Mary's earthly mission was complete, her entry into heaven would be as special as her risen, ascended Son could make it, for the woman who had been so special to him. May God even give us time to meditate on Mary's ongoing activity there, as today we link her life with that of our own mothers, and of Holy Mother Church: all one in the heart and love of God.

For the beauty of the earth; For Mary, Mother of the Lord; I'll sing a hymn to Mary (*Westminster Hymnal*); O Lord of heaven and earth and sea

Fourth Sunday of Lent *Second Service*
Giving the Best Num. 21:4–9; Ps. 107:1–3, 17–22; Eph. 2:1–10; John 3:14–21

'For God so loved the world, that he gave his only Son, so that everyone who believes in him may not perish but may have eternal life.' John 3:16

Giving above the norm
God loved us so much, that he gave ... And he gave the best he had. He always gives beyond what is merely necessary. The giving of Jesus – the setting aside of his divinity for thirty-odd years, taking the restrictions of flesh and blood, as well as the terrible suffering at Calvary – was an extraordinary way God chose to show his love for us. At times we may miss out on a lot of God's love, simply because we are not expecting it to be shown in the way it is. We can read the gospel accounts of Jesus' life, and wonder why so many people rejected him, and why the disciples were so often caught on the wrong foot. With hindsight, wouldn't we have reacted more positively! Are we currently spending so much time – even in prayer – looking for the ordinary ways of expressing love, that we still fail to appreciate God's extraordinary methods of operating?

What is life?
The English language is impoverished when it comes to 'life'. We say a criminal has been given 'life', and we mean he has been sentenced to years behind bars. We say we have 'life', and we mean that one day this living, breathing body will die. We say Jesus came to give us 'life', and we mean that because of this we shall never die. To clarify matters, we have to use more language: who can mistake a life sentence for human life, or eternal life? Yet the life here and now, is really the proving ground for the eternal lifetime – which is actually time*less*! The life that Jesus came to

bring is not bound by time or space; and while it is offered freely to us, its providing cost God an unimaginable figure.

The longest life sentence
John 3:16 is the longest life sentence ever – yet not to a life behind bars, but to one of limitless freedom; and the Bible gives us precious glimpses of this infinite life. Jesus told his disciples: 'God is the God of Abraham, Isaac and Jacob – yet he is not a God of the dead, but of the living' (Matthew 22:32). Our identities survive the grave, and we do not remain in limbo after death, but carry on living. We live, moreover, with Jesus; he promised his friends: 'I am with you always' (Matthew 28:20). With life or death set over against each other, one may marvel that anyone could ever reject a belief in Jesus. Yet many in first-century Palestine could meet him face to face, hear his teaching, see his miracles, and still reject him. He once told his listeners: 'If people do not listen to Moses and the prophets, neither will they be convinced even if someone rises from the dead' (Luke 16:31). Can we imagine the additional agony this realization gave to Calvary's torture?

No clause of exception
Eternal life is offered to everyone who believes in Jesus. To the Jews of his day, the absence of exclusivity in his teaching must have been a problem. Here was a rabbi who recognized no difference between Jew and Greek, slave and free, male and female (Galatians 3:28). To have the hedge you have built up around you so thickly over centuries of Yahweh-worship, metaphorically torn down before your eyes by the Son of Yahweh, must have been one of the greatest culture shocks of all time.

Into the world
Let us thank God that the gospel eventually left Jerusalem and Galilee: that the earliest, Jewish, disciples were inspired to put the message of Jesus before patriotism. Our debt to Judaism is incalculable. May we never forget our shared theology, in our meetings today with Jewish brothers and sisters.

Suggested Hymns
Eternal light! Eternal light!; To God be the glory; There's a wideness in God's mercy; Jesus, the Name high over all

Fifth Sunday of Lent (*Passion Sunday*)

9 April *Principal Service*   It Had To Be

Jer. 31:31–34; Ps. 51:1–12 or Ps. 119:9–16; Heb. 5:5–10; John 12:20–33

'Jesus said, "And I, when I am lifted up from the earth, will draw all people to myself."' John 12:32

The Passion

How can we fathom the Passion of Christ, as one Man took on himself the sins of the world that had been, the world that then was, and the world that was still to come? Passion Sunday brings into focus the fact that God did not spare his own – and only – Son. His had to be the most awful Passion, to bring about the salvation of countless millions. It had to be. There was a terrible, inexorable inevitability about it. We may sigh, and say, 'Well, if only Judas had realized in time ...' 'If only the Pharisees and Sadducees had recognized Jesus as Son of God ...' 'If only the disciples had not deserted him ...' 'If only Pilate had done what his wife asked him to do ...' No amount of 'if onlys' would have made an atom of difference: in Gethsemane, at Gabbatha, and at Golgotha. Yet we still question, for it goes against the grain to acknowledge that some things are inevitable – that we have not got the answer every time!

Hope ahead

When one is learning a new language, it is a good idea to listen to tape recordings of grammar and conversation. The words sound strange at first: combinations of letters which are pronounced one way in English assume new identities in the other tongue; yet we persevere, because ahead is the hope of victory. Similarly, in a spiritual sense, the Passion is traumatic, yet hope shines ahead. Paul told the Corinthians: 'If for this life only we have hoped in Christ, we are of all people most to be pitied' (1 Corinthians 15:19). Yet some would say it was relatively easy for Paul to preach this, in the dangerous years of the first century. He was old, battered, beaten, persecuted, without a settled home, hated by many, hounded by his own people and the Roman empirical power alike: no doubt Paul often thought longingly of the bliss of eternity.

How much harder it is for today's Christians to long for translation to the heavenly realms. What a lot more we have to leave behind! – things we value as essential, but not one of them carries a passport to eternity.

Emblem of suffering

If nothing else, the Victory of the Cross puts into perspective our journey, our much lesser crosses. Whether we see the cross shrouded (as now on our Lenten altars), or with the crucified figure of our Lord, or as an empty cross, there is an awesome simplicity, a barrenness, even in those two pieces of wood, which never varies. Just an upright and a horizontal – the 'emblem of suffering and shame', as we sing in the old hymn. One piece of wood laid across another, symbolizing the Friday in history when the world's greatest negative force clashed with heaven's greatest positive – and when the two were fused into the greatest victory either earth or heaven had ever known. The cross still points in triumph to the heavens.

> *The head that once was crowned with thorns*
> *Is crowned with glory now;*
> *A royal diadem adorns*
> *The mighty Victor's brow.*

> *Thomas Kelly*

The magnet of the cross draws people to Jesus, where in his body the scars are still visible. Let us, on this Passion Sunday, marvel again, in reverent wonder, that time does not operate where Jesus is now: there is no time available (or necessary) to heal his wounds. They are there, as fresh as the day when they were inflicted: for there is still evil and suffering in the world.

Suggested Hymns

Meekness and Majesty; O my Saviour, lifted; The head that once was crowned with thorns; When Christ was lifted from the earth

Fifth Sunday of Lent *Second Service*
Passover Preparations Ps. 34; Ex. 7:8–24; Rom. 5:12–21;
Luke 22:1–13

'Say to the owner of the house, "The teacher asks you, Where is the guest room, where I may eat the Passover with my disciples?"' Luke 22:11

A tense situation
Jesus knew his crucifixion was imminent. He knew Judas was about to betray him. He knew Peter – the rock on which the Church was to be built – was to deny him before the night was over. All through Jerusalem tension was high. As at every Passover, the Jews were keyed to fever pitch. The Roman army of occupation had had reinforcements drafted in, to cope with possible crowd violence, demonstrations and the like – for militant Jewish groups invariably took advantage of Passover conditions to make trouble. Pontius Pilate, the Roman procurator, had travelled up from Caesarea, as had Herod Antipas, Tetrarch of Galilee. Alongside all of this, God's major work of salvation was being calmly, deliberately worked out.

The Holy Supper
God allows to happen what is meant to happen. It was vital for Christians that the Holy Supper was instituted, for we find Jesus saying: 'Very truly I tell you, unless you eat the flesh of the Son of Man, and drink his blood, you have no life in you' (John 6:53). We are not all called upon to hang physically on a cross; but we are bidden to share in the Lord's Supper, and to become one with him in the bread and wine. That night, the eleven disciples learned many lessons; they would realize, for example, that other disciples had played important roles, apart from themselves. There was the man whom they had met, the man who owned the house, and his family who had prepared and furnished the upper room. Today, the plans and purposes which God has for our lives often include other people – sometimes people whom we should least expect to be involved. We need to be open to his directing; God's plans do not depend on coincidence; he leaves nothing to chance. Each person we meet, in every circumstance, is part and parcel of the divine purpose – brought into focus at the time, or with hindsight.

Obedience works

Another lesson from that night was obedience. The disciples carried out the instructions Jesus gave them to the letter. They did not offer another room; they did not query a man carrying a pitcher (women's work); they did not complain that Jerusalem at that Passover was particularly dangerous. Against the time we hear God's instructions, we should endeavour to keep mind and soul in readiness to respond positively. When God allots us a work, it is useless to protest we cannot do it, because with the command God provides the wherewithal to carry it through. He never asks anything of us that we cannot accomplish. He knows the scope of every talent he has given us; and if we have not realized the number of our talents, we need to go to him in prayer for a revelation of our hidden worth.

Total commitment

A third lesson from the Night of Institution was that of commitment. Jesus was honouring his Father's commitment to save the world. He was prepared to go through with giving his life for us; his body, to make our souls clean; his blood, to wash away our sins. On that night in Jerusalem, Jesus came to the most critical point of his commitment – for within hours of the Holy Supper, he would agonize in Gethsemane, and make the incalculably brave decision to go forward to the arrest, and the horror of crucifixion. It was a night when the disciples, too, were to learn something of the cost of commitment. Judas would realize how wrong he had been, and would commit suicide in despair. Peter would cry as he had never cried before, in remorse at his denials. The other disciples would be lost, bewildered and frightened, as their Master was apprehended. We know that for all, except Judas, it came right in the end – even as, today, we know that however difficult proves our Christian commitment, we shall win through because Jesus won through.

Suggested Hymns

Bread of heaven, on thee we feed; O Jesus Christ, remember; Soul of my Saviour; We hail thy Presence glorious

Palm Sunday 16 April *Principal Service*
Praising through Pain Isa. 50:4–9a; Ps. 31:9–16;
Phil. 2:5–11; Mark 14:1–15:47 or Mark 15:1–39

' "Truly I tell you, I will never drink of the fruit of the vine, until that day when I drink it new in the kingdom of God." When they had sung the hymn, they went out to the Mount of Olives.' Mark 14:25, 26

Praying twice over
The Russians have a saying: 'To sing is to pray twice.' And they have a point: it is possible to say prayers parrot fashion; it is even possible to read the Bible while thinking of something else. But it is very difficult to sing anything without being conscious of the words. Physically, we use more muscles to sing than to speak; even though we may not expend the energy of a Pavarotti, Domingo or Carrera, any singing involves an effort. In today's gospel reading, the Last Supper draws to an end in the upper room. Judas has gone out into the night, to betray his Master. The disciples are confused, apprehensive and fearful of what may be to come. Jesus knows what lies ahead, but he is still going to go through with his sacrifice; and before he leads the way out to Gethsemane, he leads them in the singing of the Hallel, the Passover hymn (Psalm 113–118). If you were on Death Row, with the execution only hours away, would you lead your companions in the singing of a hymn? The bravery of Jesus would not be fully appreciated by the disciples until later. A lesser man would surely have developed 'a lump in the throat'. But Jesus sang. Perhaps the singing gave him extra courage. Certainly God would hear and approve, for there are many instances in the Bible where we are exhorted to sing: sing with the voice of melody; sing a new song to the Lord.

God loves music
No one can read the Bible without discovering that God loves music, and that he wants us to love it, too. We may never know how much hung on that Hallel in the upper room – just as we may not know, time and again, how much hangs on the way we make music before the Lord. But we can resolve to make as much melody for him as we can; the Bible says he has put a 'new song' into the heart of each one of us. The song may be deep inside us, but it is there. Jesus' singing at such a poignant time was not

merely an observation of Passover tradition: he was leaving his disciples a lesson in confidence, to remember when the cruel mockers at Calvary had done their worst. Jesus might have been going to allow them to arrest and crucify him – but he was still in control.

Holy Week

We, too, shall be singing hymns this week – from the triumphant hymns of today, to the Passion hymns and the 'words from the cross'. May we draw closer to our Lord in this music, as it enriches our worship and focuses our minds not only on the events of Holy Week, but on how those events relate to life in the new millennium. Perhaps we can sing a 'new song' to God: a song born of our love and compassion. And, with the example of Jesus before us, can we not resolve to keep worry and grief, foreboding and fear, from depriving us of the faculty to sing? God is faithful: he will hear every note, and will appreciate, as can no one else, the effort and love behind the music.

> *Why should I feel discouraged?*
> *Why should the shadows form?*
> *Why should my heart be lonely,*
> *And long for heaven and home?*
> *For Jesus is my Saviour,*
> *My constant Guide is he;*
> *His eye is on the sparrow*
> *And I know he watches me.*
>
> *Charles H. Gabriel*

Suggested Hymns

Christ triumphant, ever reigning; My song is love unknown; All glory, laud and honour; My heart and voice I raise

Palm Sunday *Second Service* Lost Inheritance

Ps. 69:1–18; Isa. 5:1–7; Mark 12:1–12

'What then will the owner of the vineyard do? He will come and destroy the tenants and give the vineyard to others. Have you not read this scripture: "The stone that the builders rejected has become the corner-

stone; this was the Lord's doing, and it is amazing in our eyes!" ' Mark 12:9–11

A last chance
Time and again in his ministry, Jesus warned the Jews that they were being given a chance to amend their ways, accept him for whom he was, and get themselves right with God. The Palm Sunday crowds who hailed him with joy almost got there; the temple-hierarchs came nowhere near; Jerusalem, as a city, went her own way, unheeding. The tragic irony is nowhere better seen than when Jesus wept over the place he loved so much (Luke 19:41). And, in today's parable of the vineyard, he does not need to spell out to his listeners the implication of the 'tenants'' destruction: they know, but they will still not believe. That is the tragedy. People's belief cannot be enforced: it needs an effort of will, a step of faith, a decision of trust. We either accept Jesus, or we reject him. If we attempt to do both, we either end up lost to history, as were the Palm Sunday crowds – or pilloried for ever, as were the luke-warm Christians of Laodicea (Revelation 3:16).

A time of decision
Palm Sunday, at the start of Holy Week, is a time for deciding how closely we are to follow Jesus through this, the most poignant week of the Church's year. Are we to be loyal, consistent vineyard workers, or are we to avoid the tragic scenes of the Passion, only to meet up with him again in his resurrection joy next Sunday? How can we understand the joy, if we have not experienced the trauma? The disciples had been forewarned by Jesus, but still they were caught off balance. He is looking to us to be *his* salt, *his* light to a world that generally does not know her need. If Holy Week means little to us, we are sadly lacking salt and light, and are of little use to those still outside the Church.

In the vineyard
Grapes need to grow and ripen quickly, with plenty of food and sunshine. If they are short of these, the harvest is poor. They also need constant attention, or again the crop suffers, due to energy being wasted in unnecessary growth. As workers in Christ's vineyard, we are always on duty (does God ever take 'time off'?), always under orders. Holy Week – its message, services, vigils

and liturgical candles, clothes and colours – highlights the way of the Cross. Do we let Jesus tread this way alone, again? Do we try to go it alone? Can we not introduce someone to Jesus, as he undergoes so much, as one of us, for us? Let the pathos, the cruelty and the eventual triumph speak to those who as yet have not committed themselves to God. Every vineyard needs its journeymen and apprentices: they are the next generation of professionals.

The 'A' team?
And how professional is our Christian status? God asks for a tenth of our time and talents, but do we give it grudgingly, or do we give more than the basic requirements? When we have become serious in our Christian walk, and give our utmost for the sake of the Christ who gave his all in Holy Week – well, then we are being businesslike with God. We are honouring our contract of divine employment: not like the fickle crowds that first Palm Sunday; not like the carping, vindictive ecclesiastical hierarchs of the Jerusalem temple; not like the wicked tenants of the vineyard in today's parable – but as salt and light to a world desperately in spiritual need of both.

Suggested Hymns
Ride on! ride on in majesty; Christ is our cornerstone; We have a gospel to proclaim; Ye that know the Lord is gracious

Monday of Holy Week   17 April   Great Love
Isa. 42:1–9; Ps. 36:5–11; Heb. 9:11–15; John 12:1–11

'Jesus said, "Leave her alone. She bought it so that she might keep it for the day of my burial. You always have the poor with you, but you do not always have me."' John 12:8

Mary, a sinner
St John says the woman who anointed Jesus was Lazarus' sister Mary. St Luke in his gospel tells us she was a sinner (Luke 7:39). Some believe she was Mary Magdalene, who had been a prostitute in Magdala, and had later been healed and forgiven by Jesus. Now her dark days are over. Lazarus, her brother, has been raised from

the dead, and apparently their house at Bethany is the nearest to a 'home' that Jesus enjoyed in his ministry years. Mary has been forgiven so much, she wants to give generously; so she chooses the most expensive oil she can buy. Her loving act made such an impression that it has been recorded in each of the four Gospels (Matthew 26:6–13; Mark 14:3–9; Luke 7:36–50; John 12:1–11). Some of the details vary – as stories in our newspapers differ according to the memories, data and observations of individual reporters.

Judas the treasurer

From John we learn that Judas was the treasurer of Jesus' ministry team. He had charge of the cash, and distributed some to the poor, and some for the disciples' housekeeping. But he was a thief, and misappropriated funds from the bag. Therefore it was sheer greed and hypocrisy, when he complained that the expensive perfume could have been converted into funds for the poor. It can be very hard, when we decide to do something really special, in God's name, and our motives are misunderstood and criticized. Until Jesus expressed his appreciation of Mary's loving act, she would feel very small and confused; probably she wished to be anywhere else, as the scent filled the room, every eye turned in her direction, eyebrows went up and tongues began to wag. Sometimes God allows us to work for him in secret. At other times, he makes sure our work is known abroad. As Mary found, it is at times like that when God has to know best. Magdala and Bethany were small places: many at the meal would still think of 'Mary the Prostitute'. But now she was to be known for a very good reason.

Friend of sinners

Jesus, as the Friend of sinners, gives everyone a chance of redemption – otherwise, with our very first sin we would all be beyond the point of no return. Mary had had much forgiven. In gratitude, she gave of her best while the opportunity was there. 'You always have the poor with you,' said Jesus, 'but you do not always have me' (v. 8). It can be difficult to put God's work even before helping others. Both are important. But we need to be sure which comes first. These are uncomfortable words of Jesus: while this earth is extant, we shall have poor people around. Why does it have to be? Often folk say – at times jokingly, at times with no humour: 'There is no justice in this world!' They are quite right. There is not. And God never said there would be. 'The poor will always be with you . . .' 'In the world you face persecution . . .' 'You will hear of wars and rumours of wars . . .'

> *Trials dark on every hand,*
> *And we cannot understand . . .*
> *And we wonder why the test,*
> *When we try to do our best . . .*

> When morning comes

Yet Jesus tells us to get our eyes off the problems, and to seek first God's kingdom. A Chinese pastor, who spent more than twenty years in prison for his faith, once said: 'In approving Mary's action at Bethany, the Lord Jesus was laying down one thing as the basis of all service; that you pour out all you have: your very self, unto him. And if that should be all he allows you to do, that is enough. It is not first of all a question of whether "the poor" have been helped or not. That will follow. But the first question is: Has the Lord been satisfied?' (Watchman Nee, *The Normal Christian Life*)

Suggested Hymns
All for Jesus; Blessed are the pure in heart; What a Friend we have in Jesus!; Said Judas to Mary

Tuesday of Holy Week   18 April
Life Springs Again   Isa. 49:1–7; Ps. 71:1–14;
1 Cor. 1:18–31; John 12:20–36
' "Very truly, I tell you, unless a grain of wheat falls into the earth and dies, it remains just a simple grain; but if it dies, it bears much fruit." '
John 12:24

The falling grain
Jesus did not say, 'Except the wheat is sown . . .' or 'unless someone sows it'. God's purposes will go on, whether or not we are a part

of them; but in his love, through the indwelling Holy Spirit, when we do become involved, he can use our participation to work out what he has already worked in, and in his good time great things can happen; so long as we do not tell ourselves that we are indispensable, God will use us in ways we could not ever have imagined were possible. We are wonderfully made, with a potential so great we cannot reach it this side of the grave. Our faith can be made to blossom into a beauty so far removed from our present state – just like the lovely shoot that emerges from the seemingly inert, bare grain.

Dormancy or death?

The poppyseeds in Flanders' Fields, buried under stones, buildings and machinery from warfare, laid dormant in dark, dry conditions until warmth, moisture and light, with man's intervention – and without it – broke their dormancy, and beauty came to cover what was dreadful and sepulchral. The first-century Jews saw the seed 'dying', because it was buried in the earth, and never re-emerged. Instead, what came up was a green shoot bearing no resemblance to the seed. Up it came, thrusting through the soil above where the seed had been interred – to all intents and purposes, a new thing. It is the same, says Jesus, with our harvest. We sow seed. Something more beautiful comes to light. Can we not recall an instance in our life, when from a very small (perhaps unwelcome or misunderstood) beginning, emerged something really beautiful for God? – something to which we can now look back, and say: 'God redeemed that situation in a truly wonderful way.' As the grain of wheat dies and is seen no more, so the body that dies will be seen no more. But from it, building on what it contained, will be something so much more beautiful, as to be a new body. Yet, as we learn in many places in the Bible, recognition of the person whom we are, survives. And why not? The little grain of wheat may die; but the lovely fresh shoot that emerges is not barley or rye or sorghum or maize: it is still wheat. Our identity, the person we are, all the characteristics by which people have known us on earth: this is the artistic painting of our lives; but the picture frame, the body surrounding the person, will change.

The Russian wheat bowl

In the house of Russian Orthodox Christians stands a little bowl of wheat grains, as a continual reminder of John 12:24. The

Russians look at these grains, and are reminded daily that the family and friends laid to rest in the churchyard are not completely dead, but live on as the people whom they are; and will one day be clothed with a different body, to be re-united with their loved ones. The little wheat grains, so closely associated with harvest on earth, speak more clearly than words of the greater harvest of heaven. We plant our inherited grains – our time and talents – in fertile soil, with prayer. God will give the increase: he will effect the resurrection. It is our job to see that we bring in the best harvest we can.

Suggested Hymns
Fill thou my life, O Lord my God; Lord, through this Holy Week of our salvation; Sow in the morn thy seed; Will you come and follow me?

Wednesday of Holy Week   19 April
The Betrayer is Known   Isa. 50:4–9a; Ps. 70;
Heb. 12:1–3; John 13:21–32

'After he received the piece of bread, Satan entered into him. Jesus said to him, "Do quickly what you are going to do."' John 13:27

All is known
Had Judas imagined Jesus did not know of his treachery? Probably so, since the receipt of bread, after Jesus' statement that he was giving the food to the betrayer, caused Judas to lose his head – 'Satan entered into him'. By his singling out of Judas Jesus brought the matter to a head. He was doing what his Father required. Judas now had to do what Satan was telling him to do. There was a hideous inexorability about it all: so horrible, that to the other disciples it was unthinkable. We must not judge them: so often we shut our eyes or walk away from unbelievable horror and trouble, for all the world as if that will make it go away. Today we are just hours away from the yearly remembrance of the betrayal. Had it been a stranger who fell so low, the crime would have been bad enough: that it was a member of the innermost circle of Jesus' friends, plumbed the depths of evil. The Psalmist

100

had also known a friend to play him false: 'It is not enemies who taunt me . . . But it is you, my equal, my companion, my familiar friend, with whom I kept pleasant company; we walked in the house of God . . .' (Psalm 55:32–34).

God's gift of free will

Note that Jesus did not attempt to dissuade Judas. The betrayer had chosen to steal from the ministry funds; he now chose to go through with Satan's temptation to betray Jesus. He could have chosen otherwise; but God, who had known him from before he was born, also knew that Judas would listen to Satan first. We are not automatons: every day we make choices, some good and some bad. That is part and parcel of our Christian life. And it is disturbing to realize that someone as close as Judas was to Jesus, could nevertheless make such accommodations to Satan. It is a lesson against complacency: there, but for the grace of God, go we. So where does the gift of free will take over from our destiny? Or, are the two inextricably intermingled? Jesus said: 'The Son of Man goes as it is written of him, but woe to that one by whom the Son of Man is betrayed! It would have been better for that one not to have been born' (Matthew 26:24). It had been prophesied that Jesus would be handed over to the authorities. Yet, how precise was the identification? We can reverently posit that Judas had not been singled out from the beginning, though of the Twelve it would seem that he showed the greatest tendency to sin. We trot out statistics for aircraft disasters, and predict the likelihood of engine failure. And the disasters occur – seemingly at random, for we cannot predict that a certain aircraft, at a certain time and place, will come down, nor the number and extent of injuries or fatalities.

Prayer makes a difference

If we catch ourselves compromising with Satan, we need to leap back on to the straight and narrow, with the agility and skill of an Olympic athlete. The first step along the Devil's way is all too rarely the last. Judas' example is a terrible warning. From what we read of him, his prayer life cannot have been very strong. Let us not lose our contact with God. But let us also cherish our free will. With God's grace, it can make this world a better place, and survive into the next.

Prayer is the soul's sincere desire; Jesus, grant me this, I pray;
Praise and thanksgiving, Father, we offer; Thy way, not mine, O
Lord

Maundy Thursday   20 April   Washing the
Disciples' Feet   Ex. 12:1–4 [5–10], 11–14; Ps. 116:1–2,
12–19; 1 Cor. 11:23–26; John 13:1–17, 31b–35

*'And during supper Jesus, knowing that the Father had given all things
into his hands, and that he had come from God and was going to God,
got up from the table, took off his outer robe, and tied a towel around
himself. Then he poured water into a basin and began to wash the
disciples' feet . . .' John 13:3–5*

Why their feet?

Rabbi Jochanan used to say: 'If one rises, and a verse comes into
his mouth, behold, this is like a little prophecy' (TB *Berakot*, 3a);
and a verse from Ephesians seems to link itself with this gospel
reading: 'As shoes for your feet put on whatever will make you
ready to proclaim the gospel of peace' (Ephesians 6:15). It is, at
least in part, an answer to the question: Why, at the supper in the
upper room, did Jesus not anoint, or wash, the disciples' heads,
if this was to be a symbol of their baptism-for-mission? Why their
feet? It was because, prior to this, the disciples had been arguing
about their social status in heaven. The foot-washing was to teach
them humility and service. Had Jesus anointed their heads, this
would more clearly have defined the 'master-servant' relationship;
instead, the foot-washing showed to the disciples that the man in
high office was the servant of all.

The time of testing

In this humble act, we see something of Jesus' awareness of what
is to come. For the past six months or so, he has been warning
the disciples that his 'hour' is coming. It has now come. But,
instead of dwelling on his own agony, he concentrates on preparing his friends for the job they will have to do. Though he had
prepared the disciples for a major event in store, he had not dwelt

on the cross. He emphasizes it now – but they don't understand. From this point on, we can sense an estrangement: the disciples are suddenly unsure of their Lord, of themselves, of their position. They don't understand the foot-washing. They sense something awful is about to happen. Their time of testing has begun. And now Jesus opens his heart to them: from now on, until the last verse of his long exhortation and prayer, John has Jesus time and again warning of his cross – but never without also foretelling his resurrection.

Slaves' work
The washing of the master's feet was a menial task not required of the Jewish slave, but of the slaves of other nationalities (*Mekhilta*, Exodus 21:2). We live in a world where convention, despite free thinking and a lot of licence, still rules society to a large extent. According to the gospels, Jesus was not overburdened by convention – and nowhere more so than in the upper room that night. The disciples were embarrassed. Peter, as usual, protested, only to call forth the rebuke: 'Unless I wash you, you have no share with me' (v. 8). Today, we too need to let Jesus make close contact with us. We need the contact, and the cleansing it brings. We may be Christians, but there is no automatic switching on of God's power in us, or his love for us: we can block the power, and negate the love, by refusing to let him come close. To the Jews of the time, symbolism meant so much. John, reviewing the life of Jesus, saw that this washing of the feet, because of who instituted it, was the only way to have fellowship with him. By the washing, Peter and the rest would be completely cleansed and prepared for their mission.

> *Wash me, and make me all thine own,*
> *Wash me, and mine thou art,*
> *Wash me, but not my feet alone,*
> *My hands, my head, my heart.*
>
> *The atonement of thy blood apply,*
> *Till faith to sight improve,*
> *Till hope in full fruition die,*
> *And all my soul be love.*
>
> Charles Wesley, 1707–88

For ever here my rest shall be (*Methodist Hymnbook*); Let us break bread together; O thou, who at thy eucharist did pray; Love is his word

Good Friday   21 April   *Principal Service*
'I Have Written'   Isa. 52:13–53:12; Ps. 22; Heb. 10:16–25 or Heb. 4:14–16; 5:7–9; John 18:1–19:42

'Then the chief priests of the Jews said to Pilate, "Do not write, The King of the Jews, but, This man said, I am King of the Jews." Pilate answered, "What I have written I have written."' John 19:21, 22

Procurator Pilate
Pilate had been procurator of Judaea since AD 26. There had been blips along the way – as, for instance, at the outset of his tenure, when he had marched his troops into Jerusalem under cover of darkness, with the Imperial standards raised; when dawn broke, and with it the storm of Jewish protest, the standards had had to be lowered; and again, when he had ordered a Galilean bloodbath, having misread the situation and inflamed anti-Roman feeling even more. But in general Pilate seems to have trodden the Judaean minefield with commendable skill, and with more understanding of the Jewish mindset than is sometimes allowed him. Philo tells us that Pilate was 'by nature obstinate and stubborn'. He must also have been an opportunist, to have survived for so long in one of the most difficult and least desirable positions of the time.

At any cost?
Pilate knows the chief priests have brought an innocent man to trial: for a death sentence, at any cost. He has no love for this complicated, volatile, religious race. They want a conviction, at any cost? He will make them pay. His contempt for the Jews is heightened by the realization that he has been cleverly 'set up'. Much of the charge is mysterious to him; but he latches on to the 'kingdom', and uses it repeatedly: 'Are you the King of the Jews?' (John 18:33). 'So you are a King?' (John 18:37). 'Do you want me to release for you the King of the Jews?' (John 18:39). 'Shall I

crucify your King?' (John 19:15). This last elicits the strange reply: 'We have no king but the emperor.' And with this, the hunter has been snared; Pilate has scored what to his Roman mind would seem a valuable point.

The titulus

As Jesus is led out to Calvary, Pilate sees an even better chance of venting his anger and frustration on the Jews. He orders the titulus to be written: 'Jesus of Nazareth, the King of the Jews.' Now no Jew can run to Caesar with a complaint against Pilate: the titulus ensures the implication of attempted Jewish insurrection. It also means – and more importantly for us – that Jesus is crucified under a valid legal, and regal, title. He will, in effect, reign from the tree. In the end, the people did 'take him by force to make him King' (John 6:15). The titulus was in Hebrew, in Latin and in Greek – the national, official and common languages (or, the religious, social and intellectual ones). Pilate almost certainly went to especial trouble over it – even though polyglot notices were then fairly common – for we do not hear of a titulus on either of the other crosses.

Paradise today

If Pilate's titulus had not been written, we may never have known the precious words of comfort from Jesus to the penitent thief (Luke 23:43). Once dictated, the wording on the titulus was irrevocable. The three languages proclaimed to the crowds gathered in Jerusalem for the Passover, the universal Kingship of Jesus. Unconsciously, Pilate had confirmed Jesus' own words: 'You say that I am a King. For this I was born, and for this I came into the world' (John 18:37). All four evangelists mention the titulus, but it is John who draws out the difference between the Jews (who present Jesus to the procurator as a 'criminal') and Pilate (who consistently calls him a King).

Did it have to be?

Was it all predestined? Jesus knew in advance that Judas would betray him. Are we to believe that the actions of Caiaphas, Herod and Pilate were predestined? Surely not. We may have a fair idea of what a close friend may do in a certain situation – but he is still a free agent, and responsible for whatever action he takes. While the events in Jesus' life were inevitable, the individuals acted according to their inclinations, each man knowing that he could do otherwise. God's most daring and dangerous gift to us is free-will. But would we respect a God who shackled us? Yes, we may well respect him – but we should find it hard to love him. 'What I have written I have written.' There is a dreadful, sonorous finality in the two perfects; and they teach us the need for constant awareness that our words – spoken and written – have the potential to outlive us on earth. What we have written so far in our own Book of Life,

we have written.

Suggested Hymns
Beneath the cross of Jesus; Man of sorrows! What a name; O sacred head; There is a green hill far away

Good Friday *Second Service* What is Truth?
Pss 130, 143; Gen. 22:1–18; Col. 1:18–23; John 18:38–42
'Pilate asked Jesus, "What is truth?"' John 18:38

The sinless One
Paul, quoting Psalm 14, tells the Christians at Rome: 'There is no one who is righteous ... all have turned aside' (Romans 3:10, 12). Each of us has a character that is flawed. Only one Person was truly sinless through and through: and it was perfect humanity which stood before Pilate that morning, and baffled the procurator with his purity. We do not know how 'truth' was defined in Jesus; but somehow it set him apart. Pilate was out of his depth, and he knew it. Whether his was a cry of anguish, despair, desperation, anger or contempt, after he had faced Jesus with the question, he turned and went out. 'What is truth?' No, it is not merely the opposite of falsehood. John tells us in the Prologue to his Gospel: 'The word [Jesus] was full of grace and truth' (John 1:14).

Truth is ...
The ancient Greek philosophers called truth 'the sum total of the reality of the universe of God, and the correspondence of the

known facts of existence with that reality'. We can see it a little plainer in the New Testament, where (particularly in John's Gospel) truth is represented in the life and person of Jesus. In spite of his silence when Pilate asked the question, Jesus is seen as living truth, truth-in-the-flesh. Not only was he 'full of grace and truth' – he was 'the way, and the truth, and the life' (John 14:6). Jesus was, at one and the same time, the goal (life) of our perfection, the path (way) by which it was attained, and the reality (truth) undergirding that life. It was his purpose to teach his followers truth, in order to make them free. They were to worship God in spirit and in truth.

The comforting truth

The 'Spirit of Truth' was the Comforter, whom Jesus promised to send to us after he had returned to the Father; but the world would not recognize the Spirit of Truth, because it neither saw nor knew him. Jesus, the 'true vine', told his followers that they were branches of that vine; and because of this link with him the Spirit of Truth would be able to lead them into all truth. Today, it is easier to focus on Jesus on the cross, than as a sort of spiritual amalgam of grace and truth. But John, in recording this strange question from Pilate, intends us to try. 'Everyone who belongs to the truth listens to my voice,' Jesus told Pilate (John 18:37). Pilate did not belong. Truth stood before him, bruised and bleeding, and the Roman could not understand.

Truth's opposite

Since the opposite of truth is falsehood, it comes as no surprise to find Jesus in John's Gospel defining the Devil as 'a murderer from the beginning, [who] does not stand in the truth, because there is no truth in him. When he lies, he speaks according to his own nature; for he is a liar and the father of lies' (John 8:44). But we, says Jesus, will know the truth, and the truth will make us free. Yet often, it seems, lies and falsehood surround us, while truth is at a premium. The world understands those who compromise. But with those who stand with Jesus, the world had a problem; it misrepresents, ridicules, cold shoulders, and even does its best to 're-educate' them. There is still a Pilate waiting to meet us, at every turn, with the now despairing, now sneering question: 'What is truth?' We can pray that God will lead these questioners to a knowledge of the truth, through us – even as Pilate, having come into contact with Jesus on that fateful Friday morning, was moved to write the titulus which so truly gave Jesus his kingly title. Then the question will not have been asked in vain.

Suggested Hymns
Alas! and did my Saviour bleed; At the cross, her station keeping; Glory be to Jesus; When I survey the wondrous cross; His are the thousand sparkling rills; Forgive them, O my Father

Easter Eve 22 April (*Any service other than the Easter Vigil*) The Sealed Tomb Job 14:1–14 or Lam. 3:1–9, 19–24; Ps. 31:1–4, 15–16; 1 Pet. 4:1–8; Matt. 27:57–66 or John 19:38–42

'Pilate said to them, "You have a guard of soldiers; go, make it as secure as you can." So they went with the guard and made the tomb secure by sealing the stone.' Matthew 27:65, 66

A time of respite
The trauma of Calvary is over: the revelation of Easter Day is not yet here. Today is a time of hiatus, of respite. If we have followed our Lord along the Via Dolorosa, we shall stand in need of the quietness and suspense of Easter Eve. Pilate is still wondering: 'Make it as secure as you can,' has an implicit doubt that anything they do will not be effectual. Jesus had promised the penitent thief: 'Truly I tell you, *today* you will be with me in Paradise' (Luke 23:43). If, therefore, we are to believe that the soul is translated into Paradise immediately at death, then however the remaining body is disposed of – whether by burial on land or sea, or burning – is immaterial to the purpose of God. In the case of Jesus, the same would apply, even though there was to be a bodily resurrection: if the tomb had been an underground cavern, infilled by tons of masonry after the burial, the purpose of God would not have been affected. This is one of the saddest portions of scripture. The people for whom Jesus had suffered so much are suspicious even of what might happen to his 'lifeless' body. Do they think Calvary was not the end? Is there a doubt that, perhaps, even now, something will happen in the tomb?

The canker of suspicion

Jesus had told his friends that he was 'the truth': perfect simplicity and integrity – the very opposite of suspicion and falsehood which now racked the Jews. Today, in this time for reflection between tragedy and triumph, let us take stock of our spiritual integrity. How single-minded for God are we? If we are harbouring suspicions about others' intentions, or even questioning our own beliefs, can we not bring these into the open before God, and allow him to guide us into the truth of the matter?

There were no winners in the machinations to seal the tomb: the chief priests and Pharisees lowered themselves still further in Pilate's estimation; they were forced to admit the possibility of a resurrection, albeit obliquely; and, as we know, their efforts were wasted labour; and after the event they were forced into another tissue of lies and intrigue, in perpetuating the falsehood that the disciples had stolen the body while the guards slept on duty.

A tangled web

They had trapped Pilate into ordering the crucifixion; they had seen Jesus die on the cross; they had marked the tomb of Joseph of Arimathaea; and yet all this tragedy had not washed out the venom from their hearts. There is much to be learned here, about the dangers of allowing a grain of suspicion into our minds: one grain can mature into a plant that can twist its poison into every fibre of our being in a very short time.

Waiting for the morning

We cannot mourn as Mary and the disciples mourned that first Easter Eve, because we know what tomorrow will bring. But we can wait, as the body of Jesus waited in the tomb; we can wait, and use this time to reach out in prayer for any we know who are in trouble, who do not yet value the cost of Calvary, for whom tomorrow will be like any other day. Especially, we can lift in prayer those recently bereaved, for whom Easter can be a time of bitterness. But, because a certain grave could not remain sealed against God, no other grave can ever be permanently a home for the dead.

> *Where, O death, is your victory?*
> *Where, O death, is your sting?*
>
> *1 Corinthians 15:55*

Easter Vigil 22/23 April **Easter Joy** Ex. 14:10–31; 15:20–21; Ps. 114; Rom. 6:3–11; Mark 16:1–8

'They had been saying to one another, "Who will roll away the stone for us from the entrance to the tomb?"' Mark 16:3

God ahead of us
The problem of the great stone had not prevented the women from setting out for the tomb; but it loomed larger, the closer they came. 'Who will roll it away for us?' We can only admire the faith that kept them walking. Would the guards be there? A disciple? Not knowing how they would get past the boulder, they nevertheless kept on. When we have a problem that we know is beyond us, do we keep pressing on, or do we right-about-turn, and leave it to someone else to solve? Or do we carry on in faith that, because we have shared it in prayer with God, we can have confidence that he will be one step ahead of us, all the way through?

The empty tomb
To those who query the empty tomb, we can reply: the Jews had the choice of believing in the resurrection or producing the body of Jesus. If, as the Jews alleged, the disciples had stolen the body, how could a Man bearing the crucified's wounds appear to several hundred people and convince them? Much has been written and debated about how the image of a crucified man was impressed on the Shroud of Turin: how were the wounds preserved on the resurrected body, if the body was not that of Jesus?

Easter celebrations
Much of the world celebrates Easter, though to many of them it is a secular holiday. Yet as the morning lightens the long dark night, we get a glimpse of the joy those women experienced as they saw the stone had been rolled back; they met the young man; and they were told the good news. God had truly been ahead of

110

them, all the way: the young man was full of the new future, and who they were to meet. Already the tomb was past history; life had left its wrappings there, and had moved on, never to return. Jesus many times had foretold his resurrection. Had the disciples agreed it was so unlikely as to be impossible? And would we, if faced by an unlikely act of God, also deem it impossible, not worthy of belief? The candles, flowers, cards, coloured eggs, lengthening days, a long weekend holiday, and spring growth brightening the gardens . . . all make Easter special. It is easy to forget that the first Easter Day's joy only began to dawn towards evening for most of the disciples, when Cleopas and his companion returned to Jerusalem from Emmaus. The women's news, earlier in the day, had been rejected as impossible.

Peter remembered
Despite gaining the victory over death and hell, Jesus could remember Peter, in torment after his threefold denial. When the women repeated the young man's message to the disciples, what would be Peter's reaction? Almost certainly, a numbed disbelief. Peter, the rock on which the Church would be built, did not accept the resurrection joy until that evening. It reminds us of Pharaoh, in the days of the plagues, asking Moses to beg God to take away the plague 'tomorrow' (Exodus 8:10). Who in his right mind would voluntarily endure a plague for an extra day? Can we not marvel that the disciples, longing for their Master's return above all else, similarly chose to postpone their acceptance of it for nearly twelve hours? May we have the grace and courage to accept God's gifts as soon as they are given. Can we *now* share the Easter joy with others?

Suggested Hymns
Early morning. Come, prepare him; Good Joseph had a garden; Light's glittering morn; The day of resurrection

Easter Day 23 April *Principal Service*
'I have seen The Lord' Acts 10:34–43 or Isa. 25:6–9;
Ps. 118:1–2, 14–24; 1 Cor. 15:1–11 or Acts 10:34–43;
John 20:1–18 or Mark 16:1–8

*'Jesus said to her, "Do not hold on to me, because I have not yet ascended
to the Father. But go to my brothers and say to them, 'I am ascending
to my Father and your Father, to my God and your God.'"' Mary
Magdalene went and announced to the disciples, "I have seen the Lord."'*
John 20:17, 18

A converted woman
From the depths of depravity and sin, Mary had been cured by
Jesus: raised by grace to friendship with Christ himself. He had
removed her sins, so far as the east is from the west; and she loved
him so much, she came back to the tomb as soon as the sabbath
was over. In a city packed to the walls with passover crowds, and
the problems that such crowds always bring, Mary had the courage
to go out alone in the dark of early morning, to a tomb which she
would still believe was being guarded by unfriendly men. She
came, she saw a dark hole where the stone should have been, and
she ran, in panic and terror, until she found Peter and John. Yet
her courage and love made her return with them to the tomb. This
was a woman who owed all her life to Jesus. Would we have
returned, through crowds where some would be sure to say:
'There's the prostitute Magdalene. What's she up to, now?' And,
when Peter and John had returned to the city, would we have
stayed, with only abandoned grave clothes and a gloomy cave for
company?

True discipleship
We can call it love, or faith. Whatever it was that kept Mary at
the tomb till her risen Lord arrived, it was the stuff of true discipleship: the love and faith which, while not understanding, yet
remains firm. And Mary's discipleship received the great reward
of her being the first to see the resurrected Jesus. What a confirmation of her loyalty and devotion! What a divine assurance, if
such were still needed, that her sins had indeed been forgiven!
Lazarus – raised to die again – had come out of his tomb still

wrapped in grave clothes. Jesus would never need his winding-sheet again. The linen had served its short purpose, and now lay neatly folded on the slab in the tomb. There was a finality about the orderliness which spoke louder than words.

The resurrection body
It was Jesus who met Mary: of that she had no doubt. Yet he had changed: she was not allowed to hold him to a certain place. For thirty-odd years he had been restricted to earth's environment: but now he was free, to come and go between earth and heaven, through time and space, just as he had been since the world began. It was going to take his friends some time to come to terms with his resurrection body: a body that bore the wounds of Calvary, could still operate through the senses, could assimilate food – and yet could appear and disappear at will. They had had a foretaste of this on the Mount of Transfiguration: now it applied all the time.

Christ is life
Once we are born into this life, we have no option but to die. When the time comes for our transition to the next life, Christ (Life itself) takes care of the change-over. We do not usually dwell on the thought of our death: our long-range schemes give us implicit hope of being around long enough to fulfil them; but Easter Day brings into sharp focus the end of one stage and the beginning of the next. When Jesus met Mary outside the tomb, he was already looking forward to his ascension; but he wanted his friends to know and to share the experience with him. Easter's joy is not solely concerned with the past, but with the present and future – in the realization that because of the resurrection the divisions that man places between these three periods have been rendered obsolete.

Alleluia! Christ is risen!
He is risen indeed! Alleluia!

Suggested Hymns
Ye choirs of new Jerusalem; Now the green blade riseth; Alleluia, Alleluia! Hearts to heaven; Jesus Christ is risen today

Easter Day *Second Service* **The Lord Has Risen Indeed!** Pss 114, 117; Ezek. 37:1–14; Luke 24:13–35

' *"The Lord has risen indeed, and he has appeared to Simon!" Then they told what had happened on the road, and how he had been made known to them in the breaking of the bread.'* Luke 24:34, 35

The empty tomb

There had been plenty to talk about, as these two disciples set out for Emmaus; but their mood was glum, for they believed the body of Jesus had been stolen. Worry had them so tightly by the throat that they could not recognize Jesus when he joined them – until he re-enacted the Last Supper. But we might have been no quicker on the uptake. It is easy to allow worry to paralyse our minds. Hindsight is a wonderful enlightenment; but we are treading on dangerous ground if we depend on hindsight. Jesus was quick to remind Cleopas and his friend that they should have used the scriptures properly; read them, learned them, and applied them. This is a vital lesson for us today; for while the earth endures, the scriptural truths and prophecies are no dead letter.

The women's testimony

The women had not been believed. What does it take, to induce belief? Jesus had said, so truly: 'If they do not listen to Moses and the prophets, neither will they be convinced even if someone rises from the dead' (Luke 16:31).

Zeal for the truth

The Jesus of the Emmaus road was not the calm, impassive figure of Veronese, or Leonardo, but the vibrant, risen Christ, burning with holy zeal – not for the nominal allegiance of his followers, not for Christians with a 'faith of convenience' – but for whole-hearted, fully committed disciples, who could believe when belief seemed out of the question. We read in the gospels about his compassion, tenderness and long-suffering; but we also read of times like this, when he could be impatient, especially when he found those who by intellect, integrity or from long association with the things of God, were well equipped to believe, but who did not.

Jesus the teacher

Yet even on these occasions, he gives us a chance: he took time to explain the scriptures to the two disciples; from Isaiah, he would show the necessity of his suffering; from Daniel, he would explain how the Messiah had had to be sacrificed, in order to fulfil his destiny. He would show how the sacrifice and exile of the goats on the Day of Atonement had been superseded by his greater, once-for-all, sacrifice . . . 'This man knows his scriptures!' Yet still they did not recognize him.

Revelation

Lessons learned at Emmaus are lessons also for us today, if we are to recognize our risen Lord. God chooses the times of his visitations. He is always there in time of need. Sometimes his greeting is a justified rebuke. If we welcome him, he will teach us. When we are back on course, he retires and gives us space to share and deepen our faith; but in his good time, he returns. Cleopas and his friend were disciples, even as we are. But we would not have earned the rebuke: 'How foolish you are, and how slow of heart to believe!'

Would we?

Suggested Hymns

The Lord is risen indeed; Come, ye faithful, raise the strain; Jesus lives! no longer now; The strife is o'er

Second Sunday of Easter   30 April
Principal Service   **'My Lord and My God!'**
Acts 4:32–35; Ps. 133; 1 John 1:1–2:2; John 20:19–31

'Although the doors were shut, Jesus came and stood among them and said, "Peace be with you." Then he said to Thomas, "Put your finger here and see my hands. Reach out your hand and put it in my side. Do not doubt but believe."' John 20:26, 27

The answer to doubting

Sometimes God asks us to do the most extraordinary things. We may do them without seeing their strangeness, until, as we look back in wonderment, we say: 'It must have been God-in-me doing that. *I* should never have dared!' Who, after all, would ask to thrust a hand into a gaping incision somewhere behind a person's ribcage? Yet Jesus took Thomas' request literally. But when the time came, Thomas found he could not touch the precious wounds. He had asked to do something so great, but when commanded to do it, he broke down. 'My Lord and my God!' And Jesus is stern with him: stern, but still loving.

Bargaining with God
Sometimes we are like Thomas: perhaps not so daring, but nevertheless trying to strike a bargain with God: 'Lord, I will do this – if you give me a really clear instruction – if you sort out this other problem first – if I find I can't do it my way . . .' It may be that God replies by giving us such a clear instruction that, like Thomas, we take spiritual fright. One day, like Thomas, we shall come face to face with those same wounds. We can become sophisticated, sanitized, in our religion, away from the impact of the wounds. But Easter shows us we need the shock of the wounds, to recognize the resurrection. Without sight of them, the disciples may have thought he was someone else – or a ghost.

A Father's love
God loved us so much, not only to be wounded for us, but also to carry those wounds for ever. We have been bought with a price that is greater than we can imagine. For our sakes, God became vulnerable. Something of the shock of this realization is surely seen in Thomas' 'My Lord and my God!' Until that day, not one of the disciples had called Jesus 'God'. Centuries before, in the time of Moses, the people had been told that no one could see the face of God, and live. Did those words race through the minds of the disciples, as they stared on their risen, wounded Lord?

Easter's message
Easter and its message is not the stuff of which 'rational' explanations are made. It is, rather, the opportunity for God to give us answers to prayer. A research scientist from mainland China was recently asked: 'How do you know there is a God? How do you know Christianity is real?' His answer was brief, but hard-hitting: 'By the way prayer is answered, it is obvious that God exists.' At Easter God answers our prayers, not as an ethereal ghost, aeons

116

away from human experiences, but as a Man who voluntarily stooped so low as to live life on our level for a time; a Man who still, and for ever, bears the scars to prove it.

Suggested Hymns
At the Lamb's high feast we sing; Come ye faithful, raise the anthem; This joyful Eastertide; Good Christian men, rejoice and sing

Second Sunday of Easter *Second Service*
Christ Resurrected Ps. 143:1–11; Isa. 26:1–9, 19; Luke 24:1–12

' "Why do you look for the living among the dead? He is not here, but has risen. Remember how he told you, while he was still in Galilee, that the Son of Man must be handed over to sinners, and be crucified, and on the third day rise again." ' Luke 24:5–7

Remember how he told you
When we are planning a journey, usually much preparation is involved. If, for one reason or another, the trip is postponed or cancelled, we feel, justifiably, that the preparation time has been wasted. But there is one journey where preparation time is never wasted: one journey which at times may appear to have been postponed, but which will not be cancelled. Yet often we avoid preparing for this particular journey. Before Christ's resurrection, there may have been some excuse for going towards death without much preparation, yet people did debate the subject: the Pharisees of Jesus' day, for instance, believed in life beyond the grave, while the Sadducees denied it. After the resurrection, the apostles, particularly Paul, were plied with questions on the subject.
Q. Who actually saw Jesus after his resurrection?
A. Peter; the other apostles; more than five hundred disciples (many of whom were still around when Paul wrote); James, and many others; Paul himself (on the Damascus Road); and, on the resurrection day itself, Mary Magdalene, Mary the mother of Joses, Salome and Cleopas and his friend at Emmaus. This is an impressive range of witnesses.

Q. Accepting Jesus was resurrected, does this mean that others will rise from the dead?

A. Yes – it cannot be otherwise, or Jesus' resurrection would not have been necessary. 'If for this life only we have hoped in Christ, we are of all people most to be pitied,' is how Paul puts it (1 Corinthians 15:19). Jesus is the first, but not the only one, to rise from the dead.

Q. What will be the sequence of resurrections?

A. Jesus, having risen already; then those who belong to Jesus – those who have already died; and then those who are still alive when he comes, 'will be caught up in the clouds together with him to meet the Lord in the air' (1 Thessalonians 4:17).

Q. Who are Christ's?

A. Those who have been baptized. Paul tells us there would be no reason for baptism, if there was to be no resurrection life. And Jesus tells us that those who believe and are baptized will be saved (Mark 16:16).

Q. How are the dead resurrected?

A. By the old body finishing its earthly existence, and being translated by God into another existence.

Q. What other existence? (i.e. What body shall we have in the resurrection?)

A. The body decided for us by God. Paul gives us the illustration of wheat. Bare grain is sown; a more elaborate harvest is reaped: much more beautiful, bountiful, useful and mature. Flesh and blood cannot inherit the kingdom of God: in the resurrection, we shall all be changed. This is a fact, but it is also a mystery. Can we not look at the beautiful flower which has grown from a bare seed, and have faith that our transformation will be correspondingly more lovely than what we see, and are, now?

Search the scriptures

The fact that such questions and answers are part and parcel of holy writ shows that God appreciates we are inquisitive and exploratory by nature. He made us that way, and he wants us to have more than a passing interest in the eternal life Jesus has made possible for us. It is, after all, one way of acknowledging our gratitude for the effort Jesus cared enough to make. One day we shall certainly make the transition from this life to the next; our reservations have already been made, our visas written, in the garden of Joseph on the first Easter Day.

Third Sunday of Easter   7 May
Principal Service   **Why are you Frightened?**
Acts 3:12–19; Ps. 4; 1 John 3:1–7; Luke 24:36b–48

*'Jesus himself stood among them and said to them, "Peace be with you."
They were startled and terrified, and thought that they were seeing a
ghost. He said to them: "Why are you frightened?"' Luke 24:36–38a*

God sees to the heart
Man looks on the outward appearance, but the Lord looks on the
heart. Why, then, if God knows us so well, does he allow us to
be afraid of so much, so often? It is because, having given us the
gift of free will, he does not impose his will; he does not compel
faith. If we are afraid, it is because we have chosen to fear. Paul
told Timothy: 'God did not give us a spirit of cowardice, but rather
a spirit of power and of love and of self-discipline' (2 Timothy
1:7). In today's text, Jesus might have appreciated the shock his
resurrection appearance would give his friends: the amazing thing
is, he does not expect them to be afraid. He even asks them to
look at the ghastly wounds. Dare we ask: 'Why should not the
disciples be frightened?' We are told that the 'cowardly' will head
the list of those who earn the 'second death' in the lake of fire
and brimstone (Revelation 21:8). It is a sobering thought that the
fearful will go into the fire ahead of the 'faithless, the polluted,
the murderers, the fornicators, the sorcerers, the idolators, and all
liars'. On the night of the Galilean storm, Jesus asked the disciples:
'Why are you afraid? Have you still no faith?' (Mark 4:40). According to this, faith and fear cannot co-habit in a person.

The Psalmist's commitment
The Psalmist's confidence is good for all seasons: 'With the Lord
on my side, *I do not fear*' (Psalm 118:6). The Church world-wide
is battling physical persecution as well as apathy and indifference;
but on the home front are countless lesser fears that try to eat

away our faith daily: fear of failure, of pain, of losing a friend, even of strange noises in the night.

The Easter challenge
Jesus had only a short time left on earth after the resurrection; that he used so much of it in telling people not to fear shows the importance of this question. We must pray for help and strength to banish fear; the harder we pray, the less we can fear. Concentration on Jesus and his point of view can oust fear; the disciples had learned this lesson by the time Jesus left them; instead of being devastated at the loss of their Master, they were able to return to Jerusalem 'with great joy, and they were continually in the temple blessing God' (Luke 24:53).

> Give to the winds thy fears;
> Hope, and be undismayed;
> God hears thy sights, and counts thy tears;
> God shall lift up thy head.

Paulus Gerhardt, 1607–76, tr. John Wesley, 1703–91

Suggested Hymns
Alleluia, alleluia, give thanks to the risen Lord; Commit thou all thy griefs; To the Name of our salvation; How firm a foundation

Third Sunday of Easter *Second Service*
Convincing Faith Ps. 142; Deut. 7:7–13; Rev. 2:1–11; Luke 16:19–31
'"If they do not listen to Moses and the prophets, neither will they be convinced even if someone rises from the dead."' Luke 16:31

Faith – or reasoning?
It is taken for granted in today's world that the intellect is important on every occasion. We argue interminably, sometimes over the silliest matters, to score a point: not to lose face. Since it takes two to argue, one is going to lose face, whatever the outcome.

Theological students analyse the word of God, blue-pencilling, red-pencilling – until it is something of a miracle that any emerge with faith at all; yet God is there, in the seminar and tutorial, working out his will through men and women from varying backgrounds, countries, cultures. He – perhaps he alone – knows what he is about. Those who listened to Jesus were on the same tack. 'You will not truly believe in me, even though I were to rise from the dead!' This was Jesus' message, though he wrapped it up in the parable of Dives and Lazarus.

Wesley's faith

Faith is not come by lightly. It needs to be pursued; no one has ever been handed faith on a plate. And there is no guarantee if one is in the Church, that the battle has been won. John Wesley lived and died in holy orders; but there was a time when he almost went under through lack of faith. Peter Böhler, a Moravian, strengthened him: 'Do not, on any account, neglect the gift you have been given,' he counselled. 'Preach faith, until you have it; then preach it because you have it.' Aldersgate, and Wesley's 'second conversion' followed soon after this; but many of his writings deal with the pre-Aldersgate period of blackness – a time called, centuries earlier, 'the dark night of the soul' by St John of the Cross. Was that the price Wesley had to pay, for a fertile, muscular mind? It was a price, certainly – but surely not inevitable.

Catherine's faith

Catherine de Hueck Doherty – Russian Catholic missionary, nurse, writer and founder of the Madonna House chain – used to say: 'To press into the will of God, we need to fold the wings of our intellect, until God in his richness fills us with himself, until he tells us what he wishes our work to be.' As Christians, we are in the hot seat: just like Catherine, Wesley and Jesus. The rest of the world is watching us. It knows we are different, but it doesn't know why. It watches as we meet trouble, sickness, death. With the over-intellectual mind that the world prides itself on having, it is forever analysing, calculating, weighing our words and actions. Often it is as far from the truth as was Dives, in his assessment of Lazarus, Abraham and the whole question of morals, neighbourliness, goodness and faith.

The value of the intellect
God has given us minds to get alongside his thinking, not ours; his way of working, not ours; his laws of love, of freedom, service and commitment – not ours of self-seeking, bondage to convention, earthly logic and self-will. We must be thankful for these vibrant, thinking, reasoning minds: thankful for our robust mental health. Here is Catherine again: 'If we give up our intellect to God, at his request, he will return it to us, cleansed of all that is not of him.' But if our intellect comes between our seeing God at work in us and others, then may God in his mercy put before us yet again this parable of Dives and Lazarus; and may we get our priorities firmly back on to Christian rails.

Suggested Hymns
I know that my Redeemer lives, what joy; Have faith in God, my heart; Christ triumphant; God's Spirit is in my heart

Fourth Sunday of Easter   14 May
Principal Service   **The Good Shepherd**
Acts 4:5–12; Ps. 23; 1 John 3:16–24; John 10:11–18

' "I lay down my life for the sheep. I have other sheep that do not belong to this fold. I must bring them also, and they will listen to my voice. So there will be one fold, one shepherd." ' John 10:15, 16

New life
As a shepherd in first-century Palestine daily led his flock to new pastures, so Jesus daily leads his followers towards new life. When the shepherd leads his flock, the animals do not start arguing whether or not they have come to the right field; nor do they go into a huddle over the precise botanical definition of each grass blade. They accept the change in their life, and adapt to it. What is behind, is behind: they can never eat that particular food twice over. So it is with our spiritual lives: if we make ourselves available to God, he will lead us on to new experiences and situations. Perhaps the new experience is painful, and brings us (spiritually, if not physically) to helplessness and confusion for a while; but

then we discover that God is with us in the new situation, and joy replaces tears.

The Easter experience
Mary Magdalene's was a tearfulness that turned to joy at the tomb. Thomas' was a doubting which took a week to be resolved. We, too, may find that getting to grips with a new experience takes time: we agonize, and pray, and seem to lose spiritual ground. Then, often when least expected, there is God showing us the very thing we had longed to see . . . and the way ahead is clear. In sheer joy and relief that God loves us more than we had thought possible, we step out in faith along the road where he is leading. However we respond, may it not be like Caiaphas – so wrapped up in the suffocating mass of man-made regulations, that spiritual vision is severely restricted. The truth of a new situation may be staring us in the face, but because it is different from our preconceived notions, we do not see it.

> *If our love were but more simple,*
> *We should take him at his word;*
> *And our lives would be all sunshine*
> *In the sweetness of the Lord.*
>
> Sir Frederick Faber

Accepting the Shepherd's gift of life
This acceptance seems to be so difficult – because it is so simple! Why do we put obstacles in the way? Why cannot we simply believe that Jesus rose, to give us Life? Why does the human mind have such a problem with what is not seen, unmeasurable – something that survives the human frame? It rests deep within us, this indefinable 'something', this strange, enigmatic part of us which no bullet, persecution, poison, pain or disease can touch. To the Hebrews, it was *nephesh*; to the Greeks *pneuma* or *psyche*; to the Romans, *spiritus*. And we? The English language speaks of the *soul*. It is the 'spark of pure life': invisible to human eye, incapable of measurement; unknown to science; unidentifiable by DNA count. Yet we know it is in us, or we should not be able to relate to God.

123

Pure life
As the shepherd calls each of his sheep by name, and they respond;
so, when God calls to us (through the Bible, worship, prayer,
people, situations), we respond, by means of the spark of pure life
inside us. Pure life calls to pure life – on earth, and beyond, as
the shepherd's care for his sheep is translated into Jesus' care for
our souls: 'I came that they may have life, and have it abundantly'
(John 10:10).

Suggested Hymns
Loving Shepherd of thy sheep; The Lord's my Shepherd, I'll not
want; How sweet the Name of Jesus sounds; There's a wideness
in God's mercy*

Fourth Sunday of Easter   *Second Service*
The Sign of Bread   Ps. 81:8–16; Ex. 16:4–15;
Rev. 2:12–17; John 6:30–40
*'So they said to him, "What sign are you going to give us then, so that
we may see it and believe you? What work are you performing?"' John
6:30*

Signs for belief
When John was in prison, he sent his disciples to ask Jesus if he
really was the Messiah. 'Go back and tell John what I am doing,'
Jesus replied. The signs spoke for themselves. Similarly, when
Nicodemus came to Jesus, he opened the conversation: 'Rabbi, we
know that you are a teacher who has come from God; for no one
can do these signs that you do apart from the presence of God'
(John 3:2). Nicodemus, the intellectual, believed on Jesus *because*
of the signs. John the Baptist had doubts *despite* the signs. The
people in today's gospel reading, who had been fed from a minus-
cule five barley loaves and two fish, did not believe they had been
candidates for a miracle: they saw Jesus as a sort of first-century
caterer – a provider of physical food, rather than heavenly bread.

* In some hymnals, this begins: 'Souls of men, why will ye scatter'.

Five thousand people had received a sign – and they merely translated it into a free meal. No one in the crowd is recorded as having expressed surprise at the miracle; only the disciples recognized it for what it was.

The true bread
Jesus is at pains to explain to his listeners the difference between earthly and heavenly bread, but there is an underlying impatience in his words. Mark records more of his explanation: 'Why are you talking about having no bread? ... Do you not yet understand?' (Mark 8:17, 21). Surely it is thrilling to know we have a Saviour who gets excited about our progress in faith; who gets impatient when we are slow to grasp his message; who loves us intensely; who cares, and watches, and prays for us ... rather than an impassive God who merely gives us our Bible rulebook and then sits back and allows us to muddle through as best we can, not caring if we go astray.

Our reading of God's signs
How God must love it when we respond by getting really enthusiastic in our determination to know Jesus and to read correctly the signs of God's will for us! Apart from Judas, the disciples made good in the end. As Paul said – truthfully, if not too modestly, of himself: 'By the grace of God I am what I am, and his grace towards me has not been in vain' (1 Corinthians 15:10). It is only by God's grace that we are given the ability to discern his signs. The old prophets were fond of praying: 'Lord, if I have found grace in your sight ...' It is a good way to approach God at any time: 'If I have found grace in your sight, Lord, reveal to me your will ...' We need to pray for right discernment: Paul warns us, 'even Satan disguises himself as an angel of light' (2 Corinthians 11:14).

The signs are there
Jesus has guaranteed not to leave us to fend for ourselves (Matthew 28:20); so his signs are there, if we can only find them. And still he may become impatient if we fail to see or to act on them. Once missed, a particular sign may not be repeated – or it may be given in a different form. As ever, God reserves to himself the right to do the unexpected.

I saw the grass, I saw the trees (*Celebration Hymnal*); At even, ere the sun was set; Praise to the Holiest in the height; Thou didst leave thy throne

Fifth Sunday of Easter   21 May
Principal Service   **The True Vine**   Acts 8:26–40;
Ps. 22:25–31; 1 John 4:7–21; John 15:1–8

'"*I am the true vine, and my Father is the vine-grower. He removes every branch in me that bears no fruit. Every branch that bears fruit he prunes to make it bear more fruit.*"' *John 15:1, 2*

The grower's care
In the true vine, every branch comes under the divine scrutiny of the grower: no unfruitful growths are allowed to remain, and those which are producing a crop are trimmed in order to do better. This is viticulture at its best, but it is lovingly ruthless. God is not tender-hearted enough to work on the premiss that 'while there is life, there is hope'; we are here to produce fruit for his kingdom. As James says: 'Faith without works is dead' (James 2:17, 20, 26). When Jesus sent out his first gospel preachers he told them firmly to meet unbelief by shaking the dust from that place off their feet and going on to the next town (Matthew 10:14). The branch has had its chance. This is caring, at its holy best. But, how can we practise it? Are we really to share the gospel, and then to leave the rest to God? What about our elaborate 'follow-up' procedures, or week-by-week nurturing?

Ecclesiology has its place
Christ came to found the Church, and it has – by and large – done him proud, in two thousand years. Its structures are stronger than its divisions. Yet we can become so used to the intricate workings of parochial religion, that missionary outreach takes a back seat. There are still many millions of people in the world to be evangelized before the Parousia. God is no respecter of persons: he will get the work done; if we do not do it, someone else will:

someone who has been inspired to respond to the vine-grower's pruning.

> *Now the pruning, sharp, unsparing,*
> *Scattered blossom, bleeding shoot;*
> *Afterward the plenteous bearing*
> *Of the Master's pleasant fruit.*

J. R. Miller, DD, Come ye Apart

Encouragement through pain

Pruning does not invariably mean pain. The main pruning of a vine takes place in the dormant, winter season, when the branches can be cut hard back to the main stem, without the risk of 'bleeding' which would deprive the plant of vital sap. So God can train his fruiting branches in a painless way, depriving us of nothing that will injure us. But there is also a summer pruning, when excess growth is trimmed back, so as not to waste the vine's energy, and also to allow sunlight on to the ripening fruit. There is often some bleeding of sap at this pruning – but the improved harvest more than compensates. So at times we can bleed, spiritually, if not physically, when God's pruning knife cuts into our excess zeal, or when he allows a searingly honest light to show up facets of our lives we would rather remained hidden. Even our well developed structures – of church, business and family life – may come under the vine-grower's knife; and it can be hard to accept that a time has come to jettison or modify a tenet, habit or tradition that has outgrown its usefulness.

Always a greater harvest ahead

Fruitful branches are pruned regularly: while they live, they are always in need of training. We can never sit back in satisfaction that we have realized our full spiritual potential. This should keep us always alert; always keen to experience more of God's love; always ready for yet another challenge. Is this year going to see our best harvest yet?

Suggested Hymns

Love's redeeming work is done; Love divine, all loves excelling; Now the green blade rises; Within our darkest night

Fifth Sunday of Easter *Second Service* Go and Tell Ps. 96; Isa. 60:1–14; Rev. 3:1–13; Mark 16:9–16

'And he said to them, "Go into all the world and proclaim the good news to the whole creation." ' Mark 16:15

And can it be?

Written at some remove from the earlier part of Mark's Gospel, these verses tell of a Christ who rose from the dead – and of disciples who at first refused to believe he was still alive. Even so – however strong or weak their faith – they must take the gospel out from Judaea to every country in the world. Their message must be the good news of Jesus, giving people hope of remission of sins and eternal life. And the reason for this hope? – because the Man with whom they had lived for three years was none other than the Son of God. People would be saved from eternal oblivion by accepting baptism and believing in his Name. Condemnation – in the simplest terms, to be cut off from the love of God – waited for those who rejected the gospel message. The writer is brutally frank.

From east to west

Jesus had said, Go into all the world; but he had also told them to wait in Jerusalem until the Holy Spirit had been given (Luke 24:49). And obediently the disciples stayed in Jerusalem. Sure enough, at Pentecost the Spirit came down (Acts 2); but then, in the euphoria following the drama, they continued to stay . . . until such terrible persecution hit Jerusalem, they were forced to flee to Pella; there, they fully woke up to the missionary call, and began to take the gospel further afield. By that time, God had raised up a man brimful of missionary fervour, a man who had taken up the challenge with so much zeal, he could later with justification say: 'I am the least of the apostles, unfit to be called an apostle, because I persecuted the Church of God. But by the grace of God I am what I am, and his grace towards me has not been in vain. On the contrary, *I worked harder than any of them* – though it was not I, but the grace of God that is with me' (1 Corinthians 15:9, 10).

God with us

Jesus did not send out his disciples without spiritual back-up. He promised to be with us always (Matthew 28:20); he gave us the Holy Spirit (John 15:26); and he assured us that the Father is with us, because Jesus and the Father are one (John 17:11). This is a great power source combination to tap into: it is still here for the claiming, though many would-be Christians still refuse to accept and avail themselves of what is on offer. This power is a multiplied power: the power of Father, Son and Holy Spirit – without division, separation or contamination – and without end. Our scientists wax enthusiastic about DNA: chains of cells in our bodies, which can break, or be altered or destroyed by the forces of sickness, disease or decay. But our spiritual DNA is permanent: the absolute, unending power of God. Why is it, then, two thousand years after Jesus gave the great commission to evangelize the world, we have not yet managed the work?

Suggested Hymns

From Greenland's icy mountains; Lord, her watch thy Church is keeping; Tell out, my soul, the greatness of the Lord; We've a story to tell to the nations

Sixth Sunday of Easter   28 May
Principal Service   **Chosen by God**   Acts 10:44–48; Ps. 98; 1 John 5:1–6; John 15:9–17

' "You did not choose me but I chose you. And I appointed you to go and bear fruit that will last, so that the Father will give you whatever you ask in my name." ' John 15:16

To one and to all

The Greek may be plural: 'I chose *you* [all]', but the message is also to the individual. God is no respecter of persons; whether he is speaking to Peter, Augustine, Francis, Martin Luther King, Reinhard Bonnke or John Smith, he says: 'I chose you.' Each of us has been chosen to do a job, and to play a part in his Church, that no one else has been called to do. We can choose whether we respond, or not; if we accept the challenge, God will expand our calling; if we reject it, God will choose someone else (who will not fulfil the calling precisely in the way that we would have done, but God will still get his work done). It is not our job to fulfil someone else's mission, or to copy their particular calling. When Peter, flushed with enthusiasm after receiving his unique, triple commission, asked about someone else's work, Jesus told him to mind his own business. Perhaps Paul had something of this in mind, when he wrote: 'The body does not consist of one member, but of many ... But, as it is, God arranged the members in the body, each one of them, as he *chose*' (1 Corinthians 12:14–18f.). Everyone, each in his own way, is needed in the body of Christ; but we are not to jockey for the positions of other members – just as the ear would make a poor job of seeing, the nose of hearing, or the legs of smelling. Yet we all belong to his body (Ephesians 5:30); we interact, but do not take over another's function.

Christ's body, the Church

The Church of Christ, with its divisions and tensions, its varying observances and the so-called 'insuperable' obstacles against unity, still comprises people whom Christ has 'chosen'. What a great heart of love he has! Were he other than Christ, surely he would have given up on us long ago! We do great work, by the wonderful grace of God; but how much greater work could we do, if we had unity in this vast body of Christ! Unity between east and west, Catholic and Protestant, Evangelical and Charismatic! As chosen individuals, can we not pray ever more fervently for guidance from God as to how we, each in his own vocation and ministry, can help to achieve that unity for which Christ prayed (John 17:11)? James tells us: 'The prayer of the righteous is powerful and effective' (James 5:16); and Jesus himself tells us in today's reading: 'The Father will give you whatever you ask him in my name.' In the Bible we find God's ear being bent; God even changing his mind about a matter; great things being brought to pass – by the persistent, fervent prayer of his chosen ones: not always of a nation, or a township, or even a household – but an individual. In the blessed realization that individuals matter to God, may we use to the full the authority, privilege and honour God has given us, in the power of prayer in Jesus' name.

Come down, O Love divine; Jesus, the name high over all; Prayer
is the soul's sincere desire; The Church of God a kingdom is

Sixth Sunday of Easter   *Second Service*
Servus Servorum   Ps. 45; Song of Sol. 4:16–5:2; 8:6–7;
Rev. 3:14–22; Luke 22:24–30

' "The greatest among you must become like the youngest, and the leader
like one who serves. For who is greater, the one who is at the table or
the one who serves? Is it not the one at the table? But I am among you
as one who serves." ' Luke 22:26, 27

Greatness is service
St Teresa d'Avila was more than a match for the bishops of her
day, who tried to prevent her founding one Carmelite monastery
after another; and she was one of the most devout mystics of six-
teenth-century Spain; but she was also bountifully endowed with
humility, and would not only set starry-eyed postulants scrubbing
the monastery floors, but would also get down to the work herself: a
true servant, serving God and those around her. There is an ongoing
danger today of being so heavenly minded, that we end up being
no earthly use to ourselves or others. Jockeying for status did not
die out with the first generation of Christian disciples.

At several points in his ministry (e.g. Mark 9:34; Luke 9:46),
Jesus warned against pride; and nowhere more clearly than in his
parable of the two men going to the temple to pray (Luke 18:9–
14); but he delayed the most poignant lesson until the Last Supper,
when, as is variously reported in the gospels, he not only taught
the lesson in today's reading, but also took a towel and water and
washed the disciples' feet (John 13:4–16). With hindsight, the force
of the lesson would be apparent to the disciples, whose self-
seeking, betrayal, denial and disbelief had been met with sacrificial
love and service.

Broken bread and poured-out wine
There are some who believe that a Christian is misguided in working at full stretch for God: that 'burn-out' is a danger of the Devil;

131

that Jesus did not demand such fervour from the first disciples; that Christians should save 'something in reserve' – as though the length of our life here was more important than its quality. Such views could be more dangerous, if more people stood in danger of overworking for God, consistently going the extra mile, and not counting the cost. This was pointed up in 1997, when, within days of each other, a princess in her mid-thirties, and a nun more than twice her age, died. Who was to say that Princess Diana, in her love and service to the deprived and vulnerable, had accomplished any less than Mother Teresa, in her work with the poor and sick of India? Each woman had been preparing for what God had prepared for her; and God is not in the business of indiscriminately operating a 'cut-off date' for everyone on her seventieth birthday. If we take up the challenge to serve, God will give us all the time necessary to do the work: not one minute more or less.

The value of others
Age and experience can be of great value; but equally important are youth and innocence; and we are well on the way to learning today's lesson, when we can value whatever others have to offer: when we can allow everyone the dignity of being God's son or daughter. And if in our serving we are met with contempt, we can take heart from the equanimity with which Jesus met the far greater contempt from those he came to save.

> Do thy friends despise, forsake thee?
> Take it to the Lord in prayer!
> In his arms he'll take and shield thee,
> Thou wilt find a solace there.
>
> Joseph Scriven, 1819–86

Suggested Hymns
Ubi caritas et amor; Strengthen for service, Lord, the hands; 'This is my Body, broken for you'; What a Friend we have in Jesus!

Ascension Day 1 June Carried into Heaven

Acts 1:1–11 or Dan. 7:9–14; Ps. 47 or 93; Eph. 1:15–23
or Acts 1:1–11; Luke 24:44–53

'Then he led them out as far as Bethany, and, lifting up his hands, he blessed them. While he was blessing them, he withdrew from them and was carried up into heaven.' Luke 24:50, 51

Test of faith

Ascensiontide is a real test of faith. Many who accept the Bethlehem birth of Christ, and the Jerusalem resurrection, have reservations when it comes to the Bethany ascension. They look vaguely up into the sky, and because they can only see with their mind's eye as far as the farthest star, or the longest space journey, they hesitate to affirm that heaven – and God – are 'up there'. They query the biblical accounts of the ascension, seeing them as carrying fundamentalism too far. Yet the denial of Christ's ascension still has to be supported by reasonable, plausible defence. Do we, for instance, accept the building of Hezekiah's defensive water system (2 Chronicles), merely because archaeologists have discovered the site, and irrefutable evidence is carved on the tunnel wall? Are we to allow that this part of the Bible is true, while something like the ascension is false? Well, it is possible to treat the Bible in that cavalier way: a man called Marcion tried it, in the second century – and ended up in trouble.

The world's wisdom

It doesn't do to be too wise before God – to say that we know best what we should, and should not, accept in the Bible. Remember John's caution: Revelation 22:18, 19.

Old Testament assumptions

There were two men in Old Testament times whom the Jews believed God held in high esteem because he saved them from death. One was Enoch, the other Elijah. 'By faith Enoch was taken so that he did not experience death' (Hebrews 11:15). And in assuming Elijah bodily into heaven (2 Kings 2:11), God honoured him above the other prophets. Elijah was not perfect, but his dedication to the cause of God saved him from death. Perhaps God took Elijah's extraordinary courage into account; perhaps he

133

thought the faithful needed added impetus; perhaps he was simply anticipating Christ's ascension, and the opening of the kingdom to all believers. For Christ's ascension, too, capped a life of courage and faithfulness; gave the disciples encouragement to launch the Church; and signalled the opening of the kingdom to Gentiles as well as Jews. Enoch's appears to have been a private assumption; Elijah's and Christ's, relatively public.

The message for today
1) Jesus is alive. He left the earth – not passively, as a coffined corpse, but in the full strength of resurrection life.
2) He is with God. He had come from God, and returned to God; and today we have no reason to believe he is anywhere other than with God.
3) He is in heaven. Each time we pray 'his' prayer, we affirm that God is in heaven. Since wherever God is, Jesus is, he is there, too.
4) He has promised to return, as he left. And he will come; for God is faithful to what he has promised.

Suggested Hymns
Alleluia! sing to Jesus; Christ triumphant, ever reigning; Crown him with many crowns; See, the Conqueror mounts in triumph

Seventh Sunday of Easter (*Sunday after Ascension Day*) 4 June *Principal Service*
Safe in the Lions' Den   Acts 1:15–17, 21–26; Ps. 1; 1 John 5:9–13; John 17:6–19

'"*I am not asking you to take them out of the world, but I ask you to protect them from the evil one.*"' *John 17:15*

Confident prayer
There is always confidence when prayer is on the lips of Jesus. 'Jesus never mentioned unanswered prayer; he had the boundless certainty that prayer is always answered' (Oswald Chambers, *My Utmost for His Highest*). We need a similar confidence: 'scattershot'

prayers are unworthy of the Lord to whom they are addressed. Jesus was not asking God to do a great work in keeping the disciples away from trouble; but for the even greater work of protecting them in the midst of trouble. The coward with no faith stays clear of the den of lions: the Christian with God's protection goes in boldly.

A special protection
What is this all-powerful protection for which Jesus asked? It is the same that he had used to such good effect against Satan in the wilderness: the word of God. 'The words that you gave to me I have given to them, and they have received them' (v. 8). It is effective, strong, and many-faceted; but it needs to be used prayerfully and carefully, for Satan also knows it, and can try to turn it back on us (Matthew 4:6). How, then, can it be of such great use to us, if Satan is as handy with it? Simply because, since Calvary, Satan quells before the Name of Jesus. Our Lord has added that sacred caveat which spells defeat to Satan: 'I will do whatever you ask in my name' (John 14:13); 'If in my name you ask me for anything, I will do it' (John 14:14); 'these signs will accompany those who believe by using my name' (Mark 16:17).

> Jesus! the name high over all,
> In hell, or earth, or sky;
> Angels and men before it fall,
> And devils fear and fly.
> Jesus! the name to sinners dear,
> The name to sinners given;
> It scatters all their guilty fear,
> It turns their hell to heaven.
>
> Charles Wesley, 1707–88

The challenge yet to meet
Life would have little value if the Christian were to be removed from any aura of temptation; the power of God's protection in such a case would be a dead letter. As it is, we have it available on request, which ensures that it is not wasted. God gives with no niggardly hand, but he does not expend his power unnecessarily. We are not expected to engage in single-handed combat with

the Devil. Learning when to ask takes time; but God allows for that. Knowing us so well, he knows we shall get the balance wrong, on occasion! Love cared so much, that he interceded for his friends. Can we marvel at the trust that Jesus placed in mere men? Can we grasp this same love and trust – and return it in good measure? Only by the grace of God, and in the power of Jesus' Name.

Suggested Hymns
Hail the day that sees him rise; Jesus, the name high over all; The head that once was crowned with thorns; O for a heart to praise my God

Seventh Sunday of Easter (*Sunday after Ascension Day*) 4 June *Second Service*
The Jesus Custom Ps. 147:1–11; Isa. 61:1–11; Luke 4:14–21

'When he came to Nazareth, where he had been brought up, he went to the synagogue on the sabbath day, as was his custom. He stood up to read, and the scroll of the prophet Isaiah was given to him.' Luke 4:16, 17

The best example
Luke gives us here a nugget of insight found nowhere else in the gospels. Perhaps the other writers took Jesus' regular worship for granted. But it is significant that, while Jesus emphasized mission and outreach, he did not neglect weekly church attendance. The Church today stands in ever as much need of this vital combination: a strong, regular home base, and world evangelism. We have the mandate, the manpower, the technological resources. We only need the will. The sermon that followed his reading from Isaiah is a model for all, as we seek to interpret scripture in the light of modern experiences. Koheleth sagely remarked that 'there is nothing new under the sun' (Ecclesiastes 1:9); and the Bible has prophecies, advice, encouragement and support for every circumstance that can ever come our way. The word of God is our rulebook for life, life in all its complexity of adventure.

The Church's mandate

The disciples and their spiritual heirs and assigns were to carry on the work of Jesus, after he had ascended; and he promised: 'the one who believes in me will also do the works that I do and, in fact, will do greater works than these, because I am going to the Father' (John 14:12). In today's reading, our mandate is clear: 'to bring good news to the poor ... to proclaim release to the captives, and recovery of sight to the blind, to let the oppressed go free, to proclaim the year of the Lord's favour' (Luke 4:18, 19).

The poor

Jesus promised that we should always have the poor with us, with opportunities for us to do them good (Mark 14:7). Bringing the gospel to them does not make them instant millionaires, but it gives them hope, confidence, and the ability to realize their spiritual potential.

The captives

Whether bound in a spiritual, mental or physical way, we are under orders to free the captives from bondage: to care enough to make the effort, rather than to assume the work cannot be done, or is not worth doing. It may be assisting those held captive by physical disability; or those suffering mental sickness or incapacity; or it may be those restricted by a lack of faith. St Francis de Sales, the courtly Bishop of Geneva in the seventeenth century, used to say: 'These, too, are sheep for whom the Shepherd died,' and he constantly shared his episcopal advantages with the poor, the sick and the dispossessed.

The blind

Both the physically and the spiritually blind need our help – whether it is by the laying on of hands, the supporting of ophthalmic research, or bringing the light of the gospel to non-believers. 'The hearing ear and the seeing eye – the Lord has made them both' (Proverbs 20:12); and he made them to be used in his service.

The oppressed

These have never been more numerous than they are today. We can reach out in mission across the world, or we can find them in our street or village: weighed down by financial, social or family problems; being exploited by unscrupulous manipulators; or suffering actual physical oppression under regimes anathema to Christianity. Again, Jesus says: 'You can show kindness to them whenever you wish' (Mark 14:7). It's known as 'the Jesus custom'.

Suggested Hymns
All hail the power of Jesus' name; Come, let us join our cheerful songs; This is the day the Lord has made; Lord, enthroned in heavenly splendour

Day of Pentecost (*Whit Sunday*) 11 June
Principal Service **The Spirit's Coming** Acts 2:1–21 or Ezek. 37:1–14; Ps. 104:24–34, 35b; Rom. 8:22–27 or Acts 2:1–21; John 15:26–27; 16:4b–15

'And suddenly from heaven there came a sound like the rush of a violent wind, and it filled the entire house where they were sitting. Divided tongues, as of fire, appeared among them, and a tongue rested on each of them.' Acts 2:2, 3

A unique visitation
The coming of the Holy Spirit is impossible to replicate. One would have to be in the middle of a tornado, the building would be shaking on its foundations, fire would be perilously close to everyone present, and it would be inextinguishable. There would also be a cacophony of languages. Mayhem. Chaos. This is the picture that the down-to-earth physician, Luke, gives us. But the people who had the wonderful experience went out from that place renewed. They had received peace; they had prayer; they had promise; and they had power. Some of them would suffer, because of what they had received. Many would die the death of a martyr.

Our own visitation
We have not experienced the tornado, or the fire; yet to us, as believers, God has given the same peace, the same prayer, the same promise, and the same power. We may not see it, but we have it. Neither age nor time condemns the peace, prayer, promise or sheer power of the Holy Spirit. Recently a scientist was trying

to describe the vastness of the universe, and the portions of it that have so far been discovered. World upon world lies out there, beyond what we once imagined were the borders of space. Then, virtually in an aside, the scientist concluded: 'And Jesus came down to this earth, to bring us the knowledge of the love and the saving power of God. He cared so much for us, when it would have needed just a movement of his little finger, to ignite this globe and obliterate it for ever – and the universe at large would not even have noticed the act.'

God's world-wide care

God cared so much for everyone on this earth. That was the dilemma which brought about the Passion, and necessitated the coming of the Holy Spirit: the Jews, looking for the deliverance merely of their own nation, could not take on board the love of God who cared for everyone on earth. When the Holy Spirit came down, he saw to it that people from many nations were there to receive him. Judaea had its Hebrew, Latin and Greek languages; but the Holy Spirit equipped the Pentecost assembly with many more. Now the disciples had no excuse: their gospel could now be understood by more nations than they had thought possible. Invested, then, with peace, prayer, promise and power, just one thing still stood between them and their mission: will-power.

Are we willing?

A willingness to be open to God's guiding opens the way for God to accomplish great things. As Peter quoted to the assembly, from Joel: 'I will pour out my spirit upon all flesh, and your sons and your daughters shall prophesy, and your young men shall see visions, and your old men shall dream dreams' (Acts 2:17). May we endeavour to use the power, prayer, peace and promise given us by the Spirit, which changed the first-century Pentecost assembly into world-changing people. Who knows, with God's grace, what twenty-first-century people will yet accomplish?

Suggested Hymns

Breathe on me, Breath of God; Come, Holy Ghost, our souls inspire; O, Breath of life, come sweeping; O Holy Ghost, thy people bless

Day of Pentecost *Second Service*
Freedom from Fear   Ps. 139:1–12; Ezek. 36:22–28;
Acts 2:22–38; John 20:19–23

*'"You have made known to me the ways of life; you will make me full
of gladness with your presence."' Acts 2:28*

Full of gladness
There is no room in a joyful heart for fear: no room in a praising
heart for anxiety. Even though there was plenty to wonder at, in
that Spirit-filled house at Pentecost, it was joy that won the day,
as Peter, intoxicated with spiritual joy, addressed the crowd. In
today's gospel reading, we find the disciples assembled behind
closed doors 'for fear of the Jews' (John 20:19). Their fear was
natural: only a little time before, Jesus, who had gone about doing
nothing but good, had been roughly arrested, tortured, tried and
crucified. Each disciple knew that his own life had not been blame-
less – so what was there to stop the bigoted, unpredictable temple
hierarchs from arresting those who were known to have been with
Jesus? Yet this is the last time where the disciples of Jesus are said
to have succumbed to fear. That is what the gift of the Spirit did
for them. And what it did for the disciples, it can do for us.

One permitted 'fear'
God allows only one 'fear' – and it is not so much fear, as honour
and respect: Godly fear. If we could all but take on board this
great promise, that the gift of the Spirit is an antidote to fear,
many of the world's psychiatrists would have far fewer patients
to monitor. Paul tells the Galatians precisely what the Spirit brings
into our lives: love, joy, peace, patience, kindness, generosity, faithfulness, gentleness, and self-control (Galatians 5:22). This combination of gifts did wonders for the disciples, changing them from
ordinary, fearful people into powerhouses of Christian energy,
resourcefulness and courage.

Holy-Spirit-filled
As the Pentecost wind shook the house, the tongues of fire came
down, and everyone began shouting in foreign tongues, why were
the disciples not afraid? Because they were 'filled with the Holy
Spirit' (Acts 2:4): completely empowered, completely equipped

against fear – filled in good measure, pressed down, shaken together, and running over, literally, with superhuman power. Can people look at us, and say we are Holy-Spirit-filled? For God is no respecter of persons; if we believe this, we cannot say: 'It is impossible for me to be filled with the Spirit.' If God could go to work so powerfully on the disciples, he can go to work equally powerfully on us – or do we believe God has lost some of his power over the last two millennia?

God is consistent
God is the same – yesterday, today and for ever. Let us make sure we make the most of him, if we have the courage to issue this challenging invitation:

> *Come down, O Love divine,*
> *Seek thou this soul of mine,*
> *And visit it with thine own ardour glowing;*
> *O, Comforter, draw near,*
> *Within my heart appear,*
> *And kindle it, thy holy flame bestowing.*

> *Bianco da Siena, tr. R.F. Littledale*

Suggested Hymns
Come down, O Love divine; Spirit of mercy, truth and love; Spirit of the living God, fall afresh on me; When God of old came down from heaven

Trinity Sunday   18 June   *Principal Service*
Do You Not Know?   Isa. 6:1–8; Ps. 29; Rom. 8:12–17; John 3:1–17
'Nicodemus said to him, "How can these things be?" Jesus answered him, "Are you a teacher of Israel, and yet you do not understand these things?"' John 3:9, 10

141

A professor of divinity

Probably Nicodemus felt hard done by, to receive such a rebuke. Yes, he was a teacher of Israel, a Pharisee, a theological scholar of the first rank, entitled to wear elaborate, tasselled robes which marked him out to everyone as a don. People revered him, and asked his opinion on innumerable theological matters, and believed what he said. He had been intrigued by the latest theologian – a Man who had appeared from Galilee; some said he was a carpenter; others said, No, the son of a carpenter. Either way, he appeared not to have been to university – yet he was preaching to some effect, and drawing large crowds. So Nicodemus came to check him out. And Jesus launched into advanced doctrine of the Holy Spirit, and re-birth – and then was surprised when Nicodemus floundered. 'You – a teacher of Israel – you should know all this!'

Looking in the wrong place

Nicodemus and his fellow Pharisees were conversant with the old scriptures; but their view of a priestly Messiah, a kingly Messiah, a glorious Messiah, did not square with a carpenter – or even the son of a carpenter. But, recognizing that in Jesus is someone who knows something better than all his book knowledge, Nicodemus is man enough to stay and hear more.

The ear of the Sanhedrin

At a time when those listening to him were largely simple, country crowds, Jesus must have appreciated the opportunity of getting his message across to a member of the prestigious Sanhedrin (Council). At last the true gospel was going right to the heart of the nation. Yet Nicodemus was not a 'one-off': throughout Christian history, there have been those who have long been deeply entrenched in their beliefs – yet who, on coming to Jesus, find that there has been something missing in their religion.

The turning-point

The turning-point may be a new version or translation of the Bible, which brings to light a truth they had not previously recognized. Or it may be a meeting with someone whose theological outlook is different; suddenly a new slant on an old truth comes into sharp focus . . . and we hear God telling us, as Jesus told Nicodemus: 'Ah, but you should have known this all along!' And – like Nicodemus –

we should not become affronted or despondent: it is God's way of leading us on. As a child learning to walk is not required to scale Everest, so the Christian is on a learning curve from the cradle to the grave. Like Nicodemus, we have a future of learning ahead of us. This side of death, no one is justified in believing he knows all there is to know.

> *A man's reach should exceed his grasp,*
> *Or what's a heaven for?*

> Robert Browning, Andrea del Sarto, 1.97

God, being God, teaches us in his own way, in his own time. When a particular truth does strike us, God still drives the point home with that extra challenge, keeping us on our spiritual toes to meet the next challenge. Instead of merely saying: 'Well done!', God has the habit of chiding, if ever so gently: 'Are you a master of Israel, and don't you know this already?'

Suggested Hymns
Holy, Holy, Holy, Lord God Almighty; Three in One, and One in Three; Father of heaven, whose love profound; Most ancient of all mysteries

Trinity Sunday *Second Service* **You are My Son**
Ps. 104:1–9; Ezek. 1:4–10, 22–28a; Rev. 4:1–11;
Mark 1:1–13

'And just as he was coming up out of the water, he saw the heavens torn apart and the Spirit descending like a dove on him. And a voice came from heaven, "You are my Son, the Beloved; with you I am well please."' Mark 1:10–11

Spiritual confirmation
For John, that day at the Jordan saw a wonderful event; wonderful, too, for the crowds gathered on the bank – but mainly for Jesus himself. Recognized by John, baptized before everyone, confirmed by the Holy Spirit, and thundered over by God himself. Then – the

surprising sequel: driven by the same Spirit into the wilderness. He had to go. He had to meet Satan, to pit his strength against the powers of evil.

Death in a gift-wrapper
He met, and overcame, Satan every time with the same weapon: God's word. At one point, Satan quoted scripture back at him; but Jesus could out-quote the Devil. Yet this warns us to be extremely cautious when Satan tries the same tactics with us. He can quote scripture with panache; for before he fell from grace he was with God. He knows, far better than we often give him credit for, how to gift-wrap suggestions of death, to resemble suggestions of life. A couple of friends stopped by a funeral parlour, in Virginia, to look through the stock of coffins on display. Their eyes lit on a real beauty – polished oak with silver filigree mountings, and lined with oyster-silk. 'My!' one exclaimed. 'And it's six thousand dollars! Ain't that real livin'!' We may smile, but this is exactly what Satan does so often to us. He spruces up deadly temptations, under a glitzy veneer. And sometimes we fall for the glamour.

The best available
Satan had chosen the wrong person, in Jesus, to quote from scripture. Jesus had just been confirmed by the Spirit, and fortified by God to withstand any onslaught. Yet the devil was trying to use the best weapon in his armoury. If he approaches us with the same weapon, we can at least recognize the compliment he is paying us, as Christians – while ensuring we have an ample stock of scripture to counter the temptation.

Hear Jesus
On the Mount of the Transfiguration, God told the disciples: 'This is my Son, the Beloved; listen to him!' (Mark 9:7). Listen to Jesus, for he is the word of God; he is the author, subject, object and essential element of all holy writ. Listen to the word. Hear Jesus. Let your first thought on waking each morning be a message of God. Carry portions of scripture along with you through the day. Meditate on a verse, a phrase, a text. And at night, as your head meets the pillow, drift off to sleep with a word from God. John Wesley made a point of praying himself to sleep – and how mightily God's grace worked through him!

The Bath Qol

Confirmation of Jesus' mission came in the form of a dove; and the *Bath Qol* (Heb. 'daughter of the voice') thundered from heaven. By grace, if not as a visible dove, the Holy Spirit still descends, when we take the major step of acknowledging Christ as our Saviour and Lord. It is by the operation of the Spirit that we gain insights into the word of God: as Jesus told his disciples, the Holy Spirit makes plain the holy truths. With the power of the Spirit, we can have Satan at the same disadvantage as Jesus had him. Let us take this challenge into the coming week, certain that we cannot fail. We have Jesus' word on it.

Suggested Hymns

Holy Spirit, Truth divine; How shall I sing that majesty; May the mind of Christ our Saviour; We give immortal praise

Corpus Christi (*Day of Thanksgiving for Holy Communion, Thursday after Trinity Sunday*)
22 June   *Principal Service*   **The Body of Christ**
Gen. 14:18–20; Ps. 116:12–19; 1 Cor. 11:23–26; John 6:51–58

Jesus said, 'I am the living bread that came down from heaven. Whoever eats of this bread will live for ever, and the bread that I will give for the life of the world is my flesh.' John 6:51

Broken for us

There is a majesty in these words from today's gospel, as Jesus calmly, deliberately goes forward in the will of God, with full knowledge of the cost of his sacrifice. He is giving all he has – his very body – for the life of the world. If we do not share his body and his blood, we do not involve ourselves in that sacrifice, and therefore will not be involved in the life that the sacrifice has bought. Have we become so sophisticated, so anaesthetized against this very basic truth, that the full impact of the enormity, the awfulness, of Christ's sacrifice passes us by? Our hymnbooks of a generation past, for instance, had many more hymns dealing with this subject than is the case today. Perhaps our congregations could once again rejoice to sing:

> There is a fountain filled with blood
> Drawn from Immanuel's veins;
> And sinners plunged beneath this flood
> Lose all their guilty stains.

William Cowper, 1731–1800

It is at Calvary, as his body was broken, his blood was shed, that we truly and fully meet Jesus in the Eucharist. 'I counsel you to go back to the cross, and begin again as a penitent sinner to put your trust in a pardoning Saviour. Full many a time I have to do that' (C.H. Spurgeon, *Christian Festivals*).

In the synagogue
Today's gospel reading was first given when Jesus was teaching in the synagogue at Capernaum (v. 58), probably at least eighteen months before the Last Supper. Was he preparing the people for what was to come? Were they ready for such amazing doctrine? It seems they were not: to play for time, they reduced his teaching to anthropomorphism (v. 52), in much the same way that Nicodemus had asked: 'How can anyone be born after having grown old?' (John 3:4).

Body and blood
In virtually any line of communicants at the sanctuary rail this morning, there will be some who see the Eucharist purely as an act of memorial; those who see in the bread and wine the very body and blood of Christ – and a range of beliefs somewhere between these two poles. Comparatively few sermons are preached on this subject, and an equally scarce number of Christians ever publicly define their position regarding belief in the sacred elements. That such should be the case, is strange – for it is this sacrifice which is at the heart of our faith. Yet so much mystery surrounds the Eucharist; there is so much that is undefinable, our language falls short of doing it justice every time.

Jesus in us
We can be certain of this, that in accepting the bread and wine, we are accepting Jesus into our bodies, in true food and true drink

(vv. 55, 56); and we shall continue to live because of this divine intake. Calvary's physical sacrifice was made once for all time; the spiritual sacrificial memorial of the Eucharist is an ongoing divine implantation of the life brought into being on the cross. How can we cope with all of this? In sheer, naked faith, with the confidence that the Christ who asks for such faith is the One who paid the ransom, and the One who promises that those 'who eat this bread will live for ever' (v. 58).

> *Bread of the world, in mercy broken;*
> *Wine of the soul, in mercy shed;*
> *By whom the words of life were spoken,*
> *And in whose death our sins are dead:*
> *Look on the heart by sorrow broken,*
> *Look on the tears by sinners shed,*
> *And be thy feast to us the token*
> *That by thy grace our souls are fed.*

> *Bishop Reginald Heber, 1783–1826*

Suggested Hymns
Bread of the world, in mercy broken; I watch the sunrise (*Celebration Hymnal*); Draw nigh and take the body; O thou, who at thy Eucharist

Corpus Christi *Evening Prayer* Feeding the Crowd
Pss 23, 42, 43; Prov. 9:1–5; Luke 9:11–17

'Taking the five loaves and the two fish, he looked up to heaven, and blessed and broke them, and gave them to the disciples to set before the crowd.' Luke 9:16

Jesus' compassion
Jesus had withdrawn with his disciples to Bethsaida for a quiet time; but the crowds had tracked him down, wanting healing and teaching. Instead of reprimanding them, he had 'welcomed them' (v. 11), and had attended to their healing and their hunger for the gospel. Even then, his compassion was not exhausted: he saw to

their physical sustenance as well. It is a lesson to us, as Christians, always to be available on demand. For one thing, we do not know if it is Christ himself who seeks our attention, our love, our help, our time. How terrible it would be, if we were to turn our Lord away, because of our own tiredness or busyness!

Earthly bread, heavenly food

Primarily today we are celebrating the Institution of the Eucharist; but this gospel reading also shows us how concerned God is for our physical well-being. 'Come, eat of my bread, and drink of the wine I have mixed', says Wisdom (Proverbs 9:5); and as Jesus calls us to his table, he knows that we come not only with spiritual, but also with physical hunger. One day, in another, heavenly body, we shall not need earthly food; but for now we are dependent on it – for our work for God, our very existence. In order to employ the talents God has given us, 'between two Masses', we must eat and drink – sensibly, and in moderation.

Guests at the Lord's table

Corpus Christi is a good day for considering how we come to the Eucharist. We are guests at our Lord's table – and guests do not come empty-handed. What do we bring to Jesus, out of love and gratitude for all he has given? Our time, certainly; our loving, thankful hearts; our prayers and intercessions and thanksgivings – for others, as well as for ourselves; and our intentions: to lead a better life, to love and serve him better. We may come with a prayer for healing, as did the crowds in our reading:

> 'Lord, I am not worthy so much as to gather up
> the crumbs under your table; but speak the word
> only, and your servant will be healed . . .'

Do we also, as the crowds, come for his teaching? No one yet knows all there is to know of Jesus' teaching – even though we may have committed the New Testament to memory.

> Lord, teach us – to pray, to reach deep into your holy
> word.
> Teach us, good Lord, wonderful things out of your law.
> Jesus, teach us, teach us – for it is in your word that we
> have eternal life.

148

ATOL
4030

FREEPOST
Christian Tours

ORDER FORM
CHURCH PULPIT YEARBOOK 2001

Please supply .... copy(ies) at the special pre-publication price of
£14.99 Incl. UK postage. Thereafter published price of £15.99 Incl. UK
postage.
Overseas postage extra - a quotation will be supplied on receipt of order

Name: Revd/Mr/Mrs/Ms/Miss ....
(Please print clearly)

Delivery address ....

....

.... Post code ....

Tel. No. ....

**This order form should be returned, with your payment
to the address below:
G. J. Palmer & Sons Ltd, 16 Blyburgate
Beccles, Suffolk NR34 9TB**

If, as did the people who came to Bethsaida, we hunger and thirst for the words of Christ, as well as for his healing and the food he gives, we shall find in the Eucharist not only what our souls and bodies require, but also our minds. God wants the complete, tripartite person we are, in his service. Have we yet given him our selves, our souls and bodies, in full and true commitment for whatever he is preparing for us?

> I hunger and I thirst;
> Jesus, my manna be:
> Ye living waters, burst
> Out of the rock for me.
> Thou bruised and broken bread,
> My lifelong wants supply;
> As living souls are fed,
> O feed me, or I die.

John Samuel Bewley Monsell, 1811–75

Suggested Hymns
I hunger and I thirst; Give me Yourself; Let all mortal flesh; My God, and is thy table spread

First Sunday after Trinity (Proper 7)   25 June
Principal Service   **Let Us Go**   1 Sam. 17:57–18:5, 10–16; Ps. 133; 2 Cor. 6:1–13; Mark 4:35–41
'On that day, when evening had come, he said to them, "Let us go across to the other side." Mark 4:35

Divine orders
There could come a storm, an earthquake, famine, plague, pestilence or any other hazard; but, once Jesus had issued the order to cross the Sea of Galilee, nothing in the natural or the supernatural could have prevented him from reaching the opposite shore. The disciples should have known this, but they panicked. Today, often when we believe we are doing what God has directed, all hell

appears to come against us – and, if we fall to wondering whether it really is God's will for us to continue, we end up like the disciples, in a real tizzy, with the original purpose lost: just as happened to Peter, when Jesus asked him to walk on the water (Matthew 14:30).

The long green road
From Advent through to Corpus Christi, the liturgical calendar has been filled with major feasts, fasts and festivals. Now, as we begin the long green road of the Sundays after Trinity, there are fewer landmarks; and in the imperceptible slackening of fervour, in the enervating temperatures even of a British summer, it can be easy to allow ourselves a spiritual holiday. Yet the Lord who never sleeps, continues on the long green road to say: 'Let us go ... let us grow ... let us progress together.' And as soon as he has spoken, we can be sure Satan, too, will move into action. It has always been so, from the days of Eden onwards.

Have you still no faith?
This was Jesus at his most scathing. Had the disciples – fishermen though they were – not justification for feeling alarmed? No. Once the Master of the sea had ordered the crossing, theirs was merely the work of getting the boat across; landfall was guaranteed. We have an even more challenging rôle than those early disciples. They could see Jesus, to rouse him. We have to have faith that not only does he know our predicament, but also that he will hear our prayers and will answer. Nothing the disciples could have done that night would have made any difference, except the exercise of faith. The storm was beyond their seamanship; the boat was taking water faster than they could bale it out. They had no power over the wind. Nothing in the natural order of things could help them. Only faith – faith in their Passenger, who calmly lay sleeping.

Look to God
We are sometimes up against natural disaster or chaos on the grand scale. We realize that nothing we can do is going to be effective. Do we, at such times, turn our faith full on? Or do we panic, and look for another way of getting to where we want to go? Keeping on keeping on, relying only on God, is so often the hardest thing to do. Bringing faith to bear on a problem does not mean praying to God and then sitting back and waiting for

something to turn up. We need to pray, certainly, and then to expect God to answer: to believe that he has given us the answer for which we asked. 'Whatever you ask for in prayer, believe that you have received it, and it will be yours' (Mark 11:24). It is not our ingenuity that wriggles us out of a tight corner, but faith in God's ability.

> *Not mine, not mine the choice*
> *In things or great or small;*
> *Be thou my Guide, my Strength,*
> *My Wisdom, and my All.*

> *Horatius Bonar, 1808–89*

Suggested Hymns
Eternal Father, strong to save; Thy way, not mine, O Lord; Fierce raged the tempest o'er the deep; O sing a song of Bethlehem

First Sunday after Trinity *Second Service*
Asking the Lord to Leave Ps. 49; Jer. 10:1–16; Rom. 11:25–36; Luke 8:26–39

'Those who had seen it told them how the one who had been possessed by demons had been healed. Then all the people of the surrounding country of the Gerasenes asked Jesus to leave them, for they were seized with great fear. So he got into the boat and returned.' Luke 8:36, 37

The saddest verse
Verse 37 here is probably the saddest verse in the whole Bible. Jesus is being asked to leave, to take his love and healing power away from people who do not know their desperate need. He goes, and we are not told that he ever went that way again. True, the demoniac had been cured – but the rest had forfeited their own chances, in the day of their visitation. They had seen a herd of pigs fall off a cliff to their death, and fear had taken hold of those people, to the point where it clouded their judgement. 'Leave, Rabbi, *now!*' And Jesus, always the gentleman, gave them

151

his company no longer, turning back to the boat, climbing aboard, and sailing away out of their lives for ever.

Shaking off the dust

It was the same when he sent out his disciples on mission. If anyone did not welcome them, they were to shake off the dust of that place, and to go on to the next village or town (Luke 10:11). God gives us the chance to hear his word, and then it is up to us. If we reject it, we must not grumble if the opportunity is not repeated. When the Gerasenes passed up their opportunity, it was not because they were antagonistic towards him. Nor was it because they were wrapped up in their own culture and beliefs. Nor was it even because they were too apathetic to take on anything new. It was, according to Luke, simply because what Jesus had done had frightened them. He was operating at a level which was beyond their comprehension.

What do we expect?

Perhaps we can review our comprehension, our expectations of God. Do we expect him to do great things in our lives, or little things? Do we expect him to let us career along in a way that is convenient or familiar – or do we want him to stir us up? If he allows us to carry on in our own sweet way, do we feel aggrieved and complain he is not using us to the full? If he does intervene, and bring us into new, disturbing, challenging circumstances, do we (like the Gerasenes) take fright, and pray to be left alone?

The one who knew

Those Gerasenes had worked themselves up into such fear that they could not focus on how, or even why, Jesus had acted. But someone could: the man who had been healed. After Jesus had left, the ex-demoniac proclaimed 'throughout the city how much Jesus had done for him' (v. 39). In Mark's version, the man then went further into the mission field, through all the Decapolis (the 'Ten Towns', of which Gerasa was one) (Mark 5:20). Now the Decapolis area was regarded by orthodox Jews as being beyond the pale. It had been a region of Greek influence, from the time of Alexander the Great, four centuries before Christ: non-Jewish, with an alien culture and population. Yet God had not given up on it; and, if their first missionary was unusual, having so recently been out of his mind, so be it.

Only trust Jesus
The Gerasenes had not believed that Jesus wanted them to hear his word and to receive all that he had to offer. He had been prepared to tax the very last grain of salt in the vast Dead Sea reserves, to get the Decapolis converted. But they were scared of what he might do next. They did not trust him. And when a person finds he can no longer trust God, there is not much even God can do about it.

Suggested Hymns
Have faith in God, my heart; Lead us, heavenly Father; Put thou thy trust in God; As the hart pants for the water

Second Sunday after Trinity (Proper 8)   2 July
Principal Service   **Your Faith has Made You Well**
2 Sam. 1:1, 17–27; Ps. 130; 2 Cor. 8:7–15; Mark 5:21–43
'His disciples said to him, "You see the crowd pressing in on you; how can you say, 'Who touched me?'"' Mark 5:31

Divine sight
Problems tend to concentrate our minds, even if they are not already focused on ourselves. The disciples found it difficult to believe that Jesus could attend to individuals *en masse*, yet still see them as individuals. He was no less concerned about Jairus and his problem, than about the woman needing immediate attention. And his extra-sensitivity could distinguish between the jostling of the crowd, and a clutch of faith. We may not be able to comprehend his cosmic overview of humanity; but we can walk through today's gospel reading with him, and appreciate how carefully and considerately he deals with all concerned.

A humble fear
The woman, knowing Jesus had recognized her touch, 'came in fear and trembling' (v. 33), but Jesus does not chide her – for this is a fear of humility and faith. He knows, too, that she has suffered for twelve years, and that she has bankrupted herself in an effort

to get healed. Nor does he need to tell her her sins are forgiven; but he praises her faith, and gives her the health for which she has been longing. It is a beautiful scene.

A father's fear
The most austere father will falter if his little girl is in danger; and Jairus must have been anguished to hear his daughter had died (v. 35). Anticipating his fear, Jesus is quick to reassure him. It is a command we can take into every emergency. *Only believe* that Jesus is, and that he is there. The Jewish *shivah* (period of mourning) had already begun when he reached the house, and he lost no time in evicting the weepers, knowing that there was no need for their services.

The Lord's timing
Jesus could have stopped to heal another hundred patients on the road, and the result would have been the same: the girl would have been raised. We fret and worry about time, or lack of it; about what work we can get through; about what may, or may not, happen. God has no such problems. Jesus never hurried, never dawdled, never wasted time, never lost time – because he was the Master of time.

All sorts and conditions
The woman with the haemorrhage appears and disappears in a few verses, and we hear nothing about her background or influence. Jairus, on the other hand, is introduced as a local church leader – a man who, despite Jesus' injunction for confidentiality, obviously talked about the raising of his little girl. We can conjecture that, at least in his synagogue, Jesus would henceforward be assured of a welcome.

Jesus hears
Whether we approach Jesus 'head on', as did Jairus, or in fear and trembling, our fingers clutching at the hem of his robe, we can be sure he hears, and will respond. The woman did not expect to be the cynosure of all eyes – nor did Jairus expect his daughter to die before Jesus reached her; but both, in the end, received the answer to their need.

She only touched the hem of his garment,
As to his side she stole;
Amid the crowd that gathered around him,
And straightway she was whole.
Oh, touch the hem of his garment!
And thou, too, shalt be free!
His saving power, this very hour,
Shall give new life to thee!

George F. Root

Suggested Hymns
A Stranger once did bless the earth; O Christ the healer, we have come; Thou to whom the sick and dying; Thine arm, O Lord, in days of old

Second Sunday after Trinity *Second Service*
A Hand to the Plough Pss [52] 53; Jer. 11:1–14; Rom. 13:1–10; Luke 9:51–62

'Another said, "I will follow you, Lord; but let me first say farewell to those at my home." Jesus said to him, "No one who puts a hand to the plough and looks back, is fit for the kingdom of God."' Luke 9:61, 62

Filial duty
He could have been the eldest son, with the duty of remaining at home until his father had died, to see to the funeral and inherit the property; or he could have been a younger brother who merely wanted to say his goodbyes. Whichever the case, Jesus' message is that filial duty to our heavenly Father comes before all else. The furrow of life has begun with our calling: who, under these conditions, can leave the plough to stand idle, or to be appropriated by someone else? This man's chance had come, and gone. Who knows what he may have accomplished, had he chosen to follow Jesus?

Sacrifice
The call of Jesus invariably involves sacrifice. If it were any other way, where would be the challenge? If entry into God's Army were easy, the world would be beating a path to heaven. Is there anything, or anyone, currently standing between us and Jesus? If there is, can we go to work on it, before God steps in and eliminates it for us? He will probe and probe, until it has been resolved, one way or another; and it must go, if we are to make real spiritual progress.

> *The dearest idol I have known,*
> *Whate'er that idol be;*
> *Help me to tear it from thy throne,*
> *And worship only thee.*
>
> William Cowper, 1731–1800

The conditions of discipleship are stern, but they are rewarded by a perpetual contract of service.

The ploughman's furrow
With his hand on the plough, a deep furrow is possible, as well as a straight one. When we have once committed ourselves and our lives to Jesus, his is the right to drive our plough as deep as he knows we can accomplish. Nothing will be asked of us that is beyond our capabilities; but God did not give us six-cylinder engines to run only on four. Are we ploughing as deep a furrow as we can; or is there a talent lying unused in our spiritual (or physical) anatomy? Is every part of us being used in God's service?

One sows, another reaps
It may not be our mission to sow in the furrows we have ploughed. That is not our business, but God's – and he may be preparing us to sow, or reap a harvest from another's ploughing. Or he may allow us to see a crop right through from start to finish. He knows what he is about, and we are not to worry.

The purposeful furrow
The furrow that we plough, from baptism onwards, may not be straight in purely physical terms, but in spiritual purpose. Think of the furrow that Jesus ploughed: from Bethlehem and Jerusalem,

to Egypt and Galilee; then for the three years of ministry through many towns and cities – cartographically, a maze of turns and crossings; but spiritually, one straight, purposeful furrow from God back to God. Our furrows will not be so perfectly straight – unless we keep our hand to the plough.

Suggested Hymns
Give me oil in my lamp; Thy Kingdom come! on bended knee; The Church's one foundation; O for a closer walk with God

Third Sunday after Trinity (Proper 9)   9 July
Principal Service   **Is not this the Carpenter?**
2 Sam. 5:1–5, 9–10; Ps. 48; 2 Cor. 12:2–10; Mark 6:1–13
'"Where did this man get all this? What is this wisdom that has been given to him? What deeds of power are being done by his hands? Is not this the carpenter, the son of Mary and brother of James and Joses and Judas and Simon; and are not his sisters here with us?" And they took offence at him.' Mark 6:2, 3

Powerful deeds
Jesus had been working miracles, but when he was treated to such offence the miracles virtually stopped. The divine power was there, as strong as ever, but because of their criticism and unbelief the people could not accept it. God does not impose his healing on those who do not believe he has the necessary power or authority. The choice is ours, to approach him in faith, or not. This does not mean that he will heal all the faithful, and leave the others to suffer. He will still operate in his good time, and for his own purposes. If healing is not experienced by a faithful person, God alone knows why: there is at least one factor in every case about which we know nothing; and one of the most poignant mysteries in the world is why God allows so much suffering.

Judge not
The unbelief shown to Jesus on his home ground is a warning to us against categorizing those whose background, intellectual and social status and family we think we know. On meeting new

people, we begin our evaluation immediately, subconsciously pigeonholing them according to appearance, diction, car, home and the rest. That done – still probably without admitting it overtly – we decide whether we are going to accept them as friends, acquaintances, or not at all: whether we shall introduce them to our particular 'circle', or allow them to go their own way. Our network of social acceptance is very well developed. Koheleth would say, yet again: 'There is nothing new under the sun' (Ecclesiastes 1:9); and his observation is borne out by the Nazarenes in today's reading. Jesus did not fit the mould of either a carpenter (Mark 6:3), or even a carpenter's son (Matthew 13:55). Preconceptions cost these people dearly: yet we still presume to categorize, and implicitly to expect that 'once a carpenter, always a carpenter' should apply, in so many cases. Where is progress here?

Grow in the faith

We are bidden to progress in every aspect of our faith, by Peter: 'Grow in the grace and knowledge of our Lord and Saviour Jesus Christ' (2 Peter 3:18). God has no limits, and he does not impose limits on his creation. Sunday School is fine for a certain age group; but Christians are to mature – on the physical, mental and spiritual fronts. The Nazarenes had limited themselves: the carpenter must stay a carpenter! How is the race of life to be won, by simply marking time in the starting-blocks?

Where do we stand?

No athlete can run at full stretch all the time, and there will be plateaux as well as gradients on our spiritual journey. Every so often, we shall either take a rest, or be forced to take one; but only to enable us to resume the journey with renewed strength. Where are we now? Is it time to be moving forward again?

Suggested Hymns

Father, hear the prayer we offer; Lord of all power, I give you my will; O Christ, the master carpenter; Thy hand, O God, has guided.

Third Sunday after Trinity *Second Service*
The Kingdom is Near Pss [63] 64; Jer. 20:1–11a;
Rom. 14:1–17; Luke 10:1–11, 16–20

' "Whenever you enter a town and its people welcome you, eat what is set before you; cure the sick who are there, and say to them, 'The kingdom of God has come near to you'." ' Luke 10:8, 9

A personal message
Each of us is responsible to Jesus all the time. We cannot delegate any of that responsibility. We can, through Christ's gospel, bring the kingdom close to others; but the response they make to that gospel is theirs. If we are to fulfil our calling as inheritors of the kingdom, we have to come as individuals to Christ: to meet him, to hear what he says – before we go, or are sent out, on his work. And it is dangerously easy to hear him without listening. When he tells us that the kingdom has come near, he is saying, basically, that it is his presence which brings the kingdom close: either physically, or through his gospel and teaching given by his disciples. And this presence is both temporal and spatial. It is temporal, in that it is here now, but it was not here before his gospel was proclaimed. And it is spatial, in that it is near to those who are reached by Christ's wisdom. Therefore, the kingdom is not a timeless reality (after all, who on earth can go very far towards understanding a timeless reality?); but it comes close to us through Jesus working in those called to be Christians.

Paul's understanding
Paul is very helpful here. He translates the kingdom into three aspects of God's love: 'For the kingdom of God is not food and drink, but righteousness and peace and joy in the Holy Spirit' (Romans 14:17). This righteousness and peace and joy come close to us with Jesus, with his gospel. The law and the prophets – religion as generations of Old Testament people knew it – operated until John the Baptist (Mark 11:13); 'since then the good news of the kingdom of God is proclaimed' (Luke 16:16). We are children of the new order, children of the kingdom of God. When Jesus came to earth, he brought something of the kingdom of heaven to us: in his prayer, he reminds us that that kingdom can 'come' on earth.

Jesus' assurance

Just as Jesus boosted the confidence of his seventy disciples, so he continues to give us encouragement, if we will but listen. He tells us we are the salt of the earth, the light of the world – the physical means by which today his kingdom spreads, by which it comes close to people. Our task is to extend this news, to bring the kingdom as close to as many people as we can. We are commissioned officers in his service, but there is no broad smooth highway laid out ahead of us: still less are people already inclined to believe. Our work demands a strenuous, concentrated moral co-operation with Jesus, in the face of all the opposition Satan can muster.

Worth the listening

There would be some, on the route taken by the Seventy, who would look askance at men who set out without money, shoes or luggage. Some would say: 'These men must be loyal to their master, to do all this!' And surely some would decide that the message the disciples brought was worth listening to. Is our message also worth the listening? Do we concentrate on sharing the 'righteousness, peace and joy in the Holy Spirit'? Or do we think our introduction to the kingdom will only come when we've left the rest of the world behind? As ambassadors for Christ, we have a mission to the world; and through us, God – if we give him the chance – can bring his kingdom close to an awful lot of people.

Suggested Hymns

Thy Kingdom come, O God; We have a gospel to proclaim; One more step along the world I go; Who can cheer the heart like Jesus?

Fourth Sunday after Trinity (Proper 10)

16 July   *Principal Service*   John Redivivus

2 Sam. 6:1–5, 12b–19; Ps. 24; Eph. 1:3–14; Mark 6:14–29

'Some were saying, "John the Baptizer has been raised from the dead . . ."
But others said, "It is Elijah." And others said, "It is a prophet, like one
of the prophets of old." But when Herod heard of it, he said, "John,
whom I beheaded, has been raised."' Mark 6:14–16

Whose resurrection?
The resurrection of Jesus had been foretold. People had been aware of the prophecy for centuries since the Psalmist's day – though many had rejected it as being too preposterous. None the less, there it stood, as part and parcel of scriptural prophecy (Psalm 16:10). So, in the days of Herod the Tetrarch the resurrection of Jesus was still current: still unfulfilled, still a possibility. Not so the resurrection of John. Yet in each of the synoptic gospels we have Herod and others suggesting that Jesus was John redivivus. Perhaps it was a simple confusion of identities. Herod, after all, was not purely Jewish, being the son of the Idumaean Herod the Great and the Samaritan Malthace. Perhaps he was also confusing the issue with what he had been told of Elijah, whom many saw as reincarnated in John. Yet his mistake shows how confused was the life and witness of John in the minds of those who did not understand the relevant authority of the Baptist and Jesus.

The worth of John
It is even easy today to reduce John to a virtual nonentity, and to concentrate on the rôle of Jesus in the gospels. How did John fit in to the incarnation of Jesus? How was he used by God? How did God's authority over him make possible the saving work of Jesus? For we can certainly believe that unless John's life, ministry and death had been necessary for the purposes of God, we should not have heard of him. It may seem that John had a raw deal: born the son of a priest, trained in the law, an ascetic, breaking off family ties and living on a scant diet in the wilderness; preaching to many who were blatantly antagonistic . . . yet for one brief, shining moment experiencing God's glory, as he baptized Jesus in the Jordan. That was the culmination of John's hard work. Then the glory faded. Jesus began travelling, and John stayed. Jesus' disciples grew, and John's began to drift away to the new preacher. Jesus and his team had a comparatively free life-style, attending feasts and functions; John and his coterie stuck to their ascetic principles: little food, simple clothing, regular fasts.

A double investment
The authority invested in John had been twofold: the gaunt ascetic was commissioned (1) to prepare the way for Jesus, and (2) to baptize Jesus. It is surely a mark of John's importance that one man was invested with such a vital, dual purpose. And it is a

mark of the mystery of his authority that God's chosen vessel was so unbecoming in the eyes of the world, and his life so tragic. Herod Antipas had imprisoned a rebel: a rough ascetic whose message rubbed many people the wrong way; a man who may have been right in what he said, but who (in the eyes of the tetrarch) compromised the success of his mission by how he said it. And yet, when Herod heard of the fame of Jesus, and of the numbers flocking to hear a preacher who had apparently none of the gaucheness of John, he decided that Jesus must be John redivivus. There is nothing of human logic here - but religious incongruity, spiritual foolishness, and divine wisdom. Such was the power of the silent tongue, the posthumous authority, of John. Herod was unconsciously admitting what the powers of evil knew was coming with Jesus' resurrection: that death was no longer unassailable, the power of the grave was not inviolate, and that God's authority was absolute. And the force of Herod's words was all the greater, considering *how* John had died. The Tetrarch was not assuming the resurrection of an entire body, but a corpse from which the head had been cruelly but decidedly severed. When we are tempted to think that God's authority has been misplaced, may we remember the life and work of John.

Suggested Hymns
Give praise for famous men; Lo, in the wilderness a voice; To God be the glory; At the Name of Jesus

Fourth Sunday after Trinity   *Second Service*
Do Likewise   Ps. 66; Job 4:1; 5:6–27 or Ecclus. 4:11–31; Rom. 15:14–29; Luke 10:25–37

' "Which of these three, do you think, was a neighbour to the man who fell into the hands of the robbers?" He said, "The one who showed him mercy." Jesus said to him, "Go and do likewise." ' Luke 10:36, 37

Learning – and doing
A Gentile once challenged Rabbi Hillel with the words: 'Make me a proselyte on condition that you tell me the whole law while I stand on one leg.' Hillel replied: 'What you hate for yourself,

do not do to your neighbour; that is the whole law. The rest is commentary. Go and learn.' (TB *Shabbat*, 31a). The head of a rabbinical school would advocate learning: daily a semi-circle of students would sit before him, cross-legged, listening to and learning the Torah. But there comes a time when theory needs to be translated into action, if it is to benefit others. Jesus tells the lawyer to put what he has learned into practice. He did not say: 'There is an important moral in this story; don't forget it. Go away and think about it; meditate a while.'

Jesus' example
At the start of his ministry, Jesus spent some time in the wilderness, overcoming Satan and preparing for the work ahead. Then he returned to civilization, and put theory into practice. Thinking about our work in order to do it, is wise, thinking about it when we should be doing it, is procrastination. So, we feel like writing a note of encouragement to a Christian in Peru or China, who has been imprisoned for his faith? Let's do it. We feel like sharing a vision for a Bible study group at the Church Council meeting? Let's do it. We feel like telephoning or visiting the lady in the parish who came out of hospital yesterday? Let's do it.

The 'meeting' mentality
We hear a lot today about the 'committee meeting mentality'; and unless we are careful, some of it can rub off on to us. A job needs doing? Let's call a meeting – and then another, to discuss it further – and another, to see where we are in the preamble . . . It all needs talking about, and consideration, and procrastination – and, who knows, it may not need doing after all; or, after the committees have had their say, someone else may do it. There are not too many committee meetings recorded in holy writ.

Jesus' special dealings
The message in today's parable was simple: love your neighbour. But Jesus dealt with his questioner in a special way – a way particularly suited to the man's calling and approach. As a lawyer, he was used to dealing with (and without) prejudice. So Jesus gave him something more than the straightforward moral to deal with: he neatly wrapped racial prejudice in and around the theme. Ever since the Samaritans had offered to help the Jerusalem Jews to re-build their temple, had been rebuffed, and in high dudgeon

163

had withdrawn and erected a rival temple on Mount Gerizim, the two peoples had hated each other. This lawyer was now expected to carry love for his neighbour even across the yawning chasm between the races. In asking for teaching, he had shown a willingness to learn; and Jesus built on this, by asking more of him. God will do the same for us, giving us answers to our prayers beyond what we have expected, if he sees we are in real earnest. Lord, make us willing to be more willing to learn.

Suggested Hymns
Forth in thy name, O Lord, I go; Help us to help each other, Lord; When I needed a neighbour, were you there?; Take up thy cross, the Saviour said

Fifth Sunday after Trinity (Proper 11)
23 July   *Principal Service*   **Healing Ministry**
2 Sam. 7:1–14a; Ps. 89:20–37; Eph. 2:11–22; Mark 6:30–34, 53–56

'When they got out of the boat, people at once recognized him, and rushed about the whole region and began to bring the sick on mats to wherever they heard he was. And wherever he went . . . they laid the sick in the market-places, and begged him that they might touch even the fringe of his cloak; and all who touched it were healed.' Mark 6:54–56

First-century problems
Without an NHS, social security, insurance system or pensions board, sick people in first-century Palestine either worked off their symptoms, or became worse. If they did not die of the malady, and the family could not look after them, there was no alternative but to beg. So when the new rabbi came on the scene, who cared about healing all in need, the people in today's gospel reading responded with alacrity.

Twenty-first century problems
Despite all our securities and insurances, health is as precious today as it ever was. There are those, however, who will tell us

that God sends sickness for a purpose. But how can this be? Jesus said: 'If a house is divided against itself, that house will not be able to stand' (Mark 3:25). So when we read of Jesus healing every sick person who was brought to him, what was he doing it for, if God had inflicted the sickness in the first place?

Satan's work
God may allow sickness, but he does not send it. According to Jesus, Satan is the culprit. Jesus taught in a synagogue on the sabbath, where there was a woman who had been bent double with spinal trouble for eighteen years. Jesus healed her, and provoked an indignant outburst from the synagogue ruler, about infringement of the sabbath laws. Angrily, Jesus retorted: 'Ought not this woman . . . *whom Satan bound* to be set free from this bondage (even if it is the sabbath)?' (Luke 13:16).

God does not set an obstacle course
God sends us nothing that will hinder us from fulfilling our mission. He wants us to make the most of our opportunities. He wants us to reach the gates of heaven, not gasping that, despite everything, we've 'only just made it' – but triumphant, joyful – 'Mission accomplished!' John spells out this philosophy: 'I pray that all may go well with you, and that you may be in good health' (3 John 2). It is God's will for us to be well – physically, mentally, spiritually. Paul told Timothy: 'God did not give us the spirit of cowardice, but rather a spirit of power, and of love, and of self-discipline' (2 Timothy 1:7). God's power to heal is constant. There is no sickness or disease that is stronger than the Creator. He heals today – though many refuse to recognize his work; and if he is not given the credit, who is to complain if he decides not to heal?

Our living dynamo
The power that is in us is the health-promoting Holy Spirit, who never gets tired, never sleeps, lies in or has time off. 'The one who is in you is greater than the one who is in the world' (1 John 4:4). If we can hold on to this truth, in every situation, we can trust God to move powerfully – not only in healing, but in every aspect of our lives. Let us use the power he has given us, whose strength far exceeds our demands.

165

Suggested Hymns
I come with joy to meet my Lord; Immortal love, for ever full;
Thine arm, O Lord, in days of old; To God be the glory

Fifth Sunday after Trinity   *Second Service*
Priorities   Ps. 73; Job 13:13–14:6 or Ecclus. 18:1–14;
Heb. 2:5–18; Luke 10:38–42

'The Lord answered her, "Martha, Martha, you are worried and dis-
tracted by many things: there is need of only one thing. Mary has chosen
the better part, which will not be taken away from her."' Luke 10:41, 42

Food most necessary
Martha, busily preparing a meal for Jesus, is told she has her
priorities wrong. On several occasions Jesus had provided food
for people's physical needs – but he makes the important distinc-
tion here, that earthly food takes second place to God. Bethany
was not the desert. No one visiting the little place need have
walked more than a couple of miles since a meal. Mary had rightly
decided that what Jesus was saying was more important than the
next meal. One could argue that the perfect guest would have
affirmed Martha in her preparations; but quite possibly her bang-
ing about with pots and pans had disturbed the couple sitting in
the parlour. And Jesus' teaching was as much for the benefit of
Martha's soul, as Mary's. His repeated use of her name shows his
affection, as well as a rebuke for her request that Mary should
leave Jesus' side and give some help with the meal. It is a signal
warning to put God and his business first. We may be accused of
religious zeal; but if it is going to be a crime to stand up and be
counted for our faith, let us make sure we give our convicters
ample material for the prosecution.

The priorities of God
The promise Jesus gave to Mary would come to pass: the 'better
part' would not be taken from her. Perhaps we have a promise
from God in our hearts – a vision we have received – a word we
have cherished, perhaps for years, lodged deep within us. It will
not be taken from us, unless we banish it. To Martha, it seemed

inconceivable that the customs of hospitality, which she had been taught from childhood, could take second place; but there are such times when God's priorities knock our own awry. Sometimes his ways appear logical; at other times we may be as mystified as was Martha. Yet there will always be those times when, like Mary, he affirms us in our present work, and life seems to run on well-oiled wheels.

Our choice
We do well to note how Jesus says: '*Mary has chosen* the better part.' God never coerces, never compels. He has given us the freedom of our will, and he is not in the business of cancelling out a gift as precious, and as challenging, as that. Mary had chosen to leave the kitchen-sinkery, and to hang on every word of Jesus. Martha had chosen to bang around with the pots and pans.

The open door
Jesus says, 'Look, I have set before you an open door' (Revelation 3:8). God is an expert at opening doors for us. Many a time, if he did not open one, we never would. But often he opens a particular door only once. If we go through it, well and good. If we do not, we may have to wait a long time before he opens another. Perhaps Martha never again put kitchen work before Jesus; and his friendship and regard for both sisters remained constant. When they appealed to him in their grief at Lazarus' death, he responded with love, and restored their joy.

At the beginning of a new week, we stand on the threshold of a time we have never lived before: a time which God will use to prepare us for what he is preparing for us – doors which have yet to open. And as God brings us to these doors, we have the choice to proceed, or not. May he give us the grace to choose wisely.

Suggested Hymns
Lord, thy word abideth; Father of mercies, in thy word; Be still, my soul, the Lord is on thy side; Be still, for the presence of the Lord

Sixth Sunday after Trinity (Proper 12)
30 July *Principal Service* **Gather up the Fragments**
2 Sam. 11:1–15; Ps. 14; Eph. 3:14–21; John 6:1–21

'Then Jesus took the loaves, and when he had given thanks, he distributed them to those who were seated; so also the fish, as much as they wanted. When they were satisfied, he told his disciples, "Gather up the fragments left over, so that nothing may be lost."' John 6:11, 12

The methods of Jesus
There is a complete mastery about the operation. Jesus takes command of the food, meagre as it seems, gives thanks, distributes all that is necessary to satisfy the crowd, and then orders a retrieval operation for the surplus. No food was to be left for the birds or scavenging animals; it was to be carefully salvaged. There is no wasting with God, though he is generous in his provision. So it is with us: he gives us all we need; and, if we do not use all he has provided, he will see that his gift benefits someone else.

God's care
God does not abandon those who trust him. Providing we put his work first, he has contracted to feed and clothe us (Matthew 6:31–33). Can we trust him so much? Or, when we are hard pressed, do we rely on our own ingenuity to extricate us – just in case God fails to come through! Are we, like the people in our reading, satisfied with less than he gives? If the disciples had not covered the ground tidying up the left-overs, twelve baskets of food would have been wasted. At times we also fail to set our spiritual sights high enough. God can work out good things in our lives, if we are prepared to take the risk. He may only ask once.

This is the prophet
As the realization of the miraculous feeding penetrated the eaters' minds, the rumour began to spread: This is indeed the prophet who is to come into the world. They have been looking for him for so long, even now they can hardly believe that Jesus is the one; yet who else could have fed the crowd with a schoolboy's dinner? We can surely sympathize with this myopic spiritual sight – for who has not on occasion been concentrating so much on a particular idea or figure, that the actual event or person has passed

unrecognized, just because it varied in some way from our expectation? But, having decided that Jesus is the prophet, the people move quickly (v. 15). The irony of the situation is that, before many months are over, the Jews *will* take Jesus by force – and, in an amazing way, they will make him king, when he is crucified under the title of Pilate's writing: 'This is Jesus of Nazareth, King of the Jews.'

Jesus' withdrawal
To prevent premature action, Jesus conveys himself away; perhaps he left miraculously, for that same evening we find him defying gravity and walking on the water (v. 19): a terrifying experience for the disciples. Jesus is used to the volatility of the Jews. He also takes our mood swings in his stride; and while he does not want us to be lukewarm in our allegiance, neither should we provoke or weary him by histrionics. The crowds were not allowed to indulge their king-making. When we feel a surge of spiritual fervour, let us pray for guidance to expand it as God wills.

Suggested Hymns
Bread of heaven, on thee we feed; For the fruits of his creation; It passeth knowledge, that dear love of thine; Let us break bread together

Sixth Sunday after Trinity *Second Service*
Teach Us to Pray Ps. 74; Job 19:1–27a or Ecclus. 38:24–34; Heb. 8; Luke 11:1–13
'He was praying in a certain place, and after he had finished, one of his disciples said to him, "Lord, teach us to pray."' Luke 11:1

The gift of prayer
Tennyson's *Morte d'Arthur* includes these lines:

> More things are wrought by prayer
> Than this world dreams of. Wherefore let thy voice
>   Rise like a fountain for me day and night.
> For what are men better than sheep or goats

That nourish a blind life within the brain
If, knowing God, they lift not hands of prayer
Both for themselves, and those who call them friends.

Paul told the Christians in Rome: 'We do not know how to pray as we ought' (Romans 8:26), but acknowledged that we can succeed in prayer through the Holy Spirit's help. And Jesus, in today's reading, summarizes the work of prayer (Luke 11:9). No prayer, therefore, goes unanswered, so we need to cultivate the habit of expecting answers to our prayers. Prayer is a meeting of spiritual persons: we pray as commanded by God the Son; we address God the Father; and the inspiration to pray emanates from God the Holy Spirit.

When does the building of the spirit really begin to appear in a man's heart? It begins, so far as we can judge, when he first pours out his heart in prayer.

J.C. Ryle, Practical Religion

'Teach us to pray'
This is the only request in the gospels for Jesus to give instruction. Why do *we* ask? Perhaps because we want to be drawn closer to God; perhaps because we want to be spiritually better equipped to help others; perhaps we want to know ourselves better; perhaps because we want to learn how to pray for the things that God is waiting to give us. God does not insist that we need a doctorate in English to pray; if your intentions are pure and good, he will take care of the actual linguistics of prayer.

History of prayer
Behind the disciples' request was a long history of prayer. The official prayers of the synagogue were obligatory; private prayer was also used; but the prime synagogue prayer, the *Shemoneh Esreh* ('Eighteen Benedictions'), was to the first-century Jew what the Lord's Prayer became to the Christian; and the *Shemoneh* is still prayed three times a day in the Jewish church. Of these eighteen benedictions, the first three deal with praise, the next twelve with petition, and the last three with thanksgiving. The *Shemoneh* is actually a prayer which Christians can use as an extended version of the Lord's Prayer.

170

Why another?

Why, then, was the Lord's Prayer given? Because it was short? Because the disciples found traditional praying difficult? Perhaps; we know they found problems with praying. When they failed to cure the epileptic boy, Jesus told them soberly that the answer lay simply in prayer (Mark 9:29). (Some texts add: 'and fasting'.)

Prayer life

In the *Miserere*, the Psalmist had prayed:

> *Give me back the comfort of thy saving power;*
> *Strengthen me in generous resolve.*
>
> *Psalm 50:12, Knox*

Prayer is a serious business, and to make it effectual it needs not only all the attention and effort we can give it, but also the grace of God. For real prayer, these must always go together, as they were always together in the prayer life of Jesus. True prayer is the result of a combined effort from God and from us: God using his omnipotence, and requiring us to use all the talents he has given us. James tells us: 'The prayer of the righteous is powerful and effective' (James 5:16). If we ask God to teach us to pray, we must be willing to learn, to work at it, to accept the grace of perfect prayer which God gives; to persevere, to be attentive pupils at the feet of the Master. Or God's lessons will be wasted.

Suggested Hymns

Lord, teach us how to pray aright; Prayer is the soul's sincere desire; Pray when the morn is breaking; Not for our sins alone

The Transfiguration (Seventh Sunday after Trinity, Proper 13)   6 August

Principal Service   **Glory on the Mount**   Dan. 7:9–10, 13–14; Ps. 97; 2 Pet. 1:16–19; Luke 9:28–36

'While he was praying, the appearance of his face changed, and his clothes became dazzling white . . . and . . . a cloud came and overshadowed them, and they were terrified as they entered the cloud.' Luke 9:29, 34

When the mists have rolled away?

Fog, mist, clouds have been with us since the world began; but on the Transfiguration mount Peter and the others experienced a particular type of cloud – a cloud so special that it is always spoken of in the singular. Centuries past, the Lord had 'descended in the cloud', and had spoken with Moses on Sinai, when the covenant was renewed (Exodus 34:5). In today's reading, Luke says the disciples were 'terrified' as they encountered this cloud; and predictably enough, since this (as on Sinai) was no ordinary, physical, rain-bearing cloud, but the glory, brightness, majesty, and beauty surrounding God himself. It hid him from the eyes of ordinary folk, because ordinary vision cannot cope with the brilliance of God's glory.

The *shekinah* glory

The Hebrews called it the *shekinah* glory; the *shekinah* which came down on Sinai at the ratifying of the Old Covenant; the *shekinah* which guided the Israelites through the wilderness to the Promised Land; the *shekinah* which filled the most holy part of the tabernacle of worship; and the *shekinah* which descended on the mount of Transfiguration. After Moses came down from Sinai, we hear that his face continued to shine with a glorious reflection of the *shekinah* glory (Exodus 34:29, 30), because he did not come down on his own: he brought with him the tablets of stone bearing God's word. On the Transfiguration mount, the *shekinah* appeared again, when God sanctioned his Son to go through to the bitter (and glorious) end, with the New Covenant: the promise to us, through the sacrifice of Christ, of eternal life.

On the mount of Transfiguration

Moses, the lawgiver of old, the partner of the first covenant, was there; Elijah, whose mission had very specially prefigured the mission of Jesus, was there; Jesus, the lawgiver and partner of the New Covenant, was there. And so were the disciples – and they were terrified. The mount in question was probably Tabor; as they had ascended, Jesus and the disciples would have seen Galilee spread out far below. Perhaps the disciples had a sense of unreality: looking down, they would see boats on the lake, going about their normal business – while up on the mount with Jesus the air was thin, they were tired and sleepy – and then suddenly jerked into panic by the *shekinah*, and the voice of God: 'This is my Son, my Chosen; listen to him!' There is a time for every purpose under heaven: this was not the time for Peter, ever impulsive, to blurt out the first thoughts that came into his mind. It was a time for listening to what Jesus had to say. The disciples will have all the time they need to speak, when they take the gospel out from Jerusalem.

Can we listen?
We may fill our prayer time with God, with a torrent of thanksgiving, adoration, intercession, confession and petition. God will listen; and he will respond. But can we also make time to listen to him? He has a voice so much mightier than ours, and he will use it. If we feel God is far away, and we cannot even visualize his *shekinah* glory; if we are finding prayer difficult; if we are worried, or ill, or in trouble of any kind; if the future is frightening and uncertain, God says to us today, as he did on Mt Tabor: '*Listen* to my Son.' Lord, give us the hearing ear, the willingness to listen.

Suggested Hymns
In days of old on Sinai; 'Tis good, Lord, to be here; Lord, the light of your love; Restore, O Lord, the honour of your name

Seventh Sunday after Trinity   *Second Service (Evening Prayer)*   **Good to be Here**
Ps. 72; Ex. 34:29–35; 2 Cor. 3; Matt. 17:1–13
[Editor's choice, not RCL!]

'And Jesus was transfigured before them, and his face shone like the sun, and his clothes became dazzling white. Suddenly there appeared to them Moses and Elijah, talking with him. Then Peter said to Jesus, "Lord, it is good for us to be here."' Matthew 17:2–4

Is it good?
There are times in our lives when, 'Lord, it is good for us to be here,' could not be further from our minds. 'Is it really good, Lord, to be in this trouble, to be struck down with 'flu, to be anguishing over relationships with family, friends, colleagues?' But there are

also times when we can say it with conviction. God is close. We have good news. We feel on top of the world. 'Yes, Lord, it is good to be here!' And God, who has brought us through the bad time, who has borne so patiently with our sighs and worries, seems to be saying: 'You see, I *love* you; I love you so much, I have waited to give you this moment – at the very best time for you!'

Back to work

Yet, as we see on the mount of Transfiguration, God loves us too much to keep us up there in an ecstasy of delight. The beautiful moment is a time for re-charging of the spiritual batteries, giving us renewed strength to return to the common tasks, renewed confidence that – whether on the mountain or the plain, or even stumbling along through the valley – we are in God's will. It helps to remember Psalm 40:8, 'Lord, I delight to do your will!' It is not an 'abracadabra' that rockets us from the valley to the peaks – heaven is not reached in a single bound – but if we can get some delight in doing God's will, it helps immeasurably.

Duty or pleasure

So often we do the will of God from a sense of duty: in fact, most of what we do for God is usually in the line of Christian duty. But to do something for him, for no other reason than that we love him – *that* gives us delight, God delight, and is the butter on the bread of duty. God took sheer delight in treating his Son and the disciples to a vision of his *shekinah* glory on the mount. He deals with us in the same generosity of love today.

A glimpse of heaven

The Transfiguration experience also gives us precious hints about the life Hereafter. We all long, at times, for someone precious to return from 'the other side', to answer questions we have on the life after death. On Tabor, God answered at least some of these. Firstly, we do not lose our identity; the identity of Moses and Elijah is not questioned. We keep our names, our looks, and our purposes. Moses was there as the great lawgiver of old; Elijah as the prophet whose mission had been predominantly fulfilled in John's preparations for Jesus. Secondly, we keep our faculties: Moses and Elijah converse with Jesus; if speech remains, can we not assume also the gifts of sight, hearing, smell and taste (as these were also preserved in the resurrection body of Jesus)? It is good

174

to know that while we may have been created from nothing, God did not create us for nothing. Whatever we do, think, say, write or pray – whatever we fill our lives with here on earth, for God – is a preparation for what we shall be called upon to do Hereafter. Jesus could have gone up the mount on his own, and the disciples could have had no part in the glory. Thank God, it happened as it did; for it strengthens our hope and commitment to make this life the best possible preparation for the life to come. God will then know that we have indeed obeyed his command from the *shekinah*: 'This is my Son . . . *listen* to him!'

Suggested Hymns
Adoramus te, Domine; Be still, for the presence of the Lord; Immortal, invisible, God only wise; Lord of beauty, thine the splendour

Eighth Sunday after Trinity (Proper 14)
13 August   *Principal Service*   **Living Bread**
2 Sam. 18:5–9, 15, 31–33; Ps. 130; Eph. 4:25–5:2; John 6:35, 41–51
'Jesus said, "I am the living bread that came down from heaven."' *John 6:51*

Divine implant
In purely scientific, physical terms, Jesus' flesh was mysteriously different from ours. It was divinely implanted in the physically sealed womb of Mary. It grew from no human origin. To the natural eye, it ceased living on the cross. It de-materialized and escaped from grave clothes and the tomb. It could appear and disappear at will, passing in a de-materialized form through doors and walls, time and space, defying gravity, yet able to imbibe food like a normal body. Jesus' body was so vitally important to us – the world and its destiny – that God chose it to be given as living bread – broken, but capable of existing eternally. It was, after all, a choice so contrary to the will of nature that its very strangeness was bound to shock, to impose upon people's sensitivity,

consciousness and emotion. It was sufficient to baffle the Jewish and Roman authorities – yet powerful enough to convert a bunch of demoralized disciples into the strongest force for good which had ever been let loose in the world.

Great power
In the days immediately following the ascension of Jesus, his power was so strong that even the shadow of a disciple falling across a sick person was enough to heal. Through the centuries that followed, miraculous healings and resurrections have been effected by this same life-giving power mediated through saints, both while they were alive, and posthumously. Where is this power of Jesus today? In the 'suffering Church'? And where is the suffering Church – in the so-called 'Third World', or on our doorstep? Which part of it is indeed showing the powerful life, the living bread of Jesus, to the rest of the world? The great power to move mountains, heal the sick, raise the dead, is still available, still as strong, after two thousand years; for the bread that was broken and scattered on the mountain was broken once and for all: its purpose has never been, and can never be, revoked. We need to forget about being timid, and instead come boldly to the throne of grace, asking and asking for yet more of Jesus' power, for more of the sustenance of his living bread.

Giving the bread
He who broke the bread for our lives is going to delight in giving us all the power, fervour, boldness and zeal we can cope with – and, at the same time, he can give us the power to cope with more. God, in his resurrected Son, is constantly saying to us: 'What are you doing about this living bread? I have made the power and life available to you. What are you going to do with them?'

Dynamic challenge
The Christian challenge is dynamic. Jesus preached a practical, hands-on, get-up-and-do gospel. He is forever telling us: 'I have given my body, the living bread for you. Go, and do . . . Go and preach, go and heal, go and raise the dead.' We like to believe we are consistent, and we'd certainly protest if anyone tried to tell us God was inconsistent. Therefore, if we are to stand foursquare not only to our consistency, but also to God's, we must believe that his word remains – yesterday, today and for ever. God is good,

and he is just. He does not promise something, and then change his mind. He does not tell us to do great things without making it possible for us to do them. All he is waiting for, is for us to accept his challenge.

Suggested Hymns
I am the bread of life; Bread of heaven, on thee we feed; Father, we thank thee, who hast planted; Make me a channel of your peace

Eighth Sunday after Trinity   *Second Service*
Be Alert   Ps. 91; Job 39:1–40:4 or Ecclus. 43:13–33; Heb. 12:1–17; Luke 12:32–40

'Blessed are those slaves whom the master finds alert when he comes . . . Know this; if the owner of the house had known at what hour the thief was coming, he would not have let his house be broken into. You also must be ready; for the Son of Man is coming at an unexpected hour.' Luke 12:37, 39–40

The tingle factor
It is God's business to keep us ready for anything, tingling with spiritual energy for whatever circumstance or situation into which he may lead us. He has harsh criticism for those who are lukewarm in their allegiance (Revelation 3:16), or who decide to take life easy (Luke 12:19). How can we rise to this challenge? By studying how Jesus lived and worked: master of time, and always having time for others. Today, so many people seem to be short of time, yet leisure activity businesses do a roaring trade. Modern days have the same number of hours as in ancient time. If we are short of time, the fault is not God's. If we have time on our hands, let us examine how we are living.

Daily duty
Filling each day as best we can means that time is given its full value. There will come a transition in our lives, when time will be no more; we shall not miss it, because then we shall not need

it. By then, with God's grace, we shall have learned to use it. Such is the 'foolishness' of God.

Our last day
If we knew when the Son of Man was coming, we should make great plans for that day, setting our affairs in order, straightening out tangled relationships, and generally getting ready for the line to be drawn under our life on earth. Can we do any of those things *before* Jesus comes? Would it not improve our spiritual quality of life in the here and now?

The servant served
Luke tells us, amazingly, that the Master will honour those servants whom he finds alert, by serving *them* at the celebratory banquet. Did the disciples recall these words, when Jesus took water and a towel and washed their feet, in the upper room? (John 13:4ff., cf. Luke 22:27). This is an indication of how God honours loyalty and preparedness. We shall not enter his kingdom as 'worms of earth', but as honoured sons and daughters of the Almighty – brothers and sisters of the Saviour. Can we fathom this? No – it is mind-blowing. We must simply have faith, and take the promise on trust.

An unexpected hour
There is the implication, in Jesus' words, that whenever the End comes, it will not be at the most convenient or likely hour. This is surely not due to any cynical or sadistic desire of God to whittle down the numbers of those who will be found ready. It will be for our good. If we have used the time we have to prepare ourselves as best we can, whenever Jesus comes will be 'convenient' for us. '*Dieu me pardonnera; c'est Son métier,*' murmured the dying Henri Heine. But God is God; he is not obliged to do anything; and it is the height of folly to presume when the End will come, or what will happen on the day it does arrive. Our job is to be faithful today – and tomorrow, if it comes.

Suggested Hymns
Today thy mercy calls us; Lord, for tomorrow and its needs; Fight the good fight; O Jesus, I have promised

Ninth Sunday after Trinity (Proper 15)
20 August   *Principal Service*
Living Because of Jesus   1 Ki. 2:10–12; 3:3–14;
Ps. 111; Eph. 5:15–20; John 6:51–58

'Jesus said to them, "Very truly I tell you, unless you eat the flesh of the Son of Man and drink his blood, you have no life in you ... Just as the living Father sent me, and I live because of the Father, so whoever eats me will live because of me."' John 6:53, 57

Jesus with us always

Jesus did not leave us when he ascended to the Father. In a mysterious way, he left us his body and his blood: more precisely, he left us the consecratory means of transforming earthly elements into his spiritual body and blood. We are not required to know or explain this mystery; just to accept it in faith. We cannot define why it is necessary to re-enact the Last Supper: why the bread and wine are changed; but Jesus willed it thus, so we can accept that it is a vital part of our spiritual journey. It is important to learn and meditate on the teaching of Jesus in the gospels. But it is not enough. It is important to put his principles into practice. But it is not enough. Unless we eat his flesh and drink his blood, we have no life in us. This is a truth so stark that it is uncomfortable. No wonder the Jews asked: 'How can this man give us his flesh to eat?'

The sacrifice of Jesus

Underlying all the teaching of Jesus is his sacrificial death. There can be no life without death. The seed falls into the ground, and 'dies', before it grows into a new plant. Jesus died on the cross, before the gates of hell could be smashed, and eternal life made available to all who would believe in him. We are to die to ourselves – to relinquish our desires and to take up the cross, in order to proceed to this eternal life. There is a death – physical, spiritual – before advancement. At the simplest level, we 'die' in sleep every night, to renew our energy for the coming day. Therefore, unless we show Jesus' death, by eating his flesh and drinking his blood, we are not accepting that he has died – that the sacrifice of Calvary has been made, the ransom been paid. If we reject his flesh and blood, we are implicitly 'relegating' him to the time before Calvary. And in so doing, we are negating our own salvation. 'As often as you eat this bread and drink this cup, you proclaim the Lord's death until he comes' (1 Corinthians 11:26). Our eating and drinking of Jesus affirms his death, his mission, his future coming.

The death that never dies
Calvary has not finished. Its memorial lives on. At every Eucharist the Lamb is still being offered; whenever there is evil in the world, the blood of the Lamb still flows. It was a life laid down 'once, only once, and once for all'; but the life that is left is the life that makes all things new, and it cannot die. The wounds remain on the Crucified's body, but the body has changed: it has mysteriously divided, and each part is a whole. Each part gives life to others. Each part is seen on the paten and in the chalice, on every Christian altar in the world. If it does nothing else, surely this tells us something of the immensity of the sacrifice Jesus made; of the love that persuades him to spread himself to preside at every Eucharist; of the solemn responsibility we have, to partake of that Eucharist. And Paul cautions us: 'Whoever eats the bread or drinks the cup of the Lord in an unworthy manner will be answerable for the body and blood of the Lord' (1 Corinthians 11:27). It is a risk we take at our peril.

Suggested Hymns
Bread of the world, in mercy broken; Father, who on man dost shower; Lord of all power, I give you my will; O bread to pilgrims given

Ninth Sunday after Trinity   *Second Service*
Fire on Earth   Ps. 100; Ex. 2:23–3:10; Heb. 13:1–15; Luke 12:49–56
'I came to bring fire to the earth, and how I wish it were already kindled! I have a baptism with which to be baptized, and what stress I am under until it is completed!' Luke 12:49, 50

For our sakes
This is Jesus at his most loving. He is not anguished on his own account, but on ours. He looks forward to the time when his baptism into death will give us the freedom to inherit eternal life. That is his one aim, in coming to earth: and he has to wait until his ministry has run its course. A lesser teacher would no doubt have employed human wisdom, logic and ingenuity to bring forward the *dénouement*; but Jesus, though eager for the outcome, will not truncate his ministry. The majesty that can bow to the will of God against such odds is awe-inspiring. How often do we try to anticipate the Almighty – just in case he were to decide against coming in time?

Holy fire
Jesus was probably looking to the cloven tongues of Spirit-fire, which were to come at Pentecost. But it was also a fire that would divide families. He could look forward through history-to-come, and see the fire of Christian fervour, and the divisions it would cause. He would see that for the cross and the Crucified there would be holy (and unholy) wars, schisms, heresies – and the greatest courage and fortitude that the world has ever known. He would appreciate that because of his great sacrifice, the world would be changed. And how he longed for it all to happen!

Looking skywards
As he visioned, perhaps he looked up; and, as a good teacher, quickly changed from the sublime-to-be, to the physical-that-was. Did the people not read the sky, to assess what they may do on any day? Why, then, could they not read what was going to happen, when he told them of his mission? The same can apply today: we rely on forecasts and computer predictions for everything from the weather to stock market movements; but do we press into the scriptures? Are we fervent in prayer, to seek God's will? Do we tune in to the spiritual forecasts?

Division, not peace
It may be that life after death will be calm and untroubled (though there is no plethora of support for this in the Bible): but Jesus warns us not to expect this earthly life to be unadulterated ease. 'I have come to bring ... division' (v. 51). Amazing words, from the Prince of peace, gentle Jesus! But it is a stern reminder that

181

nothing must come between us and the will of God: even the closest ties on earth must not part us and our Christian commitment. If they threaten to do so, we must heed their warning and take steps to straighten out our priorities. We are doing no one good service by allowing God to take second place, even on sympathetic or charitable grounds. If staying in God's will means the severing or weakening of earthly ties, the 'pulling out of an eye', or 'the cutting off of a leg or arm' must be done. As has been often remarked: 'The conditions are stern, but they are glorious.' God never asks us to give up anything that will damage our spiritual life.

Suggested Hymns
Take my life, and let it be; Strengthen for service, Lord, the hands; 'Lift up your hearts!' We lift them Lord, to thee; Teach me, my God and King

Tenth Sunday after Trinity (Proper 16)
27 August   *Principal Service*
Words of Eternal Life   1 Ki. 8:22–30, 41–43; Ps. 84; Eph. 6:10–20; John 6:56–69

'So Jesus asked the twelve, "Do you also wish to go away?' Simon Peter answered him, "Lord, to whom can we go? You have the words of eternal life."' John 6:67, 68

Offended or disheartened?
Jesus' teaching on his body and blood has either offended or disheartened many of his disciples; in the way that excuses can be found against attending worship today, perhaps some of these disciples had been looking for a reason to leave the ministry, and the difficult doctrine of flesh and blood proved the catalyst to get them on the move, away from a teacher who had become incomprehensible. Do we make mountains out of molehills, to avoid meetings, commitment or involvement in aspects of our Christian life which leave us floundering out of our depth? Or do we stay with the new teaching, the advanced study group, the

proposed development, in the belief that God is guiding us forward within his will?

New teaching
We are so familiar with the gospels, it may be difficult to realize how much of a shock the teaching of Jesus would be to many of his first-century Jewish listeners. They could refer to prophecies in the ancient scrolls, which pointed up various aspects of Jesus' life and work; but over the centuries Jewish messianic expectations had moved in accordance with their hopes: a priestly Messiah, to restore worship to its former pattern; a kingly Messiah, to restore the Davidic monarchy to Jerusalem; and a glorious Messiah – as far removed from the Son of a carpenter as it was possible to be. Small wonder, then, that when the carpenter's Son began telling them that unless they ate his flesh and drank his blood, they would have no life in him, they melted away from his side in droves.

Et tu, Brute?
And will you go as well? was the question put to Peter and the eleven. And Peter's reply was poignant in its tactlessness and insight. To stay loyal to Jesus because we have no one else to trust is perhaps not the best reason – yet because he is the one with our passport to eternity, it is the only course worth taking. Sometimes we do make a particular choice for the wrong reasons – yet it turns out to be the best choice in the end. Remember when Jesus decided to go to Bethany after the death of Lazarus. Thomas advised the others to accompany him, 'that we may die with him' (John 11:16): a brave, if desperate choice – yet how thankful Thomas and the others would be, that they had gone with Jesus that day.

Words of eternal life
'Heaven and earth will pass away, but my words will not pass away,' Jesus said (Matthew 24:35; Mark 13:31; Luke 21:33). They are indestructibly divine, dealing with a timelessness that we cannot understand; and the more of Jesus' words we have in our hearts, the better equipped we are to make the transition from time to eternity. He gives up his words, his flesh, his blood; it is an amazing love that holds nothing back. Is our Christian commitment equally unreserved?

Christ is made the sure foundation; Jesus calls us, o'er the tumult;
Oft in danger, oft in woe; Who is on the Lord's side?

Tenth Sunday after Trinity   *Second Service*
Sabbath Healing   Ps. 116; Ex. 4:27–5:1; Heb. 13:16–21;
Luke 13:10–17

*'"Ought not this woman, a daughter of Abraham, whom Satan bound
for eighteen long years, be set free from this bondage on the sabbath
day?" When he said this, all his opponents were put to shame, and the
entire crowd was rejoicing at all the wonderful things that he was doing.'
Luke 13:16, 17*

Time and chance
No one had apparently thought to heal the woman during her
eighteen-year nightmare of suffering; and Jesus castigated the
leader of the synagogue for the hypocrisy which was plainly
behind the token protest at 'work' on the sabbath. How often do
we hide similarly deep-rooted prejudices under a veneer of seeming justification? God is not deceived: he looks to the heart of the
motives that prompt us to word and action. It was no coincidence
that brought Jesus and the woman together in the synagogue, that
sabbath day. The hypocrisy of the local ecclesiastical hierarchy
was going to be shown up: Jesus did not spare the blushes of a
leader who blatantly was *mis*-leading his congregation.

Divine diagnosis
In Jesus' diagnosis of the length, severity and cause of the woman's
condition, we see a compassion and insight which is awesome in
its thoroughness and penetration. There may be times when we feel
God does not understand what we are experiencing; that if we have
largely brought the predicament on ourselves; we do not deserve
his understanding; or even that he had inflicted an illness, disability
or calamity on us, to test us. Whether we deserve his understanding,
or not, he always understands; and this reading shows it is not God,
but Satan, who is responsible for the affliction. Jesus is implicitly
telling us that it is not God's will that anyone should suffer sickness

or disability. 'I will not bring upon you any ... diseases,' God promised the Exodus Israelites (Exodus 15:26); and Matthew quotes Isaiah, that Jesus himself 'took our infirmities and bore our diseases' (Matthew 8:17). Why, then, do we still experience illness and incapacity? In much the same way that we continue to sin, even though Jesus has already borne our sins. It is because God has never withdrawn the freedom of will; we are making choices all the time, and others are also making them. Inevitably, we – and they – make mistakes. And, as others can be affected by the choices we make, for good or ill, so, also, we can be drawn into the vortex of a choice, or choices, made by them. Our case would indeed be dire, were it not for the sacrifice of Christ, which gives us hope for the Hereafter, if not a guarantee of unalloyed bliss now.

Loyal, despite everything
Though crippled for so long, the woman nevertheless did not stay away from the synagogue. Whatever calamity or trouble we face, it should not drive a wedge between us and God. Jesus showed by example how crucial was regular worship in his life; if he needed it, how much more do we. Today's pericope also demonstrates that it is by attending our place of worship that we give God a special opportunity to act in our lives. By attending to the things of God, others may be offended; but that is their problem – and it may be as short-lived as the 'rejoicing' of the crowd in the synagogue. Jesus knew what was in men's hearts: the ability to rejoice, and to criticize. May we keep our eyes on God, and not be diverted either by indulgence or opposition.

Suggested Hymns
In the cross of Christ I glory; Jesus, good above all other; Jesus, the name high over all; All for Jesus, all for Jesus

Eleventh Sunday after Trinity (Proper 17)
3 September   *Principal Service*
Abandon at Your Peril   S. of Sol. 2:8–13; Ps. 45:1–2, 6–9; Jas. 1:17–27; Mark 7:1–8, 14–15, 21–23
'Jesus said, "You abandon the commandment of God, and hold to human tradition."' Mark 7:8

Cancelling God's commandment

The Greek verb translated 'abandon' is the very strong *atheteo*, which can also mean 'to set aside', or 'to cancel'. Jesus was not wrapping up his message in cottonwool. He was accusing the Pharisees of cancelling the old laws of God, and substituting modern laws which seemed to conform better to modern circumstances. Has this not more than a hint of the twenty-first century? Are we not fond of introductions and changes and modifications – because, so we say, 'we must move with the times'? Are we not bombarded with advertisements which assure us, in one way or another: 'If it's new, it's better'?

God makes new

How often we forget that the privilege of making new is God's, not ours. He says, 'Behold, I will make all things new. I will give you a clean heart. I will renew a right spirit within you. I will give you a new commandment.' There is, by itself, no new thing under the sun. God alone gives us the new and living way. Of the Decalogue, Jesus said: 'I am not come to destroy, but to fulfil.' Yet they are the old laws, are they not? The Pharisees, who considered themselves the leading exponents of the scriptures, were very, very human in wanting to improve on those old laws. But God had said: 'Stand at the crossroads, and look, and ask for the ancient paths, where the good way lies, and walk in it' (Jeremiah 6:16). Six centuries later, Jesus tells the Pharisees, sternly and bluntly: 'You are making a good job of rejecting the commandment of God.'

Still the freedom of choice

Notice Jesus does not say: 'Stop rejecting God's commandments.' He points out the fault, and leaves it to the Pharisees to turn about and repair it – if they so choose. Jesus, out of love and concern, shows us where we have gone astray; he chastens those for whom he cares: the others do not see their faults. Ironically, the 'traditions' of the Pharisees were intended to preserve the law. In reality, they had become so overweight, that, when law and traditions conflicted, the latter often predominated by *force majeure*. So the first-century Pharisees had, however unwittingly, come to be seen as usurping the position of God. They thought, when it came to interpreting the laws, that they knew better than God. It does not do to be patronizing where God is concerned. He made the world, without our help. He made us, without our help. And he will save us, without our help. He is omnipotent, and he asks for nothing but our loyalty – loyalty to his laws, which he will preserve, without our help. God's laws are strong enough to stand alone, without any man-made protection.

Living for God
Showing loyalty to God means refusing to allow anything – traditions, influences, pressures – to come between us and our awareness of God.

> *Say nothing you would not like God to hear;*
> *Do nothing you would not like God to see;*
> *Write nothing you would not like God to read;*
> *Go to no place you would not like God to find you;*
> *Read no book of which you would not like*
> *God to say, 'Show it to me'.*

Don Bosco, Madonna

Suggested Hymns
Help us, O Lord, to learn; My God, accept my heart this day; Teach me, my God and King; The Lord is King, lift up thy voice

Eleventh Sunday after Trinity
Second Service **Salt of the Earth**
Ps. 119:1–16; Ex. 12:21–27; Matt. 4:23–5:20

'You are the salt of the earth; but if the salt has lost its taste, how can its saltiness be restored? It is no longer good for anything, but is thrown out and trampled underfoot.' Matthew 5:13

Present salt
Jesus is not saying we shall be, or even have been, salt – but that we are, in the present. We are, because he has made it possible for us to be so. We are not waiting for him to make us into special people, folk capable of flavouring the world with his love – we

are already special, salted with the tang of the gospel: at baptism, at our commitment, Jesus converted us into special people, seasoned with salt. This miracle gives us the power to walk tall and meet the world eyeball to eyeball. It gives us the courage to join any argument to put the case for God. It gives us the integrity and consistency to speak out for the truth, rather than be yes-men and go along with the crowd in the interests of 'peaceful co-existence' at any cost.

Salt cannot be overlooked
Salt, by its very nature, is not bland. It cannot be ignored. It increases the value of whatever it touches, turning the mediocre into something worthwhile. Chemically, salt can be defined as 'a body readily capable of undergoing double decomposition' – that is, a body which, when brought into contact with another, exchanges some of its elementary constituents for those of the other body: a body which is A1 at surviving. Equally, there is no getting away from the gospel of Jesus once it has knocked at a person's heart. Like salt, it is persistent; like salt, it is also aseptic, in that it cleanses from sin and the impurities that sin can bring. Once it is applied, it halts the putrefying action of sin in the human psyche. And, as salt is essential for the simplest meal, so is the gospel of Christ found in the humblest places. As far as the love of God reaches, so the undying, preservative quality of the gospel is seen.

Salt in the earth
Salt's deterioration or adulteration leaves a blank which cannot be filled. So it is with a Christian: in the Book of Life, each of us fills a gap which can be infilled by no other. If a person loses his saltiness, there will be an accusing lacuna in the book – for each of us is a 'one-off', with the responsibility such uniqueness brings. Around the year AD 90, Rabbi Yosef ben Chananiah was asked: 'If salt has lost its flavour, how will it be salted?' He answered, 'With the afterbirth of a mule.' 'But a mule,' protested the questioner, 'is barren, and can therefore have no afterbirth!' 'Neither can salt lose its flavour,' came the quiet reply (TB *Bekoroth*, 8b). In the rabbinic view, Israel, the chosen race, was incapable of becoming unsalty salt. As Christians, we dare not presume to such over-confidence, though perhaps at times our lives do reflect the standpoint of Rabbi Yosef. But in the stillness of our communion

with God this week, can we not ask: What is the percentage of salt in our spiritual make-up? What proof do we give, or seek to give, of our faith? What kind of salt are we – in our own eyes, in the eyes of the world, and in the eyes of God?

Suggested Hymns
Hark, my soul! It is the Lord; Revive thy work, O Lord; O Love, that wilt not let me go; Hark! Hark, my soul! angelic songs are swelling

Twelfth Sunday after Trinity (Proper 18)
10 September   *Principal Service*   **Asking of Jesus**
Prov. 22:1–2, 8–9, 22–23; Ps. 125; Jas. 2:1–10, 14–17; Mark 7:24–37

'They brought to him a deaf man who had an impediment in his speech, and they begged him to lay his hand on him.' Mark 7:32

Healing ministry
It was a frequent request on the part of those who wanted Jesus to heal the sick, that he would 'lay his hand' on them. We could say: 'They prayed him to lay his hand' on them. There must lie a deep meaning in the *variety* of cures recorded in the gospels: why, for example, one is healed in the crowd, another is led out of the city to be healed, while another is sent to wash in the Pool of Siloam; for one the healing is instantaneous, while another at first sees men as trees walking. Jesus leads this man away from the crowd, perhaps so that he is more receptive, perhaps out of regard for the shock that sudden healing will bring.

P-R-A-Y-E-R
Jesus answers the prayer of the man's friends convincingly, by a double miracle of healing; and the lessons we can learn from this pericope in fact spell 'PRAYER':

Personal contact
Request

189

Action
Yielding
Enlightenment
Realization

Personal contact: the friends did not let the man find his own way to Jesus; they brought him. In 'begging' Christ to effect a cure, they made their trusting *request*. Jesus tells us to ask, in order to receive; there has to be a desire for grace, then *action* by Jesus comes quickly, as the patient *yields* to whatever treatment is meted out. The cure brings freedom to the body, and *enlightenment* to the soul, as the man sees Jesus looking up to heaven, and *realizes* from where his healing comes. He sees the reaction of the crowd who have followed to witness the cure, and who now spread the news.

> *O heavenly Father, may we not only have boldness*
> *to approach Christ, but also to bring others to him;*
> *may we have courage to make our requests known to him;*
> *and in the outcome of this, may we yield to his will,*
> *and be enlightened by his grace; until at last he leads*
> *us to the fuller realization of his holy purpose.*

The wideness of God's love
The Decapolis ('Ten Towns') was not good news for Jews: a multi-racial area, it had a strong Hellenistic influence; and Jesus, not only by preaching there but also by performing miracles, was demonstrating that God's love and concern extended beyond the 'chosen race'. This seems to have been a point of recurrent difficulty for the Jews; but the decapolitans, not bound by generations of pharisaical theosophy, appear far less inhibited, and quickly warm to Jesus (v. 37), though disregarding his warning (v. 36). Their prayer has been answered, and they are intent on spreading the good news.

Listening to Jesus
We are generally far better at praying – talking to Jesus – than listening. It is not clear why Jesus cautioned the crowd against making known the miracle. Who knows what benefits were jeopardized by the people's disregard? Let us pray, let us rejoice – but let us also listen to our Lord, even when what we believe he is telling us conflicts with our inclinations.

Twelfth Sunday after Trinity *Second Service*
Kingdom, Power, Glory Ps. 119:41–56; Ex. 14:5–31; Matt. 6:1–18

*'And do not bring us to the time of trial, but rescue us from the evil
one, [for the kingdom and the power and the glory are yours for ever].'*
Matthew 6:13

God is able
God is able to deliver us from the evil one, because the kingdom
is his, the power is his, and the glory is for ever his. No one else
can deliver us; no one else is strong enough, or has the authority
sufficient for the job. Some positions on earth carry a lot of authority, but even the highest-ranking comes way below the power
and authority of God. Yet earthly power can seem impressive,
and, properly used, it can do much good; but how much more
can the power and authority of God turn the negativity of evil
into the positivity of good! Only God can deliver a person from
evil.

The presence of evil
It is not a healthy exercise – physically, mentally or spiritually –
to delve into the workings of the Devil. Yet there is evil in the
world: Satan is always on the prowl, and we do need to be aware
of him. His power is so much greater than ours, because, after all,
he is a spiritual being, not confined by time or space, never sleeping, never off duty. Therefore, if at any time we get the better of
Satan; if right is seen to triumph over wrong; if something good
that we do prevents something bad happening; if something we
say turns a bad situation around into a good one – then it is God
working in us and through us who is responsible for that, not we
ourselves. At best, we are his instruments.

191

Commitment

Jesus never wasted words, nor did he ever get his facts wrong. So, when he told his disciples to pray: 'Rescue us from the evil one,' he was looking to a twenty-four-hour commitment on the part of God, to do just that – because he knew there is no one born who can do it for himself. If we are in Satan's power, it is because we have not been keeping our prayer line to God in working order: we have taken our eyes off the word of God, our attention off his guiding. The battle goes on, every minute, from the cradle to the grave. It seems a never-ending challenge; yet when measured against eternity, even a hundred years seems to shrink to nothing. Are we living only for the present? 'If for this life only we have hoped in Christ, we are of all people most to be pitied,' Paul told the Corinthians (1 Corinthians 15:19).

Setting our sights

It is not in Satan's interests to see us set our sights on the kingdom, the power and the glory of God: these, after all, have stood between Satan and his success since Christ's sacrifice on Calvary. They are a lasting reminder to the Devil of the triumph of the cross. If we would only focus on this great truth when we are tempted, we should save ourselves a lot of trouble. Satan has been worsted, but while he can persuade us otherwise, he will try.

Inheritors

By virtue of the cross, we are legitimate inheritors of the kingdom; and by the grace of God we have the power to meet and overcome temptation – provided we give all the glory for overcoming to God. It is a tripartite phalanx of weaponry before which the Devil quails. Do we avail ourselves of these weapons? The choice is ours.

Suggested Hymns

Be Thou my guardian and my guide; Through all the changing scenes of life; Guide me, O thou great Redeemer; He who would valiant be

Thirteenth Sunday after Trinity (Proper 19)
17 September   *Principal Service*   What do *You* Say?
Prov. 1:20–33; Ps. 19; Jas. 3:1–12; Mark 8:27–38

'Jesus went on with his disciples to the villages of Caesarea Philippi, and on the way he asked his disciples, "Who do people say that I am?" . . . "But who do you say that I am?" Peter answered him, "You are the Messiah."' Mark 8:27, 29

Preparing for change
The time of Jesus' Passion is coming close. He knows it is, but as yet his disciples are in blissful ignorance. Soon, very soon, Jesus will take some of them up into the hills, where he will be transfigured. Until now, the ministry has consisted of travelling and preaching, healing and teaching. But now the mission moves into a higher gear. Jesus wants his disciples to start preparing for the change. 'Who do people say that I am?' He patiently hears them out, and then asks the crucial question: 'But what do you say?' God does not deal through a third party. We stand before him on a one-to-one basis. Jesus is our Mediator, certainly; but since he tells us that he and the Father are one (John 17), that does not alter the one-to-one relationship.

The Messiah
God prompts Peter, the unlearned, impatient, undiplomatic ex-fisherman of Galilee, to blurt out: 'You are the Messiah' (the Anointed One) – the One everyone has been expecting for centuries. Only one fisherman recognized him for what he was. We may not always realize just how much the Jews were looking forward to the Messiah. Yet it is still the case today that a great expectation can narrow our field of spiritual vision to such an extent that we fail to see the awaited outcome – particularly if it is not quite what we had envisioned.

Building for eternity
Jesus had his mind set on divine things (v. 33): on the Church that he was founding, and on how the remainder of his earthly ministry would be pointing to the setting up of that Church. Today, he continues to build for eternity: brick by brick, stone by stone, soul by soul, as his gospel spreads into ever more countries. There is

still some way to go: still many people in many places waiting to hear the gospel. Jesus has said that his second coming will not take place until that gospel has been published to all nations. On every Christian, therefore, rests the commission to share the word as much as possible.

Why so long?
Early in the twentieth century, the work of mission seemed to be gathering ever greater momentum; then came world wars, one after the other; communism, the Berlin Wall, the Bamboo Curtain – and apathy. Those wars have gone, though lesser ones remain; communism is no longer the force it was; the walls of partition have either crumbled, or are disintegrating; but we still need to fight apathy and indifference to the word of God. And in one country after another, today's missionaries are being asked: 'Why has it taken you so long to come and tell us of Jesus?' Can we, as Christians, imagine the vast Church that Jesus is still building – and yet see parts of the building growing slowly (or not at all), because the precious souls that would take their place in that portion have not yet been reached by the gospel? If, with Peter, we can affirm that Jesus *is* the Messiah, what are we doing in support of that affirmation?

Suggested Hymns
Father, Lord of all creation; There is a Redeemer; Just as I am, without one plea; Thou art the Christ, O Lord

Thirteenth Sunday after Trinity
Second Service   **The Narrow Gate**   Ps. 119:73–88; Ex. 18:13–26; Matt. 7:1–14

'Enter through the narrow gate; for the gate is wide and the road is easy that leads to destruction, and there are many who take it. For the gate is narrow and the road is hard that leads to life, and there are few who find it.' Matthew 7:13, 14

The hardest sponsored walk of all
We admire physical stamina and dedication; olympic athletes are fêted and accorded honour and attention. Yet spiritual athleticism and durability is often mistaken for eccentricity, fanaticism or misguided fervour. Somehow, sportsmen are expected to rise to a challenge, while the Christian life is believed to be a bed of roses – and when the roses prove to have more thorns than flowers, God is blamed for expecting too much. It is not God who is illogical, but we ourselves. He who did not spare his only-begotten Son will not belittle our spiritual potential by making our path to heaven a simple undertaking. Even the very entrance to the heavenly road is narrow: anyone trying to pass through the gate with a burden of fear, a bundle of worry, a load of anger, a parcel of unforgiveness . . . any excess baggage at all . . . will need to part company with that luggage before being able to pass through the gate. God asks us to part with nothing that will injure us, but with everything that will prevent our progress along his road. It is difficult to begin the hardest sponsored walk of all – and every mile we travel needs to be fought for. Were it not for the promise made by our chief sponsor, 'I am with you always' (Matthew 28:20), we should all fall by the wayside.

'Alternative route'
By contrast, Satan places alluring signs over the wide gate leading to his easy, alternative route to eternity; but none of his signs tell the whole truth, that his is an eternity in hell; so his unchallenging road is packed with folk commuting to their own destruction. It has always been easier to go with the crowd, than to stand alone; to allow one's boat to be swept along with the current, while we cannot see the dangerous weir round the bend in the river. Follow Jesus through the gospels, and you will see how he constantly spoke out against convention, mixed with the outcasts of society, championed the despised and deprived, and inveighed against injustice and bigotry in high places. And even when he meticulously observed the sabbath worship, his critics took umbrage (Luke 4:16, 28, 29). When we join the comparatively small number on God's narrow road, we can be sure the world will find something derogatory and hurtful to level against us. Jesus foretold this animosity: 'They will put you out of the synagogues. Indeed, an hour is coming when those who kill you will think that by doing so they are offering worship to God' (John 16:2). The

Devil is an expert in making white seem black, and black white.

The great search
Note that Jesus warns: 'There are few who *find* [the narrow gate].'
The onus is on us to seek for it, to search into the will of God. We
are not taxied to the heavenly entrance, with all expenses paid.
Our challenge begins not when we enter the gate, but when we
first learn of its existence. In the initial realization that Christ is
our Saviour, calling us, because he gave his blood for our sakes
... the narrow gate begins to take shape in our minds. Many
challenges may still lie between us and that gate; but once we
have seen it in prospect, life can never be the same again ...
whichever choice we eventually make.

Suggested Hymns
One more step along the world I go; Put thou thy trust in God;
The Spirit lives to set us free (Walk in the light); Let there be love
shared among us

Fourteenth Sunday after Trinity (Proper 20)
24 September Welcome to God Prov. 31:10–31;
Ps. 1; Jas. 3:13–4:3, 7–8a; Mark 9:30–37

*'Then he took a little child and put it among them, and taking it in his
arms, he said to them, "Whoever welcomes one such child in my name
welcomes me, and whoever welcomes me welcomes not me but the one
who sent me."' Mark 9:36, 37*

The Almighty
Unbelievable as it seems, we are to welcome the Lord of creation
– to open our hearts to the ruler of the universe; that he cares
enough for an individual to accept and appreciate love and greeting, is an unfathomable mystery – just as it is a mystery that we
all need to be re-born, to take up the innocence of a child, in order
to welcome Christ. Nicodemus could not understand this re-birth
(John 3:4), and his was one of the best brains in first-century
Jerusalem. The workings of God are foolishness to the sophisticated, worldly-wise. When we welcome a child (of any age) in the

name of Jesus (and thereby welcome God into our hearts), we are not operating on an intellectual level, but on the level of faith – 'the assurance of things hoped for, the conviction of things not seen' (Hebrews 11:1).

Interaction of Christ's members
The Church is Christ's body, comprising parts which need to interact in order to fulfil their mission. An arm or a leg is of no use until it works as part of a body. Similarly, a child of God is of no use to God, if he or she tries to exist in a vacuum. We need each other, to make Christ known to the world. Ours is not an ego trip: 'Not unto us, O Lord, not unto us, but unto thy name be all the glory.' A child is capable of a little love, a little learning. We need to realize that our love and learning is but a small fraction of the whole body of Christ. God could get along without us; we must be thankful that he has chosen not to. There is a place in heaven reserved for us, with our name recorded in the Lamb's Book of Life (Revelation 21:27); but God is not obliged to give us eternal life: we cannot earn heaven, or buy eternity. There is a boldness and assurance with which we can approach God (Hebrews 10:22); but still we must approach with the humility, the innocence, integrity and trust of a child.

Re-birth pangs
As a physical birth is attended by labour and pain, so is our re-birth in Christ. It is a dying to the world, a cutting off of extraneous material, a cleansing of all that drags us down to the mundane. Can we go through with it? Can we brave the pangs? Little by little, point by point, God will bring us to the place where whatever is holding us back from full commitment is seen clearly for the danger it is. The choice is ours: to reject it and move forward in freedom of faith – or to cling on to it, and forfeit an opportunity for spiritual advancement which may not be repeated.

In Jesus' arms
Jesus' body language spoke of unadulterated love. We should not be chary of giving an embrace in his name. The beggar who was embraced by an embarrassingly penniless Dostoevsky, replied that he had been given more than any money could buy. We must learn, like a child, to value what cannot be priced in the world's Stock Markets.

197

Behold, the mountain of the Lord; From heaven you came (The Servant King); Jesus, Friend of little children; O, sing a song of Bethlehem

Fourteenth Sunday after Trinity
Second Service   **What Sort of Man?**   Ps. 119:137–152; Ex. 19:10–25; Matt. 8:23–34

'Then he got up and rebuked the winds and the sea; and there was a dead calm. They were amazed, saying, "What sort of man is this, that even the winds and the sea obey him?"' Matthew 8:26, 27

Who is this man?
The question is still being asked: 'Who is Jesus?' Is he who he says he is? How can we believe it all? A man who is God? With our pitifully inadequate human understanding of love, we cannot comprehend the compassion that motivated the Son of God to leave glory for thirty-odd years, to suffer as no one had suffered before – for someone else's sin. If the very thought does not cause us to tremble, we need to get serious with God about our faith. Who do we believe, when we say we are Christians? A carpenter, whose yoke is (anything but) easy? A God who can control wind and water with a word? A shepherd, who will go to extreme lengths to rescue a single wandering lamb? A crucifixion victim, despised and rejected by all? A friend, a brother, who shares with us a common Father? Or, a Savior? Yes, surely it is Christ's saving power alone that can draw us to him in love. Were it not for that saving power, life here would be aimless, worth living only for a seventy-, eighty- or ninety-year period, and then to be snuffed out in perpetuity. Jesus is the man who stands between oblivion and eternal life? No – between eternal hell and eternal life!

Between the dead and the living
Aaron had stood between the dead and the living, and the plague was stopped (Numbers 16:48), when God had shown his anger at the revolt of Korah, Dathan and Abiram; so the crucified, resurrected and ascended Jesus stands between our consignment to hell

and our elevation to heaven. The work of salvation required one man; and only one was capable of fulfilling the operation. *This is Jesus*, whom Peter preached on the Day of Pentecost, when the Holy Spirit came in power, and the Christian Church was born. 'This man' (Acts 2:23), Jesus, had been 'freed from death' (v. 24), to bring us that same freedom. 'This Jesus' had been resurrected (v. 32), as Peter and the others could bear witness. 'This Jesus' was the man who had hung on the cross, dead, as many of those present could also bear witness (v. 36) – because they had done the deed. This is that Jesus. He still bears the scars, which mean that he is not entirely the same as he was before his great sacrifice. Our sin has effected the change in God himself: that realization should bring us to our knees – as, by the mercy of God, we cross over the divide between the dead and the living, by the bridge which those wounds have built.

For love of this Jesus
If Jesus is to be given our love, it is because his sacrifice has touched our hearts. We come to him with no other plea, for no other reason; and when our hearts have been so touched, we cannot with integrity approach him and then forget him. Once we have come, he says, 'Follow me'. We can choose to turn back ; but we then forfeit integrity and consistency. So, we must stay with him. And it is then that we learn salvation may have been free, but discipleship comes at a price – for he tells us: 'Go and make disciples of all nations, baptizing . . . and teaching . . . and, remember, I am with you always' (Matthew 28:19, 20).

'Who is this Jesus?' Whenever we are asked this question, the very life of our questioner may depend on our answer. 'Even the wind and the sea obey him.' That can be said of none but Jesus.

Suggested Hymns
Fierce raged the tempest; I love you, Lord, and I lift my voice; How firm a foundation; Oft in danger, oft in woe

Fifteenth Sunday after Trinity (Proper 21)

1 October   *Principal Service*   Salt in Yourselves

Est. 7:1–6, 9–10; 9:20–22; Ps. 124; Jas. 5:13–20; Mark
9:38–50

*'For everyone will be salted with fire. Salt is good; but if salt has lost
its saltiness, how can you season it? Have salt in yourselves, and be at
peace with one another.' Mark 9:49, 50*

Adulterated salt

Is there such a thing? Yes, in many ways. The Dead Sea is noted
not only for its high percentage of 'salty' salt, but also for a range
of other mineral deposits, including white crystals which look and
feel like salt, but have no salty flavour. These are crystals of carnallite – the hydrated chloride of potassium and magnesium, with a
bitter taste: salt which is not salty. From very early times,
unscrupulous traders would use carnallite to make their true salt
go further. Such swamping of Christian saltiness can be seen in
the case of religious persecution or harassment overcoming a
believer and causing his or her faith to waver or even succumb.
Then there was poor quality salt, such as was imported into Palestine from the vast marshes near Larnaca on Cyprus. It was stored
in houses rented for that purpose; but these houses usually had
primitive, beaten earth floors. Gradually, the salt nearest the
ground was spoilt, until the only course was to throw it out into
the streets, where passers-by trampled it underfoot. People like
this rotten salt do not take their faith seriously. Gradually other
interests take over, and their faith is not of a sufficiently-high
calibre to withstand the onslaught. Less and less time is kept for
God – until, one day, the world and its glitz have all but trampled
their faith into obscurity.

Roofing salt

In parts of the Holy Land today, as in the time of Jesus, salt is
spread on the flat house roofs. This thickens the roof which then
keeps the house cooler in summer and warmer in winter; it also
keeps the roof waterproof in the rainy season, since, when mixed
in a sufficiently concentrated amount, salt hardens a soil. As the
flat roofs are used for social gatherings, such salt is, like the Lar-

naca salt, being trampled underfoot. But this roofing salt is better salt. It began life as salt of quality, and is put to a useful purpose – but a purpose which seems to fall short of its value as a condiment. Christians like this salt may have great gifts, but use them humbly in the service of others. They play a steady, unobtrusive rôle in the community – often being so much taken for granted as, metaphorically, being trampled underfoot.

Red-hot salt
Arab bakers on occasion strew the floors of their ovens with salt, sometimes in powder form, sometimes roughly crushed or hammered from large blocks. The catalytic effect on the slow-burning fuel (dried camel-dung) increases combustion. After a while, however, the 'combustible energy' of the salt expires and it is then swept up and thrown out into the street – once more to be trodden underfoot. Such Christians play a really vital part in the Church – for a while. Red-hot with enthusiasm, they are the life and soul of worship and study group, until their combustible energy flags and, exhausted, they retire into virtual oblivion.

Skin-deep religion
In first-century Palestine, salt was heavily taxed. Dishonest merchants were prone to mix cheap white powders (often chalk) with the salt, which would then not only be pretty tasteless, but even dangerous to eat – and which had certainly lost most, if not all, of its preserving and aseptic qualities. A Christian with such contaminated salt in his make-up would be one who, while outwardly appearing a Christian, had nevertheless allowed sins and shortcomings into his life. His religion, in other words, would be skin-deep, and liable to crack under pressure.

Gospel salt
In Old Testament days, salt was added symbolically to the Jewish sacrifices, to point to their inherent incorruptibility. So the reality and permanence of a Christian life will be recognized by the fire promised at the Last Day; in the fire, that which is merely wood, hay or stubble will be consumed, while that which is of real worth will be for ever preserved. In the time of proving, may we season not only our lives with the pure salt of the gospel, but also as many other lives as God gives us opportunity to touch.

Dear Lord and Father of mankind; Father, hear the prayer we
offer; I lift my eyes to the quiet hills; When all thy mercies

Fifteenth Sunday after Trinity
Second Service   **Filled with Awe**   Pss 120, 121;
Ex. 24; Matt. 9:1–8

*' "So that you may know that the Son of Man has authority on earth to
forgive sins" – he then said to the paralytic – "Stand up, take your bed
and go to your home." And he stood up and went to his home. When
the crowds saw it, they were filled with awe, and they glorified God who
had given such authority to human beings.' Matthew 9:6–8*

Faithful friends
The Markan and Lukan accounts of this healing describe how the
paralytic's friends broke up the house roof and lowered the patient
down to Jesus in the room below. Matthew omits this, but makes
it clear that Jesus commended their faith and healed the sick man
because of it. The friends were determined to succeed in their
mission, at any cost; that is precisely the sort of commitment God
is looking for. The best evidence of faith is the effort we make to
prove our faith. How is this effort to be measured? God alone
knows our spiritual potential. He will expect from us all that we
can give. He does not give us talents to lie unused. When God
gives a command, even though it may seem impossible, he gives
also the strength to carry it through. But the strength will not
come until we try to obey. When Jesus commanded the paralytic
to get up, there was no way in the natural order of things that the
man could comply. But, as he recognized the authority in Jesus'
voice, and was willing to obey, new power flowed into his limbs.
His friends were not the only ones with faith that day.

New life on earth
God gave him renewed strength when he had heard Jesus' voice
and wanted to obey it. If we follow Jesus through the gospels, we
find that a significant part of his ministry was giving new life,
strength and joy to people while they still had a mission to fulfil

on earth. Jesus certainly preached 'the kingdom of God' – but it was a kingdom, a state of being, for our time on earth as well as our eternity Hereafter. 'Your kingdom come – as in heaven, so on earth,' he taught his disciples to pray. 'And when you go out preaching,' he told them, 'say to people: "The kingdom of God has come near you." Heal the sick, cure the blind, cleanse the lepers, raise the dead; and say: "The kingdom of God is at hand."'

Success
As we journey ever nearer to God, we can be sure of one thing: God wants us to make it – now and Hereafter. He was at pains to make us as beautiful as we are, with all the potential we have – and God deals in the business of success. If necessary, he would tax every one of those cows on his thousand hills, to get us where he wants us. All we have to do is to co-operate – as the people in today's miracle co-operated and called forth awe among the assembled crowd.

Unconventional
Those friends of the paralytic were so determined to get him to Jesus, they could break with convention when convention got in the way of their mission. And today it quite often happens that Christians, obeying what they believe is the will of God, appear – to the world – to be doing extraordinary things and letting convention fly out of the window. We must be thankful that God is not bound by what most of the world regards as 'normal', for the normal Christian life is anything but normal. When one comes to think about it, everything that God calls us to do is impossible. Was it not sheer recklessness that led those friends to move all obstacles to get the paralytic to Jesus? Yet their reckless abandon resulted in a beautiful commendation from Jesus, and in the restoration of their friend. What may we dare to do for God, that we have not already done? Has anyone yet been awed by our Christian faith and boldness?

Suggested Hymns
Help us to help each other, Lord; Thine arm, O Lord, in days of old; Fight the good fight; God sent his Son, they called him Jesus (Because he lives)

Sixteenth Sunday after Trinity (Proper 22)
8 October *Principal Service* **As a Little Child**

Job 1:1; 2:1–10; Ps. 26; Heb. 1:1–4; 2:5–12; Mark 10:2–16

' "Truly I tell you, whoever does not receive the kingdom of God as a little child will never enter it." And he took them up in his arms, laid his hands on them, and blessed them.' Mark 10:15, 16

The value of childhood

Jesus warmed to children, not only because he was wholly love, but also because he had once been a child. He knew the vulnerability as well as the value of childhood: so frail, and yet so beautifully innocent. But as the child grows, so often both the frailty and the innocence depart; and what is left in their place is something the world likes to call wisdom. When Yuri Gagarin, the first man in space, returned from his epic flight, he remarked scornfully to a priest in Moscow: 'I never found God up there!' The priest quietly replied: 'If you have not found God on earth, you will not find him in heaven.' Faith is simplicity of belief, not advanced astro-physics or telescopic vision. Paul pursues this theme: 'The righteousness that comes from faith says, "Do not say in your heart, 'Who will ascend into heaven?' (that is, to bring Christ down), or 'Who will descend into the abyss?' (that is, to bring Christ up from the dead). But what does it say? 'The word is near you, on your lips and in your heart' " ' (Romans 10:6–8). Can we not accept the proximity and provenance of God, unconditionally, as a child? Instead, we blue-pencil and red-pencil the Bible, until we have convinced ourselves that such-and-such is myth or allegory; or that Paul wrote this, but not that; or that a certain text is of doubtful authenticity ... It is good to have sound biblical scholarship, and informed discussion can do much to enrich our understanding; but let us pray for grace to season criticism with consistency; investigation with integrity; sophistication with the child-like innocence which says: 'Lord, I believe. Help thou mine unbelief.'

On fruitful ground

Jesus' teaching may not have appealed to the dedicated seminarians of Jerusalem's prestigious rabbinical schools, headed by rabbis such as the austere Shammai, or even the moderate Hillel.

He used down-to-earth illustrations, more from rural areas than the towns; and his language was unpretentious. Even a child could be held spellbound by his preaching – while, time and again, the message fell on deaf ears among the older listeners: despite the fact that, time and again, Jesus emphasized the truth of his words. It took child-like acceptance to grasp this most basic teaching. It was as a child that Jesus had been accepted by the unsophisticated shepherds, and the erudite Magi. Both extremes had acknowledged what as yet they could not see – 'something' veiled in infancy, just as a child will often recognize a subject in a drawing or painting, which to adults is merely a series of lines or splashes of colour.

The right instinct
A child is drawn by instinct to simple goodness; and so it is not surprising that children were attracted to Jesus. They did not complicate the issue by questioning his social status or religious stance. Can we not take Sir Frederick Faber's words to heart?

> *But we make his love too narrow,*
> *By false limits of our own;*
> *And we magnify his strictness*
> *With a zeal he will not own . . .*
> *If our love were but more simple,*
> *We should take him at his word,*
> *And our lives would be all sunshine*
> *In the sweetness of our Lord.*

Suggested Hymns
Christ is the world's light; There's a wideness in God's mercy; Will you come and follow me; Lead us, heavenly Father, lead us

Sixteenth Sunday after Trinity
Second Service   **The Kingdom is Near**   Pss 125, 126; Josh. 3:7–17; Matt. 10:1–22
'As you go, proclaim the good news, "The kingdom of heaven has come near."' Matthew 10:7

A soul-searching claim

The fact that Jesus chose this amazing statement, this soul-searching claim, as instruction for his first missionaries, shows the importance he attached to it. Do we consider it of prime importance today? Do we claim this truth, in his name? Do we understand what he means by it? He is telling us that it is his presence – either physically, as the disciples experienced it, or spiritually through his gospel, as we experience it – which brings the kingdom close. This presence is evidence in both time and space: in time, for it is here now but was not before his gospel was made known; and in space, for it is near to those who are reached by Christ's mission – those who are given the choice of accepting or rejecting it.

Timeless reality

Learned theologians tell us that the kingdom of heaven is a 'timeless reality'. It is a fine title, but who can comprehend it? Paul is less high faluting: 'The kingdom of God is not food and drink, but righteousness and peace and joy in the Holy Spirit' (Romans 14:17). This is a great, tripartite claim for the identity of the kingdom: it is 'righteousness and peace and joy' as mediated through the Holy Spirit – building on the righteousness, peace and joy which characterized Jesus and his gospel. 'The law and the prophets' had shown God to the people before John the Baptist came on the scene; since when, with the coming of Jesus, the kingdom of heaven is preached.

Heaven came down

We are children of the new covenant, children of the kingdom of heaven. Jesus brought something of heaven to us when he came to earth. In the special prayer he gave, he reminds us that the kingdom of God exists in heaven: 'Your kingdom come . . . on earth as it is in heaven' (Matthew 6:10). Can we preach this kingdom? To do so, we need to hear what Jesus is saying in the way of encouragement. We are his 'little flock', to whom it is our Father's 'good pleasure' to give us the kingdom (Luke 12:32). We are 'the salt of the earth' (Matthew 5:13), the 'light of the world' (Matthew 5:14) – the physical means by which his kingdom spreads today and comes close to people. Our task is to extend the news of the kingdom, and to bring it as close to as many people as we can. We, as heralds of the cross, are to be up and doing, spreading the news of the kingdom through the righteousness, joy and peace of God.

Worth listening to
There would be some, on the route taken by the Twelve, who would look askance at men who set out with no money, change of clothing or food, even given the conditions of the time. Can we not hear them saying: 'These men must respect their master, to work like this!' And surely many would decide that the disciples' message was worth listening to. Can the same be said of our message? Do we, as Christians, concentrate on showing and sharing the righteousness, joy and peace of God? Or do we think our introduction to the kingdom will come only when we have left the rest of the world behind? As representatives of Christ, we have a mission to the world, and – if we will let him – God through us can bring his kingdom near to very many people. We can perceive the kingdom – or not. Those to whom we minister can perceive it – or not. Our recognition of God's kingdom does not govern the operation of God. He does his part, he brings the kingdom close – within reach – and leaves the rest to us. We can take heart that he wants us to recognize it; he is anxious we should recognize it; he is even willing us to recognize it. Praise God, his kingdom is still on offer – still available, through you, through me, to the world.

Suggested Hymns
Tell out, my soul; We have a gospel to proclaim; Thy kingdom come, O God; The Church of God a kingdom is

Seventeenth Sunday after Trinity (Proper 23)
15 October   *Principal Service*   **Suited to the Work**
Job 23:1–9, 16–17; Ps. 22:1–15; Heb. 4:12–16;
Mark 10:17–31

'Jesus, looking at him, loved him, and said, "You lack one thing: go, sell what you own, and give the money to the poor, and you will have treasure in heaven; then come, follow me." When he heard this, he was shocked and went away grieving, for he had many possessions.' Mark 10:21, 22

207

Misplaced confidence

The man was confident that he could pass the entrance examination for eternal life. He was a good living citizen, with a clear conscience that many would envy. It had never occurred to him that his wealth would be anything but an asset. The shock of Jesus cutting through his misplaced confidence sent him away 'grieving', mourning over the very suggestion of loss. He could not understand why his balance sheet bore no resemblance to the one Jesus had. It is a lesson to us all, to run a check over the priorities in our lives: are we, for instance, trusting in money or possessions – or even friendships – too much?

Preconceptions

It can be so easy to come to Christ with misconceptions of what he really wants from us – or preconceptions of what we think we need from him. If we can come with a comparatively clear conscience because we have been honestly trying to amend our ways, he will honour the commitment. If we can come with a clear conscience because we have anaesthetized our awareness of sin, we need to attack our over-confidence very quickly. Jesus 'loved' the man (v. 21), despite his dependence on wealth. This implies that apart from his money he was well suited to the work of following Christ. How tragic to be called of God, and yet unable to take up the offer!

Real essentials

His money was not inherently evil: it could have been used to benefit the poor and dispossessed; but the way in which he was hoarding it, or lavishing it on himself or his family, was perpetuating a barrier between him and God. Money is a gift from God, which can be mis-used more easily than virtually any other gift – which is why money can be traced to the root of most troubles in this world. The ministry team of Jesus needed money for its day-to-day expenses: we are told that Judas was the treasurer, and that he misappropriated its funds (John 12:6; 13:29). No one can live without money, and God does not intend that we should try (Matthew 5:32, 33); but we are not to make a god out of it (Matthew 5:24). To put one's trust in earthly security is really to live more dangerously than God intended. Little by little, he will go to work in the life of someone who is committed to following Jesus – until that person has recognized the real essentials of life, essentials mani-

fested by the Holy Spirit: 'love, joy, peace, patience, kindness, generosity, faithfulness, gentleness and self-control' (Galatians 5:22).

How difficult!
Jesus had to reiterate how difficult entry into the kingdom of God
is for the rich (Mark 10:23, 24), because the disciples could not
grasp his message. And today the self-made millionaire, the 'rags-
to-riches' story, and a jackpot fortune of one sort or another, seems
to personify success: a fleeting, ephemeral success – but there are
many modern Esaus ready to sell their true inheritance for a mess
of potage. Let us remember to give God the things that are God's:
not a single coin or banknote has yet carried his likeness.

Suggested Hymns
God of mercy, God of grace; O God of Bethel; Come, Holy Spirit,
heavenly dove; Will you come and follow me

Seventeenth Sunday after Trinity
Second Service   **Take My Yoke**   Ps. 127; Josh. 5:13–
6:20; Matt. 11:20–30

'Come to me, all you who are weary and are carrying heavy burdens,
and I will give you rest. Take my yoke upon you, and learn from me:
for I am gentle and humble in heart, and you will find rest for your
souls. For my yoke is easy, and my burden is light.' Matthew 11:28–30

Light and easy?
These are beautiful words of Jesus – and yet, so often, the yoke
seems anything but easy, and his burden positively back-breaking.
At such times, therefore, are we making heavy weather of what
are essentially smooth waters? Does the fault lie with us? It must
be so, if we are to take these verses at face value. 'Learn from me,'
Jesus invites. Learn how to live, learn how to fulfil the will of God.
If we are honest with ourselves, we cannot learn anything worth
knowing without recourse to Jesus. The world can only teach us
how to die to God and live to self. Jesus reverses this process of
self-destruction – and he encourages us, by telling us it is easy to
abandon ourselves to him. The commitment may ostracize us from

the world, even from our family; but if Jesus is to have his way, the severance must come.

No compromise

We are to make no accommodation with lesser values. Jesus chose a yoke as his illustration advisedly; for when one is shouldering a certain yoke, it is impossible to carry any other: for better or worse, we are under that yoke. There can be no compromise: we are either under Jesus' yoke, or we are not. Yokes do not come in pairs or halves. Once we have taken on his yoke, it is all or nothing.

Wide invitation

All who are tired or over-burdened are included in Jesus' invitation. He will not refuse any who come, but we must come: we must make the first move. We must be willing to be divinely yoked. Earlier in the reading, we have heard about towns such as Chorazin and Capernaum, which had witnessed 'most' of Jesus' deeds of power (vv. 20, 23), but who had not repented. What does it take? asks Jesus: even the vice-ridden centres of Tyre and Sidon would have got the message by now! Sometimes we can be so preoccupied with what we want Jesus to do, that we fail to appreciate all he has done already. 'Learn from me,' he still insists. It needs not a heroic, but a humble laying down of our will, and a wide open listening ear, to get our priorities in line with God's. Are we prepared for what it will take? Are we willing to enrich our spiritual vocabulary by jettisoning the power-hungry 'I' and 'mine' and 'me' and 'my'? These over-used nuts and bolts play no rôle in the construction of Christ's yoke, which instead is bound together with cords of love and self-denial.

'My burden is light'

It is light, because God had taken the strain. 'Cast all your care on him, for he cares for you,' Paul directs. A burden shared may indeed be a burden halved: a burden taken, is no burden at all. God knows we have a rough ride at times: we could not survive if we took all our cares along as well. Let go grief, worry and the rest. Let them go. Let God take the strain. He is so much on top of the job, he will give us *rest* as we press on: rest in the course of the journey. Above everything else, God wants us to make it to eternity. Can we understand his loving care and concern? No, not this side of eternity. But we can take it on trust.

Art thou weary, art thou languid?; I heard the voice of Jesus say;
Come, let us sing of a wonderful love; Now, come to me, all you
who seek

Eighteenth Sunday after Trinity (Proper 26)
22 October *Principal Service* **'We are Able'** Job
38:1–7; Ps. 104:1–9, 24, 35c; Heb. 5:1–10; Mark 10:35–45

'Jesus said to them, "You do not know what you are asking. Are you able to drink the cup that I drink, or be baptized with the baptism that I am baptized with?" They replied, "We are able." ' Mark 10:38, 39

The right way of asking
'You ask and do not receive, because you ask wrongly' (James
4:3). James and John did not appreciate the enormity (or the
impossibility) of their request for special seats in glory. (In
Matthew's account, the brothers' blushes are spared, in that the
request comes from their mother, Matthew 20:20f.). Not only was
the request itself out of order, but such a special favour was not
Christ's to grant. The other disciples, predictably, took umbrage.
It could easily have been an all-round disaster; but Jesus, in his
mercy, returned the request with a question of his own: one which
James and John could answer, and which restored their confidence.

Divine PR work
Jesus affirmed the brothers' loyalty and courage, even though he
was not in a position to accede to their initial request. Today, his
divine PR work with Christians is still as delicate. We still 'ask
wrongly', time and again; our importunity is enough to try any
saint's patience. Thank God, Jesus' tolerance outweighs that of a
normal saint! If we have made a crashingly stupid *faux pas*, he in
his love will turn it round into something which affirms our zeal
and builds up our confidence. 'Yes, Lord, we can do this! We are
able!' And, this accomplished, we have the courage to progress.
God is in the business of encouraging us: were it otherwise, we
should soon lose heart. If Jesus had treated the brothers' ill-advised
request with contempt, two great saints might have been lost to

the kingdom of heaven. The other disciples were ready to mete out judgement with scant mercy, for the world has a short fuse in such matters.

We *are* able

It is a good thing to take stock occasionally of our spiritual capabilities: usually we do not come near to knowing ourselves in this field – sometimes from a sense of over-scrupulous humility. Yet God-given talents need to be realized, and can be used in his service more fully, the better we are aware of them. False modesty and humility can be ever as dangerous as over-confidence. Our reputations and dignity matter far less than our service for God. The world, in any case, will find some criticism to level at us, merely for being Christians. It has often been said that, if in Britain it became an indictable offence to be Christ's, how many of us would remain free through lack of evidence! James and John were not afraid to come out into the open; let us have a similar disregard for opposition or ridicule. God's ways and those of the world are never going to run in tandem this side of eternity. 'We are able.' Lord, let me, this week, say . . . this. I am able. Let me go . . . here. I am able. Let me take up my cross. *I am able!*

> *'Are ye able,' said the Master,*
> *'To be crucified with me?'*
> *'Yes,' the sturdy dreamers answered,*
> *'To the death we follow thee.'*
>
> *'Are ye able?' still the Master*
> *Whispers down eternity,*
> *And heroic spirits answer,*
> *Now, as then in Galilee:*
>
> *'Lord, we are able,*
> *Our spirits are thine;*
> *Re-mould them, make us*
> *Like thee, divine.*
>
> *Thy guiding radiance*
> *Above us shall be,*
> *A beacon to God,*
> *To faith and loyalty.'*
>
> *Earl Marlatt, b. 1892*

Eighteenth Sunday after Trinity
Second Service **Mercy not Sacrifice** Ps. 141; Josh. 14:6–14; Matt. 12:1–21

'I tell you, something greater than the temple is here. But if you had known what this means, "I desire mercy and not sacrifice," you would not have condemned the guiltless. For the Son of Man is Lord of the sabbath.' Matthew 12:6–8

The feel-good factor
To give something in expiation for our sins makes us feel better: we have got out of an awkward situation by our own efforts, so the good in us has once again outweighed the bad. We can look the world in the eye, and walk tall. But to confess sin to God, and receive his merciful pardon, is really hard. *We* have done wrong: *he* has crowned our repentance with forgiveness – and where does that leave us? – the recipients of a free pardon, the acceptance of which needs grace. We are used to grace from God, but often woefully inept at accepting it ourselves, much less in showing grace to those whom we have wronged, or who have wronged us.

The Church
To a certain extent, we rely on the sacraments of Holy Mother Church, as – in a rather different way – the first-century Jews relied on the temple and its ordinances. There is less danger today that we shall make a god out of ecclesiastical traditions and observances, as did the Jews of Jesus' time; yet we can fall into the trap of trying to bargain with God for favours in exchange for attending worship, even serving on committees and becoming involved to the hilt with study groups and the like. All these are good, and we should certainly take them on board; but we are not to trust in them for divine forgiveness and favour. A loving heart is better than all the possible formal observances.

213

Love of mercy

Outreach to one's neighbour, particularly under adverse circumstances, is more congenial to God than duty from a heart of stone. We rarely meet over-scrupulous defence of Sunday observance nowadays; but the Church will be criticized by inveterate carpers for too much indulgence, as for none at all. It is when 'Sunday observance' gets in the way of worship and doing God's will that we really need to worry. God deals in a merciful way with us, and desires that we in turn should be merciful, rather than censorious; quicker to help than to criticize; and always more ready to forgive than to rebuke.

> *With mercy and with judgement*
> *My web of time he wove;*
> *And aye the dews of sorrow*
> *Were lustred by his love.*
>
> A.R. Cousin

When we are spiritually mature enough to see mercy in all God's dealings with us, we shall have no room for criticism – of God, ourselves, or others. It is a condemnatory, critical spirit that seeks to atone for its own sins by mere sacrifice. The only sacrifice God is interested in is the atoning body and blood of Jesus in the eucharist, and the sacrifice of a contrite heart. Do we attempt to seek forgiveness by any substitutory sacrifice? Let us beware of even a hint of bargaining on this point.

Giving – receiving

'It is more blessed to give, than to receive.' And while God claims the right to out-give, we in turn should cultivate the blessing of giving to others, and expecting no return. God will keep a record: we can manage without our 'pound of flesh'. Today's reading points up the danger of using sabbath observance to inhibit the exercise of mercy, whether from God or man. No law on earth takes precedence over the divine blueprint for healthy spiritual living. Let us sever the connections of any traditions which endanger our walk with God, before their encroachment becomes life-threatening.

Lord, for the years; The sands of time are sinking; Father God, I wonder (I will sing your praises); When all thy mercies, O my God

Nineteenth Sunday after Trinity (Proper 25)

29 October   *Principal Service*   **A Beggar No More**

Job 42:1–6, 10–17; Ps. 34:1–8, 19–22; Heb. 7:23–28; Mark 10:46–52

'Throwing off his cloak, he sprang up and came to Jesus . . . Jesus said to him, "Go: your faith has made you well." Immediately he regained his sight, and followed him on the way.' Mark 10:50, 52

Blind belief

Bartimaeus did not need to throw off his cloak. He did it in a gesture of blind faith. That garment was his meal-ticket: it marked him out as deserving of alms, unable to earn a living by normal means. But as soon as he heard Jesus was there and asking him to come, Bartimaeus believed the cure was as good as his, and he wrenched off his cloak with reckless abandon. He knew his days as a beggar were over. No wonder Jesus commended him! 'Your faith has made you well.' It is an indication of the combination – faith on our part, power on God's part – of force that is required in a miracle of healing. We may have faith in our need to ask; we may have faith in God's power to answer; but have we also faith that he will answer? True, we cannot see God: we have to take him on trust – just as Bartimaeus did, in blind faith.

Unseen conviction

'Faith is the assurance of things hoped for, the conviction of things not seen' (Hebrews 11:1). Bartimaeus had such assurance and conviction, despite his blindness. Often, sighted Christians rely more on the things they can see. Jesus once told his disciples: 'Blessed are the eyes that see the things that you see!' (Luke 10:23). He was not remarking on the spectacular scenery of the Jordan Valley, or a golden sunrise on Galilee; but on the revelation of God as given by himself (Luke 10:22); the unseen conviction of love, joy, peace, and all the other fruits of the Spirit (Galatians 5:22). What convictions do we get from the word of God? When we read it with the eyes of faith, God undertakes to show us wonders: 'Open my eyes, so that I may behold wondrous things out of your law,' pleads the Psalmist (Psalm 119:18). And when Jesus was interceding for his disciples, he prayed to his Father: 'I desire that those you have given me, may be with me where I am, to see my glory, which you have given me because you loved me before the foundation of the world' (John 17:24). This was the *shekinah* glory of the Transfiguration, and the glory of heaven; but it was also the glory of his earthly life, the glory of his resurrection and ascension. The disciples saw it all; and we can see it also with the eyes of faith. Bartimaeus saw his cure before Jesus had opened his eyes.

Lightning cure
And his sight was immediately returned. There was no hiatus, no 'men as trees walking' (Mark 8:24). Bartimaeus' faith was so strong, it activated great power to heal. It is a lesson that the strength of our faith may produce equally quick answers to prayer – that God responds to fervour. But, how can we have such mountain-moving faith? The 'simple' laws of mathematics simply do not apply. We cannot take a figure of faith and multiply it at the stroke of a pen. 'Lord, increase our faith!' begged the apostles, on a certain occasion (Luke 17:5). And Jesus replied that faith the size of a mustard seed could uproot a mulberry-tree. What sort of a riddle is this?

Wesley's faith
When John Wesley had a crisis of belief, the Moravian Peter Böhler told him: 'On no account neglect the gift God has given you. Carry on preaching; preach faith until you have it; and then preach it because you have it.' Bartimaeus heard that Jesus wanted to see him – so he believed. We know Jesus so much better – can we, therefore, accept that we already have faith . . . and build on that foundation?

Suggested Hymns
Firmly I believe and truly; I know that my Redeemer lives and ever prays; Alleluia! sing to Jesus; Amazing grace

Nineteenth Sunday after Trinity

Second Service **Misplaced Trust** Ps. 119:121–136;
Eccles. 11, 12; 2 Tim. 2:1–7; Luke 18:9–14

'He also told this parable to some that trusted in themselves that they were righteous and regarded others with contempt . . . "for all who exalt themselves will be humbled, but all who humble themselves will be exalted".' Luke 18:9, 14

Self-belief
Jesus is criticizing those who are on an ego trip, relying on themselves rather than on God: those like the man who trusted in his fine armour for protection (Luke 11:21f.). Such people trust in their self-confidence, in the outward observance of religion, in the façade they present to the world. The proud Pharisee represented the stubborn nation who refused to recognize Jesus: the humble publican, those who believed in him, and were not forever polishing the image they presented to others.

Thanking God
The Pharisee began well enough: 'God, I thank you . . .', but he went on to thank God for the wrong things. As we might say today: 'I'm a cut above the rest, thank God!' As he cannot think too highly of himself, it follows that he cannot think highly enough of others; and he drags the publican into his prayer – not because he is a man in his own right, but simply because of his calling. The Pharisee has gone beyond the normal call of duty, as regards fasting and tithing: he is heavily committed into buying his way into God's favour. With him, money and effort count. He virtually sees God as his debtor. His sins are never mentioned: if they are in his mind at all, they are so well hidden under the veneer of respectability, as to be wholly discountable.

No pretence
The publican has no image to polish. He is a sinner, and his one aim is to come clean to God and to receive pardon. His was the simplest of prayers, but it came from the heart. And God heard, and honoured it. There was no manipulation – no doctoring of God's laws to suit himself or boost his self-importance, no pretence.

For God alone

Moses had received the commands regarding fasting and tithing, from a God who knew what men could accomplish. Life was not to be made so complicated that men agonized more over the observance of laws than over doing God's will. The Pharisee had allowed his fasting and tithing to knock his spiritual equilibrium awry. He was courting the attention and approbation of men, as well as God. And, while some Pharisees were certainly more honourable in their motives, this Pharisee was not alone: robes were made more elaborate, prayer was ostentatious rather than private, and their frequent (self-imposed) fasts were publicized by draping themselves with sackcloth and smearing their faces with ashes. Scroll after scroll of explanations, modifications and additions had been attached to the old laws, until the general public could not differentiate between the true law and later accretions. Little wonder, then, when Jesus met the Pharisees head-on with his new covenant, that tempers rose, and the battle of wills began. For he came with a new authority; he could say with justification: 'You have heard how it was said in the old days . . . but *I* say to you . . .' And he is still saying it today: he is still in his temple (the Church), listening when we pray. Do we come full of importance, or preoccupied with affairs of the world? Or do we come in quietness and humility, conscious of shortcomings and failings? The answers to our prayers will be determined by the attitude we bring to prayer, not necessarily the length: the Pharisee's prayer was five times longer than the publican's. May we re-evaluate our attitude and approach to prayer in the light of this parable, reflecting that:

> *Prayer is the Christian's vital breath,*
> *The Christian's native air;*
> *His watchword at the gates of death;*
> *He enters heaven with prayer.*

> *James Montgomery*

Suggested Hymns

Prayer is the soul's sincere desire; Meekness and Majesty; Help us to help each other, Lord; Not for our sins alone

Fourth Sunday before Advent   5 November
Principal Service   **The First Commandment**
Deut. 6:1–9; Ps. 119:1–8; Heb. 9:11–14; Mark 12:28–34

'You shall love the Lord your God with all your heart, and with all your soul, and with all your mind, and with all your strength.' Mark 12:30

God above all
We are bidden to put the Lord first, in every circumstance of our lives, every minute of day and night: the Lord alone, and above everything else.

> *The dearest idol I have known,*
> *Whate'er that idol be,*
> *Help me to tear it from thy throne,*
> *And worship only thee.*
>
> *William Cowper*

Idols come in many forms. We can easily identify the TV, the tempting luncheon concoction, the lure of nicotine or alcohol . . . Less obvious are those coated with a veneer of respectability: forms of worship and good works. We can become more devoted to these than to God himself. Oswald Chambers once said: 'Beware of anything that competes with loyalty to Jesus Christ. The greatest competitor of devotion to Jesus is service for him . . . Are we being more devoted to service than to Jesus Christ?'

Simply love him
We are simply to love God, with our whole heart, soul, mind and strength. This is total commitment. Given such complete love, everything else will follow. Given such complete love, the way to God, though narrow, is kept free. Fearing God, walking in his ways, loving him and serving him with all we have, keeps the way open not only for miracles to be prayed for, but for miracles to happen. Total love of God overrides temporal worries, tragedies and afflictions. Total love of God means learning to live as people who may one day die! For no matter the trouble, pressure, anguish, pain or trauma, it will pass. And, even before it passes, we have God's promise that it will not be more than we can bear.

It will soon pass

Every trial we face, every test we are required to meet, *will pass*. In the fourth century, the effects of the apostate Julian's policy seemed catastrophic; but in a famous verdict on the ghastly reign, Bishop Athanasius (exiled by the emperor several times for his plain speaking) wrote: 'It is but a little cloud, and it will soon pass' (*Letter* 47 to the Alexandrians; also 46 to Ecdicius, Prefect of Egypt, AD 362). The worst that can happen to us will pass, even as Julian and his horrific reign passed into history – and the Church survived. We have been promised testing – but God is a God of love. We have been promised temptation – but God is a God of power. We have been promised trials – but God, through everything, still calls for our unconditional loyalty. Job had the right attitude, when he said: 'Though he slay me, yet will I trust in him' (Job 13:15). And if anyone suffered, it was surely Job; yet he refused to compromise his faith.

War and peace

A Christian can be identified as much by the warring in his heart as by the peace of his mind. For the heart is the bedrock of emotion, where Satan constantly strives for supremacy. The mind can be fixed: 'Those of steadfast mind you keep in peace – in peace because they trust in you' (Isaiah 26:3). The peace of Christ, which passes all understanding, gives the Christian that precious equanimity at which non-believers marvel. And this peace cannot be bought – only accepted as the most gracious gift on offer from God:

> *Peace I leave with you;*
> *my peace I give to you.*
> *I do not give to you as the world gives.*
> *Do not let your hearts be troubled,*
> *and do not let them be afraid.*

> John 14:27

With hearts on 'war alert', and minds at peace with God, we are well equipped to take on the other commandments. Let us pray for grace to align our priorities with the priorities of God.

Suggested Hymns

Fill thou my life, O Lord my God; Join all the glorious names; Glory be to Jesus; O for a closer walk with God

Fourth Sunday before Advent
Second Service   **A World Upside-down**
Ps. 145; Dan. 2:1–48; Rev. 7:9–17; Matt. 5:1–12

*'Blessed are the poor in spirit ... those who mourn ... the meek ...
those who hunger and thirst for righteousness ... the merciful ... the
pure in heart ... the peacemakers ... those who are persecuted for righteousness' sake ... Blessed are you when people revile you and persecute
you ... Rejoice!' Matthew 5:3–12*

Early comment on the Church
It was said of the disciples, in the early apostolic Church: 'These
people ... have been turning the world upside-down' (Acts 17:6).
Their preaching, in so many ways, was a reversal of the values
and outlook of the world in which they operated. To the Jews,
they preached a crucified Christ: a real stumbling block, for the
Jewish mind viewed crucifixion victims as cursed (Galatians 3:13).
To the Greeks, they preached a down-to-earth gospel aeons away
from sophistication. 'We will hear you again about this,' said the
icily polite Athenians, and walked away from Paul (Acts 17:32).
And the Romans? They were saturated with power, and scornful
of a strange doctrine which did not deal in politics and cold steel.

Jesus' teaching
Nowhere better than in the Beatitudes do we see Jesus' precedent
for this 'upside-down' doctrine. Who would normally feel blessed
when suffering from poverty, or being taken for granted? Who
feels like joying, when torn apart from the inside out by grief?
Who feels like praising, when walked all over, or marginalized?
Surely only fanatics – holy Joes and Janes – people who take no
pleasure in religion, hunger and thirst after righteousness? And
who but the super-tolerant, who are accused of bending to the
prevailing wind, can be called merciful? Then, we may sing
'Blessed are the pure in heart', with great feeling and musical
expertise: but who apart from Jesus can sing it with truth? As for
the peacemakers, look at the newspapers and TV, and see *war*mak-
ers making the news. This world's business is war, not peace. And
who can be blessed when being reviled, persecuted or slandered?
Do we not immediately seek to justify ourselves, to save face, to
feel good?

By faith, we can rejoice
In all, or even any, of this, we can only rejoice by faith: faith in the Lord who issued this list of 'impossible ideals'. For with God, nothing is impossible. He made us. He knows us. He recognizes to the 'nth degree, our spiritual potential. (And let's never deceive ourselves we know it.) Let us give God best, and open our hearts to be turned upside-down by him, as he goes to work on the job of lighting us up from the inside out, so that we can in turn work on our part of the Church.

Let go, and let God
For God to move powerfully in us, to realize the Beatitudes through us to others, we need to break out of the anaesthetic of worldly sophistication and caution. Fear, suspicion, disinterest, apathy, pride – even a desire just 'to be left alone' – all deaden the working-in of God and the working-out of the Holy Spirit in our lives. And this anaesthetic does not lead to good health; it complicates our lives instead – and usually promotes spiritual deterioration. So let us take these Beatitudes, and not be afraid of applying them to our situations – in the full assurance that God knows we have the potential to accomplish all he requires of us.

Suggested Hymns
Blessed are the pure in heart; Happy are they, they that love God; Love is his word; O happy band of pilgrims

Third Sunday before Advent   12 November
Principal Service   **Fishing for People**   Jon. 3:1–5, 10; Ps. 62:5–12; Heb. 9:24–28; Mark 1:14–20

'As Jesus passed along the Sea of Galilee, he saw Simon and his brother Andrew casting a net into the lake – for they were fishermen. And Jesus said to them, "Follow me and I will make you fish for people."' Mark 1:16, 17

Preparation time
God is preparing us for what he is preparing for us. The disciples knew what it was to sail into deep water and bring to the surface

what lay hidden below. They knew the value of taking a harvest from one place, to nourish life in a different place. Experience had taught them that waters which could seem treacherous and inhospitable at times, could still yield food enough to sustain many families. Jesus was to build on this experience. He knew his men. He knew their stamina, resourcefulness and dedication. It would take several seasons, but he would convert their fishing skills into missionary zeal. And he did it. Quite possibly, he was not keen on the smell of fish; very likely, the slowness and obtuseness of the rugged fishermen got on his nerves. But he had called them, chosen them, and seen their spiritual potential. God does not give up on us when we fail to clear the first hurdle.

Spice of variety

Jesus did not fill the apostolic ranks with Galilean fishermen, but they seem to have outnumbered the other callings in the initial disciples. Why? Was it because he had grown up in the area, and knew this breed of men? Was it because their minds were more open to his message than the minds of the educated theologians who padded the corridors and courts of Jerusalem's temple? Just as we often cannot fathom why God chooses certain folk today, we can only guess at his first-century selection procedures. The ministries of Luke the physician, Paul the tentmaker, and the Ethiopian from Candace's court, were no less and no more precious.

Loyalty to Jesus

Copyright twenty centuries ago was no problem. Students would often write their masters' works; and none of the early disciples seems to have cared about becoming a best-selling author. Their aim primarily was loyalty to Jesus – following him, listening as he preached, and then eventually carrying on from where he left off. They let their ministry develop as God opened one door after another for them, or as circumstances pointed them in one direction or another. It was harder work than dredging the same waters night after night for fish, but infinitely more exciting, rewarding – and dangerous.

Our ministry

As Christians, we have all heard and answered the call to follow Jesus. And God is no respecter of persons: what he did for the Galilean fisherfolk, he can do for us. He is still recruiting troops

223

to fish for people. What skills has he already shown us we have? What do we do best? What do we like doing? Remember how the disciples went back to their fishing, in the traumatic days following Christ's resurrection (John 21:3). It was familiar work: perhaps they thought they would be doing just that for the rest of their lives. We, too, can jog along in the familiar, comfortable (or even boring) rut, of the work that comes to hand, and that pays our temporal wages. But, read on! These disciples found that they no longer had the knack of fishing for Galilean fish! They were in their home waters, engaged in a work that was second nature to them – and they could not catch a fish! Let us learn from this, and allow God to move us on, in his good time, using the skills he has given us, in a wider harvest field. There is no future in simply treading water, once God has called us to follow him – unless, that is, we do not want to fish for people.

Suggested Hymns
O happy day, that fixed my choice; Thy hand, O God, has guided; Will you come and follow me?; Take my hands and make them as your own

Third Sunday before Advent   *Second Service*
Jesus and the Father   Ps. 46; Isa. 10:33–11:9; John 14:1–29
'Jesus said, "If you know me, you will know my Father also." Philip said to him, "Lord, show us the Father . . ." Jesus said, "Whoever has seen me, has seen the Father."' John 14:7–9

Undivided

> *God always is,*
> *nor has he been and is not,*
> *nor is but has not been,*
> *but as he never will not be,*
> *so he never was not.*

> *Augustine of Hippo*

The ideas disentangle themselves in the end, but Augustine was a master of the complex: a complexity he had been driven into, for he was fighting tooth and nail for the defining of the Trinity in such a way that the whole of the Christian Church might understand. Primarily, he was attacking two heresies, those of Arius and Sabellius. Arius had tried to make the Son subordinate to the Father, with the Holy Spirit proceeding from the Father but not from the Son. Sabellius had referred to God as operating in three 'modes', though in only one mode at any one time. Much theological mileage was covered by giants such as Augustine and Athanasius, in refutation of these heresies. Jesus had kept it simple: 'Whoever has seen me, has seen the Father.' He tells his disciples: 'I am going to my Father's house. I am the way. I am in the Father.' Although, by implication, Jesus considers the disciples' questions unnecessary, his love for them gives an answer each time; and although the disciples make heavy weather of the subject, these are some of the most heartening verses of the Bible. Life goes on after death. Jesus is one with God. He is going through death to God – and where he goes, we shall go; and we shall not go alone, because he is that way through death. The mansions of heaven are not sepulchres in which lie coffins of varnished wood with brass handles; those have been left behind. At death, the spirit is freed from man-made trappings.

Why now?

Why did Jesus emphasize his indivisibility with the Father at this point? Surely because in this union there is a double reassurance. 'Do not let your hearts be troubled' (v. 1). These are really very hard words. Those who live them out are few and far between. The disciples could not understand them, and so they plied him with questions. They were all in the cenacle; Jesus had just celebrated the Last Supper. Judas had gone out into the night to set up the betrayal. The others were tired, confused, apprehensive, jittery – just as we are, so often. They were looking to Jesus for comfort, support and help – just as we do, so often. He was going to leave them. Journeys can be traumatic events, particularly if our return ticket is not ensured, or if we do not know where we are going, or if we have no place furnished, ready and waiting at journey's end.

God plans ahead

God does not deal with us in an austere, fear-provoking way. If the disciples trust Jesus, he tells them they are trusting God. There is no difference. Can they – can we – accept this? God has promised us a safe passage from this life to the next, for Jesus has gone ahead, as advance guard and guide. He knows the events leading up to death; he has experienced that 'last breath'; he has seen interment in the grave; not even there are we asked to go where he has not already been. God has promised us a second home: not a second-class home, but a better one, in Paradise – until the End of Time, when he has promised us the best home of all, in a resurrection body like Christ's own. God leaves the best wine till the last. What more can he do? When we, today's disciples, align ourselves with the disciples of two thousand years ago, and ply our Lord with unnecessary and even faithless questions, there is one more request we can make, one more request to which he will surely accede:

> Lord, we believe;
> Help our unbelief . . .

in the certainty that 'God always is'.

Suggested Hymns

I know that my Redeemer lives! What joy; We believe in God the Father; I believe in Jesus; Firmly I believe and truly

Second Sunday before Advent
19 November   *Principal Service*
Looking into the Future   Dan. 12:1–3; Ps. 16; Heb. 10:11–14; 19–25; Mark 13:1–8

'When he was sitting on the Mount of Olives opposite the temple, Peter, James, John and Andrew asked him privately, "Tell us, when will this be, and what will be the sign that all these things are about to be accomplished?"' Mark 13:3–4

A loving Master

Jesus did not castigate the disciples for wanting to see into the future, they were his closest friends. So he gave them a considered answer, yet one which fell short of telling them what they wanted to know. After the passion and resurrection, with hindsight Peter and the others would appreciate more fully the wisdom that keeps the future from us.

When (c.AD 168) the aged Bishop Polycarp of Smyrna was faced with the choice of denying Christ or suffering martyrdom, he told the proconsul: 'For eighty and six years I have been Christ's servant, and he has done me no wrong. How can I blaspheme my king who has saved me?' (Eusebius, *H.E.* iv.15.18, tr. K. Lake). We can have the same trust. God, who has brought us so far, is not likely to abandon us, when we die in the faith that we have lived.

Back from the dead

The prophet Samuel had died, and King Saul was missing his advice: the Philistines were threatening to attack, and Saul's desperate prayers to God were going unanswered. The King had expelled 'the mediums and wizards', and had no idea how to proceed; so he trekked over to see the nearest clairvoyant, at Endor, who obediently 'brought up' Samuel from the dead. But the result was tragedy: Samuel berated Saul, and told him that the next day would see his kingdom occupied and him and his sons killed. It is a disturbing account, in that not only is the wickedness of clairvoyancy implied, but also the fact that spirits are capable of being 'brought up'. We cannot condemn the 'work' of a medium on the grounds that it is charlatanism; but neither can we condone it, because it is against God's will. When Jesus faced his disciples' thirst for extra-terrestrial knowledge, that day on the Mount of Olives, he could have satisfied it – but it was not God's will. We often long for knowledge of what (we think) is to come – but God in his mercy keeps the future hidden, and an equally merciful curtain over the dead past – though who has not longed to meet again a departed soul, and to learn something at first-hand of those 'mansions in the sky'?

Life to be living

We have a life to be living here, and it is wrong to seek either communication with the dead, or knowledge of what is still to come. Can we not concentrate on the present, and consign horoscopes and magic to where they belong? There is no such pastime as 'flirting' with the occult: it is evil, dangerous, and anathema to the gospel of Christ. We can *pray* for the souls of the departed, entrusting them to the mercy of God, and in gratitude for those who have helped us along our spiritual journey. And we can *pray* for the future, that we may be kept in the will of God, with grace and strength to meet all the challenges that come our way. But our first endeavours should be concentrated on doing God's work and giving him praise, in the here and now.

> *Trust the past to the mercy of God,*
> *the present to his love,*
> *and the future to his providence.*
>
> *Augustine of Hippo*

God's love – ever present, ever strong – is the only 'sign' we need, to keep our hands on the plough. 'For Jews demand signs and Greeks desire wisdom, but we proclaim Christ crucified' (1 Corinthians 1:22).

Suggested Hymns
And can it be; From glory to glory advancing; Praise, my soul, the King of heaven; The first day of the week

Second Sunday before Advent
Second Service   Then Shall They Shine
Ps. 95; Dan. 3; Matt. 13:24–30, 36–43
'Then the righteous will shine like the sun in the kingdom of their Father. Let anyone with ears listen!' Matthew 13:43

The new heaven and earth
Can we get excited about a verse like this? Can we long to see the harvest of souls gathered in, at the end of the world? Can we thrill to think of a time when there will be no more sickness, pain or death? No Wall Street crashes, no global warning or newspapers full of doom and gloom? The Bible is strewn with references to

the time when this earth and heaven will give way to a new earth, a new heaven. The final sheaves will be brought in; we shall be re-united with our loved ones; we shall stand in the company of saints and angels; there will be music, dancing, joy . . . 'How lovely!' some say, wistfully. 'I wonder when it will come?' And others ask: 'Will it ever come?' And others shrug and say: 'Well, we can't do anything about it, anyway.' And that is not only dangerous (for it gives a person no incentive to work for the kingdom of God), but it is wrong, because it is contrary to what Jesus taught. 'The good news of the kingdom will be proclaimed throughout the world . . . and then the end will come' (Matthew 24:14). 'The good news must first be pro-claimed to all nations' (Mark 13:10).

Some way yet to go

Out of the six thousand or so languages on earth, the Bible has been translated into slightly more than one third. While these are admittedly the most widely-spoken, it still means we have to translate at least some of the scriptures into nearly four thousand languages, if we are serious about seeing the End of the world come sooner rather than later. We need to improve our record to date, of about one new translation for each year of the Christian era. It is awe-inspiring, that the Almighty Lord, Creator of the universe, can involve us in his great purposes. In the magnificent unfairness that showed a love beyond all comprehension, in giving his Son to die for our sakes, God gives us a partnership with him, in shining the gospel light to every corner of the world – not because we have earned the honour; not because he couldn't think of another way; not because he thinks we could do it better than he could himself(!) – but because our partnership was bought with a price that was greater than we can ever imagine.

Someone else?

Of course, God's magnificent unfairness has seen to it that we retain our freedom of choice; if we are not looking forward to the great Harvest, we can ignore this teaching of Jesus; we can let someone else pray for Bible translators, printers, preachers, couriers; we can let someone else share the gospel with a com-munity, a country, a continent. We can witter on about the state of the world, and the fluctuating economies, and the problems here, and the goings-on there . . . confident that the goings-on will do just that – and on, and on . . .

Lights in the kingdom

Can we imagine what it will be like to shine like the sun, when all the work is behind us? No, of course we can't: the sun is so blindingly bright. It will be a greater illumination than mere earthly sight can see. But let us not grow weary in working towards that glorious end. Let us take this vision with us into each new day – as the seasons of earth follow each other, in God's majestic ordering, let us keep our spiritual focus on the ongoing harvest of souls. Let us have more than a mere passing interest in it, for we have been recruited as workers for this harvest.

> Go, work in my vineyard, Oh, work while 'tis day!
> The bright hours of sunshine are hastening away,
> And night's gloomy shadows are gathering fast;
> Then the time for our labour will ever be past.
> Begin in the morning and toil all the day;
> Thy strength I'll supply, and thy wages I'll pay;
> And blessed, thrice blessed, the diligent few,
> Who finish the labour I've given them to do.

Anon., No. 4, Sacred Songs and Solos

Suggested Hymns

Lord, the light of your love (Shine, Jesus, shine); Light's abode, celestial Salem; Give me oil in my lamp; Lead us, heavenly Father, lead us

Christ the King (Sunday next before Advent)
26 November *Principal Service*
Do *You* Ask? Dan. 7:9–10, 13–14; Ps. 93; Rev. 1:4b–8; John 18:33–37

'Pilate asked him, "Are you the King of the Jews?" Jesus answered, "Do you ask this on your own, or did others tell you about me?"' John 18:33, 34

On our own

Others may tell us of Jesus, may share with us their experiences of his love and guidance; but no one can be a Christian by proxy. We come into the world on our own, and we leave it on our own. In the meantime, each of us comes to God on our own. Others may intercede for us: that is part of the strength of the body of Christ; but the bond with God is our responsibility. Remember when Jesus asked the disciples who people were saying he was, and followed this up by the question: 'But who do you say that I am?' (Matthew 16:15). And on that post-resurrection morning by Galilee, Jesus affirmed his faith in Peter's loyalty; but when Peter, carried away by the moment, tried to learn another's vocation, Jesus roundly told him to concentrate on his own, God-given mission (John 21:22). So here, in today's reading, Jesus is implicitly telling Pilate not to accept spoon-fed information, but to think and act for himself. But Pilate is out of his depth. He is also conscious of the precariousness of his own position. He will bow to the strongest voice – but the irony is, the strongest voice is not the loudest – and so Pilate makes the worst error of judgement in history.

The example of Nicodemus

Nicodemus is a shining example of responsible Christian enquiry. His peers had been discussing the miracles of Jesus (presumably in no very positive way), but Nicodemus sought a meeting with Jesus, to see and hear for himself, and on that one-to-one basis to make a decision. We may hear of new happenings in Christian gatherings around the world; but until we have experienced the working (or otherwise) of God in such a gathering, we should be slow to pass judgement. Let us remember Pilate's great mistake. God is a master of the ingenious as well as the simple; of the unexpected, as well as the predictable. We need to follow John's advice, to test our sources before coming to a conclusion (1 John 4:1).

Pilate's chance

Knowing what was in Pilate's mind, and anticipating the verdict, Jesus nevertheless gave the procurator a splendid chance to save his honour. If Pilate had chosen to do what was right, God could have worked mightily through him. The sacrifice of Jesus would have taken place – for that was how the world was to be saved –

but it would have involved someone other than Pilate. The Roman's freedom of choice had not been withdrawn. He had no one but himself to blame for what he did. We may also find ourselves in what appears to be an inextricable quandary; but God can always bring us through if by our own choice we refuse to compromise our faith: 'No testing has overtaken you that is not common to everyone. God is faithful, and he will not let you be tested beyond your strength' (1 Corinthians 10:13). We may still suffer in the process, but we shall not have forfeited the grace of God.

Square pegs?
There are times when we feel like square pegs in round, dark holes. It may be that a certain dark hole *needs* the friction that a square peg can give. It may be that we ourselves, in the mercy of God, need our corners smoothing off. Even if the hole has been of our own making, if God is still there with us, we can turn the experience into something not only beautiful for us, but probably also for others: such is the extent of our responsibility. Pilate could have saved many more beside himself. But he chose otherwise. Today, our Christ-King gives us our particular choices. May we do better than Pilate.

Suggested Hymns
Christ is the King! O friends rejoice; King of glory, King of peace; The God of Abraham praise; The Kingdom of God is justice and joy

Christ the King *Second Service*
Healing Ministry Ps. 72; Dan. 5; John 6:1–15
'After this Jesus went to the other side of the Sea of Galilee, also called the Sea of Tiberias. A large crowd kept following him, because they saw the signs that he was doing for the sick.' John 6:1, 2

Seeing is believing
The crowd kept following, because they saw sickness and disease being cured. They were prepared to listen to Jesus, anywhere, because they saw that he had the power to heal – and the willing-

ness. On this day of 'Christ the King', we may focus on Jesus' majestic overriding of physical symptoms which today are too often taken as a necessary part of daily life. Jesus neither accepted sickness into his body, nor did he ever come up against a disease which he could not cure. We are told, in one place, that he could work no miracles because of the unbelief of the people: the fault did not lie in him. Knowing that he had but a short time to complete his earthly ministry, Jesus had to get his message across to the crowds; if straightforward preaching was beyond them, then he would use visible signs; and, time and again, it was the signs which took their attention; if one has been healed from a chronic condition, one is certainly motivated to listen to anything the healer subsequently has to say. But surely there was more to the healing than this: Jesus came to bring life, and sickness does nothing but inhibit life; wherever and whenever he could, Jesus alleviated – no, absolutely cured – the physical defects, and then proclaimed the message he wanted his listeners to remember. Time and again, he counselled secrecy after a cure; often this was disregarded; but in his two-pronged approach, he was at pains to elevate the gospel above purely physical healing.

God wants us to fulfil our mission
God not only wants us to complete our mission, but to reach the finishing line in triumphant strength, as Jesus did (Luke 23:46). John presents it clearly: 'I pray that all may go well with you and that you may be in good health' (3 John 2). As Paul also told Timothy: 'God has not given us the spirit of fear; but of power, and of love, and of a sound mind' (2 Timothy 1:7). That is, a mind centred on the things of God: a mind that is not so naïve as to accept unquestioningly whatever drifts across its vision, but one that will not close its perception of the divine when God does act. There are those who are so determined to seek a 'rational' explanation for the inexplicable, that they try to argue God out of daily life altogether.

Constant power to heal
John tells us (1 John 4:4) that the power that is in us – the Holy Spirit – this constantly-running dynamo, is greater than anything outside us. Let us accept this truth, and apply it in every circumstance into which God brings us. The crowds who wanted Jesus to heal their sick kept close company with him. We should do the

same, feeding our inner Spirit with his word, claiming our right as inheritors of the kingdom with Christ, to the promises that comprise our covenant with him. Because they are freely available, too often we make heavy weather of accepting and applying them. Quite possibly, following Jesus meant hardship of one sort or another, for the first-century Galilean crowds. Some may have forfeited their employment; some may have gone hungry; some may have left family or friends behind. Still they followed the new rabbi with the healing power. Can we, as another Advent and new year approach, take time to clarify our reasons for following Jesus? What do we expect of him? And what does he expect of us? There is no danger of him disappointing us. Pray God we shall not fall short of his expectations.

Suggested Hymns
Jesus Christ is waiting; Thine arm, O Lord, in days of old; Restore, O Lord, the honour of your name; The Spirit lives to set us free

SERMONS FOR SAINTS' DAYS AND SPECIAL OCCASIONS

St Andrew, Apostle   30 November
Quick to Respond   Isa. 52:7–10; Ps. 19:1–6;
Rom. 10:12–18; Matt. 4:18–22

'Immediately [Peter and Andrew] left their nets and followed him.'
Matthew 4:20

Without hesitation
John (John 1:41) tells us Andrew is the first called (and so, presumably, the first Christian missionary disciple, as he straightway goes to tell Peter); but here in Matthew the alacrity of both brothers to respond to Jesus' call is emphasized. Later, at the feeding of the five thousand, it is Andrew who calls Jesus' attention to the food on offer (John 6:8f.). Andrew was one of the inner circle of the

Twelve (with Peter, James and John), and thus privileged to share, for example, Jesus' apocalyptic teaching (Mark 13:3f.); and he is given early mention whenever the apostles are listed (Matthew 10:2; Mark 3:18; Luke 6:14; Acts 1:13). His loyalty was quiet and unspectacular: he had not Peter's impulsive tongue, nor the fiery nature of James and John. Details of his later ministry are sketchy, but according to tradition Andrew took the gospel to Greece, Scythia and Byzantium. In or around AD 60, he suffered martyrdom in Achaia, being crucified on an X-shaped cross at Patras.

First things first
Andrew gave up the security of paid employment to follow Jesus. Quite possibly, his family depended on his fishing skills: we are not told whether his father Jonah was even alive at the time of Andrew's call; in fact, since Zebedee is mentioned as working with his sons, James and John (Matthew 4:21), the inference is that Peter and Andrew had lost their father by this time. Yet however great the pressures involved, Andrew did not hesitate to answer the call. He was later to hear Jesus teach, in the Great Sermon, 'Do not worry, saying, What shall we eat . . . drink . . . wear' (Matthew 6:31). God is divinely aware of our physical needs, and has undertaken to provide for us, if we have faith to put the currency of heaven before the currency of earth. It was not exclusively the financially secure whom Jesus called to the apostleship, but men such as Andrew who needed faith as well as courage; trust as well as enthusiasm; an ear for God as well as a quick eye for a catch. And whatever Andrew gave up to answer the call, would be repaid many times over, when the Auditor made up his accounts.

> *Be still, my soul: thy Jesus can repay*
> *From his own fulness, all he takes away.*

Katharina von Schlegel, tr. Jane Laurie Borthwick

Living for eternity
In the natural world, we value security – or what masquerades as security: a healthy bank balance, a good job, long-term pensions and insurance schemes; and, truly, these can make an impressive weight on one side of the scales. But in the other balance, stack the gospel and the winning of souls for Christ; add on the promise

of eternal life – and watch the first balance rocket sky-high! Yet how often we fail to appreciate how magnificently unfairly God stacks the scales! Andrew left home, family and work: we have probably forgone relatively little by comparison, in answer to Jesus' call. Yet the rewards that God holds out to us are no less than those held out to Andrew.

What is commitment?
The short answer is: it is as varied as the folk from whom it is asked. Our commitment will probably not include crucifixion on an X-shaped cross; but if it does, are we ready for it? Do we value anything, or anyone, more than the call of Jesus and what it may entail? Commitment is the signing of an invisible contract of divine employment; it is relying on an invisible Master; it is accepting an invisible salary, working long hours, maintaining constant availability – and at times suffering ridicule, pity, misunderstanding, and even downright antipathy. Are we ready, as was Andrew, to take on such commitment? Like Andrew, may God give us the grace to be ready, and the courage to accept: for we can never be certain that the opportunity will be repeated.

Suggested Hymns
Jesus calls us! o'er the tumult; A Man there lived in Galilee; Take up thy cross, the Saviour said; O Jesus, I have promised

St Nicholas of Myra, Bishop   6 December
A Man of Compassion   Isa. 61:1–3; Ps. 68;
1 Tim. 6:6–11; Mark 10:13–16

'*"Truly, I tell you, whoever does not receive the kingdom of God as a little child will never enter it."*' *Mark 10:15*

Church v. State
Born into a wealthy family at Patara in Asia Minor, Nicholas was eventually consecrated Bishop of Myra, early in the fourth century. We first hear of his compassionate zeal in his successful defence of three innocent men condemned to be executed on the orders of the Governor of Myra, who was so impressed by the bishop's

236

intervention and pleading, that he himself was converted to the faith. For other episodes in Nicholas' life, we are indebted to the writings of a ninth-century hagiographer who records the rescuing of sailors; love and care of children; helping three prostitutes to renounce their profession; and feeding the hungry.

Remembered by many

Nicholas may have suffered in the Diocletian persecution, but details regarding his death have not been preserved. However, he left a large and varied legacy: much of Europe in the Middle Ages commemorated his festival by electing 'Boy Bishops', who 'ruled' from 6 December until the Feast of Holy Innocents; Nicholas became the patron saint of Greece and Russia, sailors and children; and Dutch Protestant settlers in Nieu Amsterdam took the tradition of 'Sinter Claes' to America, from where it eventually percolated back to Europe.

Love was the key

A man of many parts; so many, one wonders why his life was not better documented, even allowing for Diocletian's persecution. Yet from what is known of him, Nicholas was a quiet, gentle man, who did not sound a trumpet before him. Perhaps it is fitting, therefore, that, among the vast hagiography, Nicholas is so well known, despite his lack of rhetoric or tomes of sermons. He was motivated by a love that could challenge unflinchingly the greatest secular powers, the worst of weather conditions, and the lowest depths of human nature. He was uncompromising not only in proclaiming but also in putting into practice the gospel of love.

> *Where is love and lovingkindness, God is fain to dwell.*
> *Flock of Christ, who loved us, in one fold containéd.*
> *Joy and mirth be ours, for mirth and joy he giveth;*
> *Fear we still and love the God who ever liveth,*
> *Each to other joined by charity unfeignéd.*

From the Office of the Mandatum, tr. R.A. Knox,
(*Westminster Hymnal*)

The Christmas saint

In the busyness of the modern Christmas, scarlet robes and white fur can easily obliterate the saint whose life gave rise to 'Santa

Claus'; but his love and care for children still help to make this season of Christ's birth special. Nicholas had experienced luxury in his own childhood, but he could appreciate the needs of children less fortunate. Like his Master, he valued the presence of young ones, and the input their innocence, vitality and joy can bring to our lives.

> *It is to such as these*
> *that the kingdom of heaven belongs.*
>
> *Mark 10:14*

Suggested Hymns
Love is his word; Jesus, Friend of little children; Eternal Father, strong to save; Love came down at Christmas

Conception of Our Lady   8 December
The Favoured One   Gen. 3:9–15a; Ps. 97;
Eph. 1:3–6, 11–12; Luke 1:26–38
'And he came to her and said, "Greetings, favoured one! The Lord is with you;. Blessed are you among women."' Luke 1:28

Theotokos
She who was to be *Theotokos*, 'Mother of God', had been favoured by God from the time of conception: God did not suddenly begin to favour her when, as a bride-to-be, betrothed to Joseph, she received Gabriel's visit. And today we focus on Mary's conception, in the womb of her mother, St Anne. Strangely, the Bible tells us more about the parents of John the Baptist than of Mary, although Christian tradition has given us some data.

A childless couple
Nazareth was the home town of Joachim, who is said to have married Anne while still quite young. They remained childless for a number of years, until Joachim, worn down by the mockery of his peers, retreated into the desert and fasted for forty days. It

may have been in answer to his prayers that an angel appeared to Anne one day when she also was praying, and told her that God would give her a child, who would be known and revered by every nation on earth. In gratitude, Anne is said to have replied: 'If I do indeed conceive, the child who is to be born will be consecrated to my God.' In due course, Mary was born, and Joachim is said to have lived to see his child's Presentation in the temple at Jerusalem. Anne at the time of conception was around forty, and is not thought to have outlived Joachim for many years. Some traditions refer to Anne's husband as Cleopas, Sadoch or Eliacim. It is possible that she married again, after Mary's birth, but there is no record of her conceiving any further children.

A devout home

We can be reasonably certain that Mary grew up in a home where God was honoured, and that sabbath attendance at either the local synagogue or the temple in Jerusalem was observed – since, in Luke 4:16, we hear that Jesus attended worship regularly. To give a child to God – whether in the Jewish 'presentation' ceremony, or in Christian baptism – is an important step, and one which today is not always fully respected. The child, once blessed and consecrated to God, is spiritually 'set apart' for whatever calls God may make on its life. There is little doubt that Anne would impress upon Mary the solemnity of her vow; and in fact this probably accounted for Mary's remarkable composure and courage when she, in turn, received the visit from Gabriel announcing the conception of Jesus. May today's parents and godparents fulfil their responsibilities by reminding their children, as they grow, of the significance of their baptismal service and vows.

God of the impossible

Throughout history, as recorded in the Bible, God intervenes when the natural laws appear immutable. Men and women well past the years of child-bearing are given children – for example, Abraham and Sarah, Zachariah and Elizabeth – and, most spectacularly, Mary herself, while still a virgin. Does God work in such ways to shock us into belief? Does he do it in response to sustained, fervent prayer? Or is it his normal *modus operandi*, and are we too slavishly bound by the natural laws not to be surprised when they are overridden? Let us pray that he will make his way plain to us, as we meditate on Blessed Mary's conception today.

Ye who own the faith of Jesus; Maiden, yet a mother; Mary
Immaculate, Star of the morning; I'll sing a hymn to Mary (*Celebration Hymnal*)

St Stephen, Deacon and Martyr
26 December   *Servus Servorum*   2 Chr. 24:20–22;
Ps. 119:161–168; Acts 7:51–60; Matt. 23:34–39
*'But filled with the Holy Spirit, he gazed into heaven and saw the glory
of God and Jesus standing at the right hand of God.' Acts 7:55*

Jesus on his feet
Stephen the deacon had been elected to serve as a table-waiter, in
the Church's daily ministration to widows and the needy. He had
matured spiritually, doing 'great wonders and signs' (Acts 6:8),
and was now being stoned for his ministry, even as Jesus had
promised: 'An hour is coming when those who kill you will think
that by doing so they are offering worship to God' (John 16:2).
Yet Stephen's ministry ends on a high note. What did he see on
looking into heaven? Luke, an educated man surely not given to
flights of fancy, tells us, simply, 'the glory of God and Jesus standing at the right hand of God' – standing to welcome the first
Christian martyr, a *servus servorum*.

Finding God
No one can prove, or physically disprove, that Stephen saw what
Luke says he saw. However, surely we can accept Luke's double
attestation, that at Jesus' ascension the disciples gazed up towards
heaven (Acts 1:10), and at Stephen's martyrdom he 'gazed into
heaven'. The Church on earth is not to look down, or even laterally,
for its final deliverance, but up: somewhere up there. That is all we
know, this side of death. But how difficult we often make this trust!

Spiritual contact
The indwelling Holy Spirit causes us to look at the world with
spiritual vision: to see Christ in others, to recognize the working
of God in our lives and the lives of others. We can accept the

Spirit, and see the gifts he gives; or we can act as though he was not there. It is that giant step of faith and trust, at which so many would-be servants of God baulk. Even the closest friends of Jesus were slow to grasp it. Jesus tried to explain the problem to them: 'It is to your advantage that I go away, for if I do not go away, the Advocate will not come to you; but if I go, I will send him to you' (John 16:7). He did not say he would send the Spirit-Advocate to one or two outstanding servants – but to all he was leaving behind, and to their heirs and assigns till the End of time. Given this, is it not strange that many of those heirs and assigns struggle through life ignoring their Helper?

> *I am the light and you do not see me.*
> *I am the way and you do not follow me.*
> *I am the truth and you do not believe me.*
> *I am the life and you do not seek me.*
> *I am the master and you do not hear me.*
> *I am your God and you do not pray to me.*
> *I am the leader and you do not obey me.*
> *I am your greatest friend and you do not love me.*
> *If you are unhappy, do not blame me.*

> *From an old French Calvary of 1632*

Beyond sense

Often the difference between suffering and not suffering lies in seeing: seeing the written word; seeing with the spirit; seeing through our physical eyes; seeing truth, revelation; seeing beyond what is normal – seeing with the insight of God. It is when we push our senses beyond sense that the Holy Spirit comes into his own. While we stay in the rut of ordinary suffering, ordinary living, we are in the case of having eyes and not seeing.

Stephen was open to the Spirit:

> *When he was shown the way, he followed.*
> *When he was offered the truth, he believed.*
> *When life was held out in hope, he sought it.*
> *When the Master called, he listened.*
> *When the Leader commanded, he obeyed.*
> *When God spoke, he prayed.*

When his greatest Friend summoned, he looked up . . .
. . . and saw Jesus standing to welcome him.

J.C.

May this be our vision, too.

Suggested Hymns
Yesterday with exultation; Hark! the sound of holy voices; Thy hand, O God, has guided; Bind us together, Lord

St John the Evangelist   27 December   One to One   Ex. 33:7–11a; Ps. 117; 1 John 1; John 21:19b–25

'Jesus said to him, "If it is my will that he remain until I come, what is that to you? Follow me!"' John 21:22

Minding others' business
Peter had suffered a terrible time of remorse following his denial of Christ. Now, in the threefold re-commitment, his self-respect and confidence had been restored. Such was his resilience that immediately he began minding John's business (and few would question that John was the 'disciple whom Jesus loved'). 'Never you mind about him,' Jesus tells him. 'Concentrate on what I've told you to do. Leave John to me!' We can virtually hear our Lord saying it, because he continues to say it on so many occasions. There is some of Peter's inquisitiveness in most of us. God did not love John more than Peter: God is no respecter of persons. But he reserves the right to deal on a 'one to one' basis, which we infringe at our peril. In high and low society, news is 'leaked', information is bought and sold: other people's business constitutes *big* business – and often produces immense heartache and anguish. When will we learn to listen to God's voice and to mind our own business – and his?

Beyond the point of no return?
Yet God is magnanimous. Jesus rebuked Peter, and that was sufficient. Peter's mission was not cancelled, nor was God's love and regard for him impaired. Moreover, the episode not only gives us a glimpse into the mission of John, but also into his character: loving,

gentle, as would befit the protector of Mary (John 19:27); and a man who was not burdened over another's business. We do not know whether the same man was responsible for the Fourth Gospel, the three Johannine Letters and the Book of Revelation. If, indeed, he wrote only the Gospel, we have a wealth of material which is unique: Jesus as the 'Word' of God, the marriage at Cana, the visit of Nicodemus, the Good Shepherd, the raising of Lazarus – and much else.

John the theologian
John in his Gospel quotes the Old Testament more than the other evangelists. He is at pains to show Jesus fulfilling the ancient prophecies, which tells us something of his immediate readership – Jews looking for answers to the questions raised by the Incarnation. John sees Jesus as existing from the beginning – deity full of grace and truth. He sees him as a living, breathing preacher who can heal even congenital disease (as in the case of the man born blind) and restore the dead to life – as well as feeding a crowd with one boy's lunch, and turning water into first-class wine. When we search for Jesus in the chapters of the Fourth Gospel, we see *God* and *Man* through the eyes of a disciple whose major aim was: 'so that you may come to believe that Jesus is the Messiah, the Son of God, and that through believing you may have life in his name' (John 20:31).

John redivivus?
There is something of John in today's Christians entrusted with the gospel. We, as Christ's ambassadors, are given life and breath to share the good news, so that others 'may come to believe . . . and may have life'. We have a God-given opportunity to change the world for Christ, as had Peter, John, and the 'cloud of unseen witnesses' whom one day, please God, we shall join. It is an awe-inspiring challenge, and one we need to meet with as much inspiration as awe, otherwise we shall faint before we have begun. As our days, so will our strength be, for with the calling God gives the grace. May we go out today inspired to fulfil our duty as those entrusted with the gospel – taking as our contract of employment one of the most precious verses in John's Gospel:

*For God so loved the world that he gave his only Son, so that **everyone who believes** in him may not perish but may have eternal life. John 3:16*

Suggested Hymns
Suggested Hymns
Word supreme, before creation; To you was given, O saint beloved;
Unto us a boy is born; Who is this, so weak and helpless?

Feast of the Holy Innocents   28 December
Fly for Your Life   Jer. 31:15–17; Ps. 124;
1 Cor. 1:26–29; Matt. 2:8–13

*'Get up, take the child and his mother, and flee to Egypt, and remain
there until I tell you; for Herod is about to search for the child to destroy
him.' Matthew 2:13*

God's great concern
God's loving care is seen not only in the command to 'get up and
go', but in the explanation. He was not asking for blind obedience,
but obedience quickened by the realization of the danger of staying. It comes as something of a shock – even though we are so
familiar with the event – to pause in our Christmas celebrations
and remember the innocent children who gave their lives, so that
one Child might live. Why did it have to be? Was it solely to fulfil
Jeremiah's prophecy? Why were these little innocents and their
families involved? Prophecy also pointed to the crucifixion of
Jesus. Surely, since the Child was destined to grow to manhood,
Herod's massacre could have been averted? Of course it could.
But God chose otherwise. The Bible is no fairy tale. God does not
only deal in 'happily ever after'.

The long trek
Mary probably rode a donkey, but almost certainly Joseph would
walk the two hundred and fifty miles or so to Egypt and safety.
How many of his carpenter's tools did he manage to take? Did
they sleep by the wayside, or find accommodation en route? What
was the weather like? And the Egyptians – did they make the Holy
Family welcome, or ostracize them? So many questions, about an
experience encapsulated in so few verses in Matthew's Gospel.
We even have no recorded words of Joseph in the Bible: yet here
he shows remarkable courage, obedience and resilience. We may
compare ourselves to Joseph, and ponder whether we should have

been so compliant – indeed, whether we are so willing to obey God now, when he seems to be telling us to do something unusual which we should not normally consider doing, and where we cannot visualize the outcome. Joseph would go, not knowing how long they would be in Egypt, or even if they would ever be able to return.

In the steps of history
As they journeyed to Egypt, would they not be thinking of another Joseph, sold by his brothers into service in Egypt: a Joseph who rose to be second-in-command to the Pharaoh of the day, and who ultimately welcomed his family to safety there? Surely Mary and Joseph would take heart that, as God had watched over the Joseph of ancient time, they need not fear. But surely, too, they would be thinking of the families left behind in Bethlehem . . . perhaps Jeremiah's prophecy came to mind. Yet it would not achieve anything to go back; they must leave those Innocents in the hands of God, and continue to Egypt as he had commanded. The pilot who sees his colleagues' planes being shot down around him, knows also he has to press on until his own mission is accomplished. One of the hardest things in life is realizing that we cannot always take on others' burdens – and allowing God the freedom to work in others' lives, as we trust he will work in ours.

Life in God's hands
We can be so conditioned into keeping alive at any cost that we fail to see life a little more from God's perspective. We cannot bear to think that he may step in and take us home before all our long-range plans have come to fruition. 'Lord, give me time – to preach, to evangelize, to bring up my children, to plant a new church . . .' Sometimes we would do well to remember that our days are still the same length as those of Paul, Peter, John and the rest. Satan was tangling with Jesus from childhood, to prevent the salvation of the world. The struggle would end some thirty or so years later, when another Joseph would provide a tomb for a corpse which could not stay dead. Jesus' life, as a child, a man, was in God's hands; just as ours are today.

Suggested Hymns
O Martyrs young and fresh as flowers; Unto us a boy is born; Will you come and follow me; Open our eyes, Lord

St Thomas Becket, Archbishop of Canterbury
29 December   This Turbulent Priest
1 Ki. 19:9–13a; Ps. 54; Heb. 13:10–16; Matt. 10:28–30

'Do not fear those who kill the body but cannot kill the soul; rather fear him who can destroy both soul and body in hell.' Matthew 10:28

Man of the world
Diplomat, administrator, lover of good living, fashion, country sport and armed conflict, Thomas had certainly no long-standing training (and perhaps no aspirations) for the archbishopric. Yet Henry II nominated him as Theobald's successor in 1161, and almost immediately the man of the world became transformed into an ecclesiastic zealous for the rights and privileges of the Church. He was to oppose kings, nobles and bureaucrats in this long-running battle, fuelled by an equally ambitious monarch, the exaggerated claims of the papacy on the world stage, and the inevitable conflicts between sacred and secular.

Man of the cloth
At Canterbury, Thomas replaced his earlier luxurious life-style, with austerity and asceticism. He was undoubtedly sincere in his aims to dedicate his life and the lives of fellow Christians, to God; but pride and a desire to override any opposition to his wishes was to sour relations between him and his king. In 1164 he fled to France for his own safety; and although Louis VII took up his cause and effected a *rapprochement* with Henry, it was to be only a temporary respite, and the King is said to have been driven to ask: 'Who will rid me of this turbulent priest?' On 29 December 1170, four knights were Henry's willing tools in this matter, despatching Thomas on the steps of his altar. The Archbishop is reported as repeating the names of earlier Canterbury martyrs, SS Denis and Alphege, and the words of Stephen, the first Christian martyr: 'Into thy hands, O Lord, I commend my spirit.'

For God and his cause
Jesus had forewarned his disciples: 'Indeed, the hour is coming when those who kill you will think that by doing so they are offering worship to God' (John 16:2). It can be argued that

although Thomas went about his mission with unnecessary pride and arrogance, if he had merely played second fiddle to the pressures of the state, the Church might have fared so badly that any damage limitation exercise would have been impossible for later prelates. Christians in every age are called to fight for what they believe to be right: God does not create plastercast saints impervious to the pressures and challenges of the times. But standing firm provokes antagonism, conflict and resistance – and the outcome may be as incomprehensible (and seemingly unjust) as the slaughter of the Holy Innocents by the megalomanic Herod, or the crucifixion of Jesus by the weak-willed Pilate.

Death not the end
To be true to ourselves and to God, we are to live as those who will one day die – yet die as those who will live for ever: to see death not as the end, but as a step along the way.

A Christian martyrdom is never an accident, for saints are not made by accident. Still less is a Christian martyrdom the effect of man's will to become a saint, as a man by willing and contriving may become a ruler of men. A martyrdom is always the design of God, for his love of men, to warn them and to lead them, to bring them back to his ways. It is never the design of man; for the true martyr is he who has become the instrument of God, who has lost his will in the will of God, and who no longer desires anything for himself, not even the glory of being a martyr.

T. S. Eliot, Murder in the Cathedral

Suggested Hymns
Christ is our cornerstone; O God of Bethel, by whose hand; Thy hand, O God, has guided; Ye watchers and ye holy Ones

Circumcision of Christ (*Naming of Jesus*)
1 January 2000   **Called Jesus**   Num. 6:22–27;
Ps. 8; Gal. 4:4–7; Luke 2:15–21

'After eight days had passed, it was time to circumcize the child; and he was called Jesus, the name given by the angel before he was conceived in the womb.' Luke 2:21

The Saviour

The conception of Jesus may have been miraculous, and the conditions of his birth unusual; but his name – 'Joshua' in earlier times – was not unique. Yet who has ever mistaken him for another? Only those, like Herod, who had their judgement clouded with guilt (Matthew 14:2). Jesus (Saviour) was the name chosen by God: this is yet another point on which we see the humble compliance of Mary and Joseph. They had not consummated their marriage; they had no choice over the time or the place of Jesus' conception and birth; and even before conception they are told what the name of the child will be. Mary, and Elizabeth, centuries before ultra-scan techniques, were privileged to know the sex of their unborn children. The Saviour of the world trod the lonely path from divinity to manhood, with the trusting compliance of Mary and Joseph, and the overriding will of God. Sometimes, when we feel God is speaking to us today, we accept his challenge with trust, even enthusiasm – only to fall prey to second thoughts and doubts as time goes on, and circumstances seem to tell against our vision. 'Lord, perhaps you didn't really mean me to do this, or say that, or go there . . . ?' We ask, like a child in the kindergarten, for repeated assurances; and if these are not forthcoming we let go the vision, and fall back on 'commonsense' – in essence, walking by sight and not by faith. Let us remember Mary and Joseph.

Family commitments

The law decreed circumcision on the eighth day; and Jesus' parents – though knowing he was no ordinary child – observed the law. We may, at times, consider a local or national law irrelevant to our position. Today's gospel is a salutary reminder that even Jesus, who had no need to be circumcized, observed this ritual. He was born a Jew, and raised according to Jewish laws and ordinances.

Thus he could say to the woman in Samaria: 'You worship what you do not know; we worship what we know, for salvation is from the Jews' (John 4:22). He was to stand before Pilate, as a recognized Jew. Pilate replied, 'I am not a Jew, am I? *Your own nation* and the chief priests have handed you over to me' (John 18:35). His own people had turned against him: 'He came to what was his own, and his own people did not accept him' (John 1:11). The Jews were his family – but when their antipathy and mistrust cost them such exclusiveness, Jesus opened his heart to all who would take the step of commitment: 'Whoever does the will of God is my brother and sister and mother' (Mark 3:35). Yet, having observed the rites of the church, Jesus was able to take a normal part in synagogue worship during the 'hidden' years of his childhood, adolescence and early manhood (Luke 4:16) in Nazareth: an example which our modern world could heed.

Early recognition

The prophet Jeremiah had been told by God: 'Before you were born I consecrated you' (Jeremiah 1:5); and when we consider Gabriel's announcement to Mary (Luke 1:31), we may believe God knows us from a time we cannot imagine; that he also knows our spiritual potential; and that it is important for us to have a name. There is everything in the Bible to suggest that, in a way we cannot yet understand, our name is something that survives the grave. Jesus showed us the importance of names. He gave special names to Peter, and James and John (Mark 3:16, 17); and, in his teaching on the Good Shepherd, he declared that he knows by name every sheep in his great fold (John 10:3, 14). Let us, therefore, on this 'naming day' of Jesus, learn to value our names, and the names of those we love, and who are known by name to God.

Suggested Hymns

To the Name of our salvation; Conquering kings their titles take; How sweet the Name of Jesus sounds; Jesus, Name above all names

St Antony, Hermit, Abbot   17 January
Length of Life   1 Ki. 17:2–6; Ps. 91; Phil. 3:7–14;
Matt. 19:16–26

'Those who love me, I will deliver; I will protect those who know my name. When they call to me, I will answer them; I will be with them in trouble. I will rescue them and honour them. With long life I will satisfy them, and show them my salvation.' Psalm 91:14–16

Here, and Hereafter
There are those whose days are prolonged on earth, to do good for many years, such as Antony, and Mother Teresa. And there are those whose lives here are relatively brief, yet who leave an equally blessed legacy, such as Thérèse of Lisieux and David Watson. If our earthly lifespan were, say, a constant seventy years, the whole challenge and excitement of the Christian life would be thrown out of kilter. Yet whenever death comes, it still seems 'too soon'. We have, it seems, much to learn about the timescale of God.

From wealth to wilderness
Antony inherited a fortune from his parents, in 276, but on hearing how Jesus had commanded the rich young man to sell everything and give his money to the poor, Antony followed the command to the letter, and went into the Egyptian desert to live an austere life of work, charity and prayer. He soon discovered that the world's temptations had followed him, even as they had followed Jesus into the wilderness. Like Jesus, Antony resisted them, and people began flocking out from the cities for his wisdom, teaching and advice. His asceticism was copied by many, living either in solitude or as small coenobitic communities. Monks from the various monasteries Antony founded went deeper and deeper into the desert, founding monasteries of their own.

A century of dedication
Antony lived 105 years, and his rules for the ascetic life were to spread and influence many religious beyond Egypt. We may not be called to a similar *modus vivendi*, but our lives may nevertheless be equally long. However, long or short, today is a good time to consider what we are going to do with the years remaining to us here on earth. Has God got our full attention, or is there something,

or someone, standing between him and us? As in every age, there were those who accused Antony and his monks of selfishness in their seclusion. Certainly the saint's life-style was a long way removed from that of an inner-city minister operating a soup kitchen for the homeless. Yet both saint and minister are doing God's work in the way each believes he has been directed. Paul went to some pains to explain to new believers that God requires different ministries from those to whom, in his diversity, he has bestowed differing gifts (1 Corinthians 12:29, 30). Provided we have God's love (1 Corinthians 13), we shall respect others' gifts, and value our own; and, though we do not understand the reasons, we shall accept and appreciate a life lived for God, however long or short this side of eternity.

Suggested Hymns
Help us to help each other, Lord; The Spirit lives to set us free; Love divine, all loves excelling; O Lord, all the world belongs to you

Week of Prayer for Christian Unity
18–25 January   **That They Be One**   Acts 16:16–34; John 17:1–19

'Jesus said, "And now I am no longer in the world, but they are in the world, and I am coming to you. Holy Father, protect them in your name that you have given me, so that they may be one, as we are one."' John 17:11

A time of transition
The Jesus who was born in Bethlehem, who walked and talked in Galilee, is going back to the absolute oneness in glory with the Father. His disciples, soon to be empowered with his Spirit, are going to be indefinably but uniquely in that same oneness. They will never again be the people they were before Good Friday.

Bungee-cord of prayer
This unity is the elastic, the bungee-cord, of the prayer which linked Jesus with the Father, and the bungee-cord which now links

us with God. We can go so far in the wrong direction, but then prayer – the gift of God through Jesus who taught us to pray – is the bungee-cord which brings us back to a realization of our one-ness with God. Because we are all God's sons and daughters, yet individuals, this oneness will mean something similar, and also something different, to each of us. In a strange way, this oneness is the most complicated unity there ever was, since it is multi-faceted to the 'nth degree. Particularly in this week of the year, it is seen in denominational terms; and in fact this is probably the simplest way to see it, even though it may be far removed from the original context. The Christian Church today is so divided denominationally – though we are less disparate today than even a generation ago.

Prayer agendas

Unity, however tenuous, between our various churches should be on everyone's prayer agenda. We do not always appreciate how negative a message our divisions present to those outside the Church; without discussion, how can we move forward? How can we ignore the shame of an altar which is still not open to all believers in every church? Does God weep? Is this what Christ died for?

The personal message

The first message we can take from Jesus' words here in John 17 was on the denominational front; the second is really personal. Self-sufficiency is good in part, but Jesus is saying: 'You cannot be wholly independent; you are not on your own; you are not your own. You must identify with the Father, as I am identified with the Father.' Are we carving out our own niche in life, or are we going God's way, aligning our wills with his? Are we so committed to God as to have gone beyond the point of no return? Such commitment is a form of spiritual 'notching-up', lifting our minds from the mundane to the supernatural, in the most positive, Christian sense of the word. It is being filled with the same disre-gard for convention and for the things of the world, with the same spiritual fighting spirit that Paul had, when he turned roundly on his jailer and said: 'Those men dealt unjustly with God's people. So let them come and do the decent thing' (Acts 16:37) – when it would have been far easier to say: 'Thank you', and slink away from the prison like a cowed animal. We are either at one with the world or at one with God. And if we want to sit on the fence between these choices, it is just not there!

Suggested Hymns
Bind us together, Lord; O thou who at thy Eucharist did pray; Thy hand, O God, has guided; We hail thy Presence glorious

Conversion of St Paul   25 January
You Did It to Me   Jer. 1:4–10 or Acts 9:1–22; Ps. 67; Acts 9:1–22 or Gal. 1:11–16a; Matt. 19:27–30

'He fell to the ground and heard a voice saying to him, "Saul, Saul, why do you persecute me?" He asked, "Who are you, Lord?" The reply came, "I am Jesus, whom you are persecuting."' Acts 9:4, 5

Just as you did
Whatever we do, or do not do, Jesus places himself before us as the recipient of our actions [or the lack of action]: 'Truly I tell you, just as you did [not do] it to one of the least of these who are members of my family, you did [not do] it to me' (Matthew 25:40, 45). So it was with Saul; he had thought he was persecuting the Christians – but on the Damascus Road Jesus firmly set him right. With letters in his pocket for Damascus, authorizing him to persecute even more Christians, Saul must have wished himself a million miles away. It is true that

> *with mercy and with judgement*
> *my web of time he wove*
>
> A.R. Cousin

– and, although Saul was severely shocked, and blinded (for all he then knew, permanently), Jesus was generous in his mercy, providing guides to lead Saul to Damascus, and Ananias to restore his sight relatively quickly. But then came the work of persuading the Christians to believe that his conversion was genuine! We may ride through a crisis magnificently, cope with a miracle of healing with thankful confidence and renewed vigour. But afterwards, like

253

Paul, we find that convincing people of the work of God is much more difficult. Jesus warned us that it would be so: 'If [people] do not listen to Moses and the prophets, neither will they be convinced even if someone rises from the dead' (Luke 16:31).

On retreat?
Paul spent some time with the disciples at Damascus immediately following his conversion. It is to the credit of these disciples that he was allowed to begin preaching in the synagogue at this early stage. Far from it being a quiet retreat, Paul was the cynosure of all eyes, and the recipient of much questioning – a test which he appears to have passed with honour. Yet certain Jews refused to accept that their most ardent persecutor had changed his stance; and they stirred up such feeling that Paul had to make a somewhat ignominious escape (2 Corinthians 11:33).

On fire for God
Lukewarmness among Christians not only escapes the headlines, but it also gives the Devil an easy ride. Satan will not trouble himself about such people. But let there come a revival, a sea change, a surge of spiritual power and fervour among a congregation, and emotions and tensions – positive and negative – are stirred. Had Saul continued his anti-Christian measures, we might never have heard again of him.

One of a family
Today, as we give thanks for the conversion of arguably the most energetic and single-minded preacher, apostle, missionary and martyr of New Testament times, let us also thank God for those Christians in Damascus (and Barnabas, in particular), who were sufficiently open to God, to believe in Paul. No medicine is more efficacious than the trust of a friend. Our greatest Friend makes us strong to face life in all its complexities; and he also works through our colleagues, family, and all who show us love and trust. There are not too many Pauls around today – but, thank God, there are the Barnabases, who quietly, loyally affirm us in our mission.

Suggested Hymns
God of grace, and God of glory; Be still, for the presence of the Lord; My God, accept my heart this day; Will you come and follow me

St Joseph of Nazareth   19 March
The Carpenter   2 Sam. 7:4–16; Ps. 89:27–37; Rom. 4:13–18; Matt. 1:18–25

'When Joseph awoke from sleep, he did as the angel of the Lord commanded him; he took Mary as his wife, but had no marital relations with her until she had borne a son; and he named him Jesus.' Matthew 1:24, 25

Man of dreams
It was in one dream that Joseph learned of his wife's supernatural conception, and in another of Herod's malevolent plans to annihilate Jesus (Matthew 2:13). His response to both was exemplary: not understanding, but trusting God, he 'took Mary as his wife'. After the birth, he heeded God's warning and took Mary and Jesus out of Herod's way into Egypt – a journey that probably meant more than two hundred miles of walking for Joseph, even if Mary and the child were able to ride on a donkey.

Twelve years on . . .
The last time we hear of Joseph is when he and Mary took the twelve-year-old Jesus to the temple in Jerusalem. They travelled in a large family group, and on the return journey mislaid the boy. Retracing their steps to Jerusalem, they eventually discovered him with the doctors in the temple. Mary was sharp in her relief: 'Your father and I have been searching for you in great anxiety' (Luke 2:48). From first to last, we hear not a word from Joseph! By the time Jesus' public ministry begins, and the first of his miracles astonishes the wedding guests at Cana, Joseph would appear to have died. Perhaps he had been much older than Mary. We simply do not know.

The carpenter of Nazareth
A painting by Holman Hunt shows the carpenter's shop at Nazareth, with Joseph busily at work, and the young Jesus standing in the doorway. The setting sun casts the shadow of a cross behind Jesus' outstretched arms – and so the traumatic future is superimposed on the otherwise peaceful scene. Jesus seems to speak from experience when in later years he tells his disciples: 'My yoke is easy' (Matthew 11:29). He must often have watched Joseph patiently smoothing the newly-made yokes until they were free

255

of any sharp edges that would have caused friction on the oxen's skin.

Example of trust and obedience
Joseph must have wondered about the meaning of his dreams; but stronger than his perplexities were trust and obedience to God. The village carpenter challenges all who may seek to be 'too wise', and who want to see the ground ahead before they leap. We are so familiar with the Christmas stories as to be in danger of overlooking the giant leaps of faith good Joseph had to make in response to each of his dreams. God knew his man. Joseph was a worthy foster father for the Saviour of the world. Jesus grew up in a stable home environment, and his subsequent teaching showed how he valued the sanctity of marriage (Mark 10:6–9).

Do not sound a trumpet before you
Joseph's quiet dedication and loyalty were the perfect combination for the foster father of our Lord. We know so little about him, yet we know enough. We know sufficient to be able, with Philip, implicitly to counter Nathanael's undiplomatic question: 'Can anything good come out of Nazareth?' by: 'Come and see' (John 1:46).

Suggested Hymns
Come, sing with holy gladness (*Church and School Hymnal*); For the beauty of the earth; Lord for the years; Lord of all hopefulness

Annunciation of Our Lord to the Blessed Virgin Mary   25 March   Mother of God
Isa. 7:10–14; Ps. 40; Heb. 10:4–10; Luke 1:26–38
'The angel said to her, "Do not be afraid, Mary, for you have found favour with God. And now, you will conceive in your womb and bear a son, and you will name him Jesus."' Luke 1:30, 31

Face to face
Mary had cause enough to be afraid. This young betrothed maid came face to face with an archangel of the celestial hierarchy. We do not know what form Gabriel took, but we can assume Mary

had not seen him before. And the message he brought would outshine even his appearance. She, a virgin, was to bear a child. She, a human, was to give birth to the divine. She, a mother, was in some strange way to mother her Creator. She, a product of time, was to hold eternity in her arms.

Athanasian theology
In the creed which, if not authored entirely by Athanasius, at least bears his stamp, the paradox is put in incomparably beautiful terms:
Jesus is:

> *God of the substance of the Father,*
> *begotten before the worlds,*
> *And Man, of the substance of his mother,*
> *born in the world:*
> *Perfect God, and perfect man,*
> *Of a reasonable soul and human flesh subsisting.*

What a message!
And what a messenger!

And Mary's response – her *fiat* which locked her irrevocably into the divine plan – is surely one of the most amazing parts of scripture.

Trusting all the way
Only rarely is it given to us to trust God as immediately and bravely as did Mary. Often we are hindered by doubt, fear, questioning. Can we have the strength of purpose to bring our doubts, fears and questions into the open, to God – and then leave them with him? God gives us time to decide, but exactly how much time only he knows. The choice is ours to make – and God is waiting.

God's choice
God had chosen Mary. Nothing like the birth of the Son of God on earth had happened before – so God chose to announce that birth in terms hitherto unknown to man. Gabriel gave notice of divine favour for a most special vocation. By the choice of Mary, God showed clearly that earthly wealth and high position count for less than humility and sanctity. Mary was to be the vehicle by

which a new nature was to be given to the Son of God – the nature of *man*, capable of suffering pain and anguish in order to meet man at every possible point. In the Marian conception, God was to be with the mother in a manner more intimate, more perfect, more divine, than he had ever been with any other creature.

Theotokos
The 'Mother of God' was the one who brought God himself into our earthly situation. The incarnation would have been impossible without Mary's *fiat*, just as it would have been impossible without the will of God. There was a total co-operation between Mary and God. There were seven archangels in the Hebrew celestial hierarchy, but God chose Gabriel (whose name means 'God has shown himself mighty') for this special mission. According to Enoch, Gabriel's main function was to pray and intercede in the presence of God, for men on earth. His other work was to show to men God's messages. He explained a vision to Daniel; he announced the coming of a son (John the Baptist) to Zachariah; and now, to Mary, he brought the greatest message of all.

Suggested Hymns
I'll sing a hymn to Mary; Tell out, my soul, the greatness of the Lord; The angel Gabriel from heaven came; Ye who own the faith of Jesus

St George, Patron Saint of England
23 April   **A Saint's Bravery**   1 Macc. 2:59–64 or Rev. 12:7–12; Ps. 126; 2 Tim. 2:3–13; John 15:18–21

'Remember the word I said to you, "Servants are not greater than their master." If they persecuted me, they will persecute you; if they kept my word, they will keep yours also.' John 15:20

The great beast of Sylene
Legend has it that George, a Cappadocian knight, rode one day into Sylene, a Libyan city in crisis. He was told of a vicious beast living in a nearby swamp, who could only be deflected from terrorizing the Sylenians by being fed on a diet of fresh meat. The

local sheep had been exhausted, and the beast was now being fed human flesh. George arrived when the king's daughter was being prepared for sacrifice. On condition that the Sylenians converted to Christianity, George killed the beast. More than fifteen thousand people are said to have been baptized.

The 'Great Martyr'
George was a victim of the Diocletian persecution, in 304; and the Eastern Church was soon referring to him as 'the Great Martyr'. It was not until after the Crusades that he succeeded Edward the Confessor as Patron Saint of England, when soldiers returning from the east brought with them the Georgian legends. His position was further enhanced when Edward III elevated him to Patron of the Order of the Garter.

Called to follow
Whether we are called to the front line in a physical battle, or to a ministry of prayer on the home front, Christ is always one step before us, and calling us to follow him. As we reflect on the great 'communion of saints', and the legacy they have given us, can we not translate this vast power of faith and trust into the even greater 'cloud of witnesses' who watch over our lives and encourage us spiritually from the Nearer Presence?

> *It may not be on the mountain's height,*
> *Or over the stormy sea;*
> *It may not be at the battle's front*
> *My Lord will have need of me;*
> *But if, by a still, small voice he calls*
> *To paths I do not know,*
> *I'll answer, dear Lord, with my hand in thine,*
> *I'll go where you want me to go.*

> *Mary Brown*

God's criteria
When our work here is done, we shall not only be asked: 'What did you do?' but '*How* did you do what you did?' We may travel the world with the word of God, and for much of the time be distracted from preaching. Or we may hold a single Bible study

group in our home – and do it excellently, for the glory of God. If we act as we are called to act, where we *are*, we can be assured that this is what God is wanting. Let us concentrate on what he is telling us to do, and not fall into Peter's trap and try to muscle in on someone else's mission (John 21:21). Even if no more than half the legends concerning him are true, St George seems to have had a life filled with Christian bravery and love for his neighbour. We can ask for no more.

Suggested Hymns
And did those feet; I vow to thee, my country; Rejoice, O land, in God thy might; For all the saints

St Mark, Evangelist   25 April
Missionary Evangelist   Prov. 15:28–33 or Acts 15:35–41; Ps. 119:9–16; Eph. 4:7–16; Mark 13:5–13

'As for yourselves, beware; for they will hand you over to councils; and you will be beaten in synagogues; and you will stand before governors and kings because of me, as a testimony to them. And the good news must first be proclaimed to all nations.' Mark 13:9, 10

Who was Mark?
It is thought he was the young boy who, slipping out of the clutches of the guards in Gethsemane, left his loincloth in their hands and fled naked from the scene (Mark 14:51). He may also have been the 'Mark', nephew to Barnabas and a companion of Paul, on the first missionary journey. Then at Perga there seems to have been an argument, and Mark left Paul and went home. Paul was indignant at this apparent fecklessness, and when planning his second journey was not willing to forgive and forget. Barnabas defended his nephew. The apostles agreed to differ, and instead of one mission team, two went out: Paul took Silas, while Barnabas and Mark went together. When time had healed the rift, Paul, now an old man, sent a message to Timothy: 'Get Mark and bring him with you, for he is useful in my ministry' (2 Timothy 4:11).

Evangelist and interpreter

Perhaps, also, the 'Mark' who wrote the Second Gospel, the earlier of the four, was this same man: a man of many parts, as useful with a pen as in the mission field. The early Church historian, Eusebius of Caesarea, in his great *Ecclesiastical History*, writing of Bishop Papias of Hierapolis (*c.* 130), records of Mark's association with Peter:

> This also the elder used to say, Mark, indeed, having been the interpreter of Peter, wrote accurately, howbeit not in order, all that he recalled of what was either said or done by the Lord. For he neither heard the Lord, nor was he a follower of his, but, at a later date (as I said), of Peter, who used to adapt his instructions to the present needs, but not with a view to putting together the Dominical oracles in orderly fashion: so that Mark did no wrong in thus writing some things as he recalled them. For he kept a single aim in view: not to omit anything of what he heard, nor to state anything therein falsely.

Eusebius, H.E. III.39.15

The preacher

Mark's gospel shows his interest in Jesus the preacher, the bringer of the good news. Those entrusted with his gospel are under pressure (unseen, yet constant) to share it, until the whole world has heard it – has been given the choice of accepting or rejecting it. Only then will the End come, when heaven and earth will give way to God's next plans, and the only survivor from this age to eternity (apart, that is, from the redeemed) will be the word of God, the gospel.

The precious word

In parts of China, and various other eastern countries, the written word is so highly valued, that no material with writing on is lightly thrown away or burned. Mark was dealing with something even more precious: the inspired word of God. His Gospel moves quickly: there are many instances of 'straightaway' and 'immediately'. The grammar is simple, the style abrupt in parts, as the writer moves rapidly from one pericope to the next. He is eager to commit the most important points (memories of Peter?) to parchment, so that many more people will be given a chance to believe in his Lord. May we pray today for equal fervour in sharing this same gospel.

Suggested Hymns
Lord, thy word abideth; Father of mercies, in thy word; From Greenland's icy mountains; Thou whose Almighty Word

SS Philip and James, Apostles   1 May
Not Afraid to be Counted   Isa. 30:15–21; Ps. 119:1–8; Eph. 3:1–10; John 14:1–14

'Philip said to him, "Lord, show us the Father, and we will be satisfied." Jesus said to him, "Have I been with you all this time, Philip, and you still do not know me? Whoever has seen me has seen the Father. How can you say, 'Show us the Father?'."' John 14:8, 9

Generosity of spirit
Philip's brief appearances in the gospels show us a man who was outgoing in thought and action. Called by Jesus, he immediately extended the invitation to Nathanael (John 1:45). Faced with thousands of hungry people, Jesus asked Philip to find a solution. Philip's mathematical mind worked out the cost – but left the mechanics to Jesus! And in today's reading, Philip's outspokenness calls forth precious information from Jesus on the Godhead.

The Lord's relation
James the son of Alphaeus (called 'the less', or 'the younger'), is thought by some to be the same as the James who was the brother of Jesus, who became head of the Church in Jerusalem, on a par with Peter in importance (Galatians 1:18f.). If this was the case, James suffered martyrdom in the year 62.

Known in part
'Now I know only in part', reflected Paul (1 Corinthians 13:12); and today as we commemorate two saints – apostles who were very close to Jesus – we can surely experience something of Paul's frustration and regret, for we know so little of the lives of Philip and James. Who does not long to know more? As we reflect on

Jesus' question to Philip: 'Have I been with you all this time, and you still do not know me?', we may treasure what knowledge has already been given us, while, taking our courage in both hands, we boldly ask for more. Jesus did not disappoint Philip, but gave him the knowledge he was seeking. He will do the same for us, if we only ask. On the day when five thousand people were hungry for the word of God, Jesus showed Philip that God is also mindful of our other, less important, needs. Surely, if we follow Philip's lead and ask for the 'best wine', that is what we shall be given.

Quiet loyalty
James the less was not the fiery 'Son of Boanerges', who wanted to call down fire from heaven on unbelievers (Luke 9:54). His was a quieter ministry, but no less loyal. It may not be our mission to chair a synod, or to design a great cathedral; but if we pursue our calling quietly and with dedication, God will bless the outcome of our endeavours. So long as we do not become agitated or frustrated because our ministry seems less spectacular than someone else's, God will gently widen our parameters to the potential he knows, yet which is hidden from us until its fulfilment. Let us get serious with God today, and ask that our progress gives him all the glory. He will take care of the rest.

Suggested Hymns
Be still, for the presence of the Lord; O, the love of my Lord is the essence; I cannot tell, why he whom angels worship; To God be the glory

St Matthias, Apostle   14 May
Chosen by God   Isa. 22:15–25 or Acts 1:15–26; Ps. 15; Acts 1:15–26 or 1 Cor. 4:1–7; John 15:9–17

'"You did not choose me, but I chose you."' John 15:16
'And they cast lots for them, and the lot fell on Matthias; and he was added to the eleven apostles.' Acts 1:26

A good beginning
Matthias did not come 'cold' to the apostolate. Peter tells us he had been with Jesus and the disciples from the beginning, and had been a witness of the ascension (Acts 1:21, 22). In the days immediately following, the eleven felt called to restore their number to what it had been before Judas' defection; and the decision to cast lots for the twelfth apostle virtually gave the decision back to God. Apart from these verses, we know nothing of Matthias, though a Gospel bearing his name circulated for a time before being lost. Paul did not confine the apostolate to twelve, or even to those who had been a part of Jesus' earthly ministry (1 Corinthians 9:1, 2b; 15:9); but Peter's parameters were more closely set.

God's choice
God chose the early apostles: chose and called them, from whatever work they were doing. His was the initiative: 'Follow me. Take up the cross. Learn of me. Deny yourself. Take my yoke on you. Love as I have loved.' There was no compulsion, yet every incentive. Those who took up the challenge gained the best and lost the worst. And God's method is still the same today. If you are a Christian, you have been surely chosen and called by God. This is his prerogative, and our privilege. We are not on our own. We are not our own.

The Almighty giver
And God does not stop at the choosing: from this time on, he gives; he is the Almighty giver. But he does not give indiscriminately; whatever gifts an individual needs, to fulfil his purpose here, God provides. Can we examine our talents, and see whether we are using them to the full, to his glory?

Rich diversity
So many people, chosen and called. So many gifts. Yet the gift that is common to all is the most daring and dangerous of all: the gift of free will. God may choose us; but he is a Gentleman: he does not force us to stay on his side. Minute by minute, the choice to go his way or ours, is open to us.

The river's pull
We need to work at going God's way, because the river of the world is constantly trying to pull us in the opposite direction. It

is hard to make a conscious decision to go God's way, but it must be done. If we did not have God on our side (Psalm 118:6), we should never make it; but as soon as we decide for him, he backs up our decision with the power to carry it out.

Generous interest
If we let God be God in our lives, he will return our commitment with a far more generous interest than Messrs Barclay or NatWest could dare to offer. Our covenant partner made the biggest decision of all, the day he chose and called us to follow him. Can we not do our best with the smaller, daily decisions – even if it takes a lifetime? Matthias, when he accepted the call to follow Jesus, would probably never have imagined that one day he would be a member of the Twelve.

Suggested Hymns
Who is on the Lord's side?; I, the Lord of sea and sky; New every morning is the love; When we walk with the Lord

Visit of the Blessed Virgin Mary to Elizabeth 31 May Sharing Good News
Zeph. 3:14–18; Ps. 113; Rom. 12:9–16; Luke 1:39–56
'In those days Mary set out and went with haste to a Judaean town in the hill country, where she entered the house of Zechariah and greeted Elizabeth.' Luke 1:39, 40

A double joy
Mary generously wanted to share the good news of Gabriel's visit with her cousin, and so to double her joy; and Luke sees also in this visit the first ante-natal recognition of Jesus by John the Baptist. Joy is infectious: some of what these two women shared can be ours as we celebrate with them today. In a fast-paced world where automation, figures and computer screens are on the increase, let us not become so caught up in the web of sophistication, that we have no time for a pleasure that comes without price.

The gospel is for sharing
From the beginning, Jesus taught his disciples to share the gospel; in the widest sense, to publish it to every person on this earth. The history of the Christian Church shows that while this sharing has been continuing for nearly two millennia, it has not been the quickest of endeavours, and there have been many times of hiatus along the way. We still have far to go, with around two-thirds of the world's languages without a complete, or even partial Bible translation. There are many things in life which we share, which are not worth sharing. Can we not make sharing the gospel our major life's work?

Devotion
Two men were walking in the spacious, well-manicured grounds of a country house in Ireland, discussing the conference that had drawn Christians from many parts of the world to that place. Suddenly, Edward Varley turned to his companion and said: 'The world has yet to see what God can do with a man who devotes himself completely and utterly to the gospel.' His friend, taken aback, did not reply immediately; but the words kept milling round in his mind. In his room that night, he made a serious commitment: 'By God's grace, I'll be that man!' His name was Dwight L. Moody, and his evangelism was to bring many to Christ, on both sides of the Atlantic.

Faith unlimited
We are so familiar with the Christmas stories that we may not always appreciate the faith 'in things not seen' shown by both Mary and Elizabeth. Here is a young woman, unmarried, telling of a miraculous conception! But Elizabeth has already experienced the marvellous working of a God who is not bound by the laws of nature: way past the age of child-bearing herself, she is nevertheless about to become a mother. God has dealt wonderfully with both these women. But God's power is not confined to a Mary or an Elizabeth, nor yet to a D.L. Moody. Yet if we pray him to move mightily in our lives – and through us to others – we must be prepared for him to take us at our word.

Suggested Hymns
Mary Immaculate, Star of the morning; Maiden yet a mother; Hail, thou Queen of ocean; Daily, daily, sing to Mary (*A Westminster Hymnal*)

St Barnabas, Apostle 12 June 'A Good Man'
Job 29:11–16 or Acts 11:19–30; Ps. 112; Acts 11:19–30
or Gal. 2:1–10; John 15:12–17

' "This is my commandment, that you love one another, as I have loved you. No one has greater love than this, to lay down one's life for one's friends." ' John 15:12, 13

Son of consolation
Luke describes Barnabas as 'a good man' (Acts 11:24), and records that he sold everything he had, to benefit the poor. His name – previously Joseph – was changed to Barnabas ('Son of Consolation'). It was Barnabas who supported Paul after Paul's conversion: Barnabas who spoke up for Paul, and had faith in the genuineness of his about-turn. It was Barnabas, too, who stood by Mark, when Paul wanted to jettison the man who went home from the field of mission; Barnabas, who let Paul set out on the second missionary journey with Silas, while he himself took Mark to Cyprus. Barnabas is said to have been martyred in Cyprus, around the year 61. Today's pilgrims can visit the little stone cupola church on the island, which houses the tomb of the apostle.

Strength of character
A man of conviction, strong enough to stand up to the wrath of Paul, and charitable enough to forgive the apparent inconsistency of a young aspiring missionary, as he had also been with the amazing about-turn of the foremost persecutor of the Church, Barnabas stands out as a man of courage and constancy: a stalwart to have at one's side on any mission. The Barnabases of this world are still hard at work, wherever the gospel is preached; they miss most of the headlines; their worth is often appreciated only by their immediate colleagues; but steadily over the years they are a force for good, in a world where quiet dedication and loyalty are too often at a premium.

Champion of others
Barnabas' championing of Paul, and then Mark, is an indication that even in the front line of evangelism there can be misunderstanding and friction. If the Church were already a communion of saints, this would not be so; but it is presently a collection of

sinners, who may be saints one day. Until then, we need to recognize our failings, and make allowances for the failings of others. Those outside the Church apparently ignore this truth, and judge us as though we already wore haloes. At least let us give them credit for acknowledging the high ideals of saintliness, while disabusing them of the notion that we have already ascended to that level. Barnabas had to do precisely this, when in Lystra he and Paul were mistaken for gods: Paul they called Hermes (since he was the main orator), and Barnabas they called Zeus (Acts 14:11ff.). 'We are mortals just like you!' the disciples cried immediately – but they had a hard job to convince the crowds.

Earthly pedestal
Sometimes a prominent evangelist or church worker may be fêted in a similarly extravagant and misguided way; and we are all in duty bound to keep well away from mounting a pedestal of the world's making. It is hard work – but if there is anyone whose example can show us how to maintain humility and dedication, then it is Barnabas.

Suggested Hymns
Just as I am, without one plea; And can it be, that I should gain; Disposer supreme, and judge of the earth; It is a thing most wonderful

Birth of John the Baptist   24 June
Pre-natally Blessed   Isa. 40:1–11; Ps. 85:7–13; Acts 13:14b–26 or Gal. 3:23–29; Luke 1:57–66, 80

'"His name is John." And all of them were amazed. Immediately [Zechariah's] mouth was opened and his tongue freed, and he began to speak, praising God.' Luke 1:63, 64

Born to be great
Yet it was not for worldly greatness that John was born, though he has become known wherever the gospel has been preached. His was to be a life of fiery dedication, impassioned courage – yet

of self-effacement. Because his birth, to a couple of advanced years, was attended with the miraculous restoration of Zechariah's speech, and his close connection with the birth of Jesus and the Christmas stories, this commemoration of 24 June tends to predominate over the death (29 August), which was horrific in the extreme.

How do we show Jesus?
John's example of humility as regards his own position (for he could have carved out for himself a successful career in oratory), challenges all Christians to review how they can point others away from themselves, and to Christ. It is not the compliment: 'Oh, what a wonderful Christian (s)he is!' that we seek, but rather: 'You have shown me what Jesus is like!' How many times have we received such a compliment? John bent all his energies, used every gift God had given him, to proclaiming Jesus. Yet he could not proclaim (as is our privilege) a Jesus who was crucified, buried, resurrected and ascended. He could not share with his listeners the parables and teaching of Jesus, or the understanding of the gospel by the Apostolic Church. He could not look back over two thousand years of Christian history, building on its successes and learning from its failures. But he did what he could with what he had. And did it magnificently.

Using our resources
In addition to the scriptures (old and new), and the wealth of supplementary history, are we using all the resources God has given us, to proclaim the gospel? Are we as recklessly abandoned to God as was John? Today's world concentrates so much of its time on planning for life before death: to live longer, to enjoy more leisure, to keep well and warm. This is prudent, and makes for a comfortable existence; but it is not the gospel which Jesus (or John) preached. The cross is not simply to be taken up on a Sunday, but daily. God's gifts for ministry are not restricted to one day in every seven.

On fire for Jesus
'Lord, send a revival, and let it begin with me!' Can we, with John's example stirring us today, really make such a prayer, knowing that God may take us at our word?

With hearts on fire for Jesus,
Brave in the Spirit's power,
Persuade us, heavenly Father,
To seek thee every hour.
Prepare us to inherit,
When every work is done,
At last the promised glory,
So let thy kingdom come.

Entrusted with thy gospel,
We'll show thy love and care,
Ambassadors for Jesus,
In duty bound to share.
For our dear Lord has promised,
The final Day will dawn,
When all have heard thy gospel,
So let thy kingdom come.

Committed, Lord, to service,
No work too great or small,
Not seeking rest from duty,
Responding to thy call.
Here, Lord, we pledge allegiance,
Hardly the work's begun;
Bring us to full devotion,
So let thy kingdom come.

J.C.

Suggested Hymns
On Jordan's bank the Baptist's cry; Strengthen for service, Lord;
Forth in thy Name, O Lord, I go; Stand up, stand up for Jesus

St Irenaeus, Bishop of Lyons   28 June
Champion of the True Gospel   Wis. 7:7–10, 15–16;
Ps. 34; 2 Pet. 1:16–21; Luke 11:33–36

' "Consider whether the light in you is not darkness. If then your whole
body is full of light, with no part of it in darkness, it will be as full of
light as when a lamp gives you light with its rays." ' Luke 11:35, 36

In apostolic succession
Irenaeus is thought to have been born at Smyrna, around the year 130. As a young man, he had learned much from Polycarp, who in turn had known St John, and Irenaeus valued the succession of teaching from an apostle who had been with Jesus. The second century was a time of many 'gospel' writers, but Irenaeus emphasized that only the four canonical Gospels should be accorded credibility.

In worthy footsteps
Irenaeus travelled extensively in Gaul, but in 177 was in Rome to hear the news of Bishop Pothinus' martyrdom, at the age of ninety. The Pope offered him the bishopric of Lyons, and Irenaeus accepted. Secular peace, of a kind, existed in Gaul, but the new bishop was quickly drawn into a defence of the faith against the gnostic heresy which denied full humanity to the incarnate Jesus. He also defended the rôle of the bishops in all heretical disputes. His correspondence was prodigious, and many of his letters have been preserved, particularly those against the Valentinian and Marcionite heresies. One of his tenets was the superiority of faith to knowledge:

> It is therefore better, as I've already said, that one should not have knowledge whatever of any reasons why a single created thing has been made, but should believe in God, and remain in his love, than that, made superior by such knowledge, he should lose that love which is the very life of man, and that he should seek after no other knowledge except the knowledge of Jesus Christ the Son of God, who was crucified for us, than that by devious questions and hair-splitting expressions he should lose his pious state.
>
> *Irenaeus, II.39.1,* Faith Superior to Knowledge

Back to basics
Irenaeus reminds us that we need to be constantly aware of the danger of allowing impurities to infiltrate our faith. One of the greatest preachers of all time, C.H. Spurgeon, humbly asked: 'Do you doubt whether you are now saved, or whether you shall hold out to the end? Then I counsel you to go back to the cross, and begin again as a penitent sinner to put your trust in a pardoning Saviour. Full many a time I have to do that.'

Legacy of truth
After about a quarter century of staunchly defending truth against
all comers, Irenaeus is thought to have been martyred in the year
200. But his teaching and writings had done much to stabilize a
furore of heresy that if left unchecked would have threatened
much of Christian Europe. The Irenaeuses of this world are rarely
popular: arguments of failing to move with the times, of backward-
ness and naïvety, are invariably levelled at them; and to support
the truth when everyone around you seems bent on distorting it,
can be well nigh impossible. Thank God, there are still those who
take up impossible challenges!

Suggested Hymns
Thou art the way; Firmly I believe and truly; In the cross of Christ
I glory; How sweet the Name of Jesus sounds

SS Peter and Paul, Apostles   29 June
Individuality   Ezek. 3:22–27 or Acts 12:1–11; Ps. 125;
Acts 12:1–11 or 1 Pet. 2:19–25; Matt. 16:13–19

*'Now when Jesus came into the district of Caesarea Philippi, he asked
his disciples, "Who do people say that the Son of Man is?" And they
said, 'Some say John the Baptist, but others Elijah, and still others
Jeremiah or one of the prophets." He said to them, "But who do you say
that I am?"' Matthew 16:13–15*

In God's image
We are made in God's image, yet we are individuals. No one can
grasp this profound truth, so we must accept it by faith. It means
we cannot come to God by proxy; we cannot be a Christian in the
name of anyone else. Peter discovered that he needed personally
to re-affirm his belief in Christ, for each time he had personally
denied him. Paul was told, as he lay blinded on the Damascus
Road, that he had not been merely persecuting Christians, but
Jesus himself – and it was to Jesus he was having to answer; and
Paul, with letters of authority to commit Christians to prison, must
have wished those incriminating letters far from himself. While
Peter had had the privilege of three years' ministry 'on the road'

with Jesus, Paul came to the apostolate almost as 'someone untimely born' (1 Corinthians 15:8). Each of us can look at another's ministry and see there a privilege we have not had; but equally, in our ministry, we have a privilege that is peculiarly ours. Some may expend much work for little visible result; others may come late to the faith – or die before their mission is hardly begun. Yet each of us, in God's image, is called to do what (s)he has been called to do.

Men of stature

We have traditional accounts of the height, colour, weight and appearance of Peter and Paul; but it does not matter one jot how they looked. They were preachers of the gospel, men of giant spiritual stature: and the message which they brought was light to a world darkened by paganism and smothered by sophistication. And what does their joint festival mean to us today? Perhaps our partially pagan world, smothered by what we now call 'technology', needs to re-discover the powerful preaching of Peter and Paul – to read again, but as for the first time, Acts and the Letters, as well as the gospels, if it is to be able to answer Jesus who continues to ask: 'Who do you say that I am?'

Martyrs for the faith

Peter and Paul are thought to have suffered martyrdom in Rome around the year 64. In our day, witnessing for Jesus less commonly leads to martyrdom, but still carries some of the same risks which threatened first-century Christians. We can be misunderstood, mocked, despised, and – certainly in some places – harassed, imprisoned, tortured or even killed. When we consider Christ's gospel of love, reflect on his sacrifice at Calvary, and realize yet again the goodness of God and his providence – is it not incomprehensible that anyone could reject all this? If man is not inherently evil, then he simply chooses to gain the worst and lose the best. That is the human tragedy. The work, worship and witness of Peter and Paul challenge us to do what we can – *all* that we can – for Christ, in the time remaining to us.

Suggested Hymns

O Rock of ages, one Foundation; Thou art the Christ, O Lord; Forsaken once, and thrice denied; Paul the preacher, Paul the poet

St Thomas, Apostle   3 July   My Lord and my God!
Hab. 2:1–4; Ps. 31:1–6; Eph. 2:19–22; John 20:24–29

'Then [Jesus] said to Thomas, "Put your finger here and see my hands.
Reach out your hand and put it in my side. Do not doubt but believe."
Thomas answered him, "My Lord and my God!"' John 20:27, 28

Is doubting sin?
The short answer is: Yes, it is, for Jesus says: 'Do not doubt.' Yet
Thomas, for all his doubting, was given his answer, in the most
convincing way possible. Jesus kept him waiting a mere week. Yet
even a week can seem a long time, if we are at a crisis point and
desperate for an answer. Why does God sometimes keep us waiting so long? It was this question that Habakkuk struggled with,
and the answer was given: 'There is still a vision for the appointed
time; it speaks of the end, and does not lie. If it seems to tarry,
wait for it; it will surely come, it will not delay' (Habakkuk 2:3).
Wait for it, as Longfellow wrote:

> *Let us then be up and doing,*
> *With a heart for any fate;*
> *Still achieving, still pursuing:*
> *Learn to labour, and to wait.*

There is a time for every purpose under heaven: a time to labour,
and a time to wait. We need to ask for grace to do each at the
right time.

The great affirmation
Until Thomas' great affirmation, Jesus had not been called 'God'
in the gospels. But now he has been through death and he is, in
the fullest, most awe-ful sense, superhuman; and Thomas gives
him a title commensurate with this. It was Thomas, earlier in the
ministry, whose question: 'How can we know the way?' elicited
Jesus' teaching: 'I am the way, and the truth and the life' (John
14:5ff.). And it was Thomas who bravely, if desperately, declared:
'Let us go and die with him,' when Jesus decided to go up to
Bethany after Lazarus had died (John 11:16). Thomas comes
across as a courageous and deep-thinking disciple: one whom
it would be good to have at one's side in a crisis, yet one who

would not acquiesce in any situation until he was sure of his ground.

Not just a doubter
These are admirable qualities, and yet it is Thomas' one great recorded doubt that has dominated his historicity. That he was not just a doubter, we can surely remember today – for in today's world, too, there is often a distortion of the facts; and many people have been convicted on a single piece of eye-catching evidence, when a much greater bulk of less interesting data has been passed over.

Thomas the writer?
There are various writings attributed to Thomas, notably the *Acts of Thomas*, which appear to date from the third century; *The Apocalypse of Thomas* (probably before the fifth century); and the best-known, *The Gospel of Thomas*, which may stem from the second century. A hymn currently in use ('They who tread the path of labour') seems to have been based on Logion 77 of *The Gospel of Thomas*:

> *'Jesus said: "I am the light that is over them all. I am the All; the All has come forth from me, and the All has attained unto me. Cleave a piece of wood, and I am there. Raise the stone, and thou shalt find me there."'*

Suggested Hymns
They who tread the path of labour; Who dreads, yet undismayed; For all thy saints, O Lord; Jesus, my Lord, my God, my all

St Mary Magdalene 22 July My Lord
Song of Sol. 3:1–4; Ps. 42:1–7; 2 Cor. 5:14–17; John 20:1–2, 11–18

> *'[The angels] said to her, "Woman, why are you weeping?" She said to them, "They have taken away my Lord, and I do not know where they have laid him."'* John 20:13

'Apostle to the apostles'

This was the title given to Mary by the Early Church. Perhaps she had been a prostitute. Jesus is reported as having cast out 'seven demons' from her (Mark 16:9; Luke 8:2), which was the recognized euphemism for the restoration of a fallen woman. Whatever her past, Mary from Magdala convincingly redeemed it by showing such gratitude and loyalty to her healer. She was rewarded by being the first woman to learn of his resurrection, and to meet Jesus on that first Easter morning. If anyone was well qualified to call him 'my Lord', it was Mary. Generously, she quickly shared her joy with Peter and the others; and it was not her fault that they did not at first believe. It is inconceivable to us, with the advantage of hindsight, that the marvellous news was spurned; yet today when God works mightily, it is not only unbelievers who seek 'rational' explanations.

Mary's courage

Such was Mary's faith and courage, she seems not to have worried about keeping the low profile expected from women in the first century, nor does the apostles' unbelief appear to have upset her confidence. She knows Jesus has risen; she has seen him, talked with him. That is enough. However complicated has been her past, it is in the past. Jesus has made a new woman of her. God is no respecter of persons.

The past is gone

Whatever we have done or said amiss, while God gives time we can seek forgiveness as did Mary. And in his magnificent unfairness, God will not hold repented sin against us. There would be women in Jerusalem who had led exemplary lives: but it was the penitent prostitute who was given the greatest gift of that Easter morning. Love had drawn her to the tomb: reciprocal love responded on the grand scale. It is not what we have done, but the love we show for Christ, that receives the munificent reward. Mary could have allowed the darkness of past sin to cloud the rest of her life; how often do we exhume confessed sin, and let it worry us all over again? If misfortune comes, it is so easy to blame it on wrong we have committed, perhaps years before: wrong which has already been confessed, wrong which God has already forgiven. If, in the divine records, our sin has been erased, why are we needlessly, sinfully re-writing it? Mary was brave enough to 'let the dead past bury its dead'. Freed from its burden, she was strong to move forward in faith.

Lack of convention
We like to feel secure – even though, at the 'best' of times, we are a mere breath away from eternity – and much time and effort is expended in hedging our lives round with the screening security of convention. But this is not God's way. Familiarity with the scriptures may blur this truth for us; but the story of Mary is a reminder of how shockingly unconventional is God's *modus operandi*. Are we brave enough to accept his willingness to work in our lives? Just what are we letting ourselves in for? What if . . . ? Mary of Magdala doubtless gave thanks many a time, that she did not do 'something more conventional', and stay at home to grieve, on Easter morning.

Suggested Hymns
My God, I love thee, not because; The day of resurrection; Lord, the light of your love is shining; O for a heart to praise my God

St James, Apostle   25 July   Son of Boanerges
Jer. 45:1–5 or Acts 11:27–12:2; Ps. 126; Acts 11:27–12:2 or 2 Cor. 4:7–15; Matt. 20:20–28
'Then the mother of the sons of Zebedee came to him with her sons, and kneeling before him, she asked a favour of him.' Matthew 20:20

Boldness of speech
Mark has the request coming directly from James and John (Mark 10:35), which is probably to be preferred, Matthew softening it to protect the disciples' reputations. Since the 'Sons of Thunder' had wanted to call down fire from heaven on a group of Samaritans, they were obviously not averse to bold speaking. James had been called by Jesus, while at work in the family boat with John his brother and their father Zebedee. Unquestioningly, the brothers had obeyed. They had been privileged to witness the Transfiguration, and also to accompany Jesus when he prayed in agony in Gethsemane.

Head of the Church

After the ascension of Jesus, James led the church in Jerusalem, and was killed around the year 44 by Herod Agrippa, in an attempt to snuff out the new religion. When he saw that the martyrdom pleased the Jews, Herod had designs on Peter's life also (Acts 12:1, 2). Still today one of the hardest of unanswered questions is: Why does sin have such power on this earth? It does not come naturally to men to follow God; but when we do convert – even become as little children, and accept the gifts our Father showers on us in abundance – still we come up against the power of evil, which at times appears to defeat all that we can muster against it. Still we fall, however hard we try not to; still we die, and no one but Jesus has yet risen from the dead.

Have faith

As did Abraham, we need to 'hope against hope' (Romans 4:18). When all the odds are stacked against us, we need to have faith in God, who then will 'reckon it to us as righteousness' (Romans 4:3). There was no one to keep reassuring Abraham, as the twenty-five years between promise and fulfilment dragged on, that he would indeed have a son, would indeed be the 'father of many nations'. He had to live by faith. James and John (or their mother) sought a cast-iron assurance, in the presence of witnesses, that their loyalty to Jesus would be rewarded with high honour. They were forced to accept no such short cuts: they must, like Abraham, live by faith. And so strongly did James' faith mature, that eventually he was able to accept the leadership of the Jerusalem Church, knowing full well that this put him in a very hot seat indeed.

High office

James' example challenges us not to reject high office in the Church if it is offered to us. The fact that much (more) is expected from those to whom much (more) is given, should increase our faith. When God calls, he gives the grace to answer. Like James, we can leave the outcome to him. High office brings recognition and problems of its own. That is not our problem. We just need to be faithful: God is capable of seeing us through whatever he has called us to face.

Through all the changing scenes of life; Forth in thy Name, O Lord, I go; Guide me, O thou great Redeemer; I will go in the strength of the Lord

Festival of the Blessed Virgin Mary (Called by some, *The Assumption of the Virgin*)   15 August

The Lord's Favour   Isa. 61:10–11 or Rev. 11:19–12:6, 10; Ps. 45:10–17; Gal. 4:4–7; Luke 1:46–55

'And Mary said, "My soul magnifies the Lord, and my spirit rejoices in God my Saviour; for he has looked with favour on the lowliness of his servant. Surely, from now on all generations will call me blessed."'
Luke 1:46–48

Marian traditions

The Bible does not tell us that Mary's childhood was spent in the temple, nor that she was always a virgin, nor that at the end of her life on earth she was bodily assumed into heaven; but these are among the Marian traditions that have long been held by many Christians. Certainly this young woman was highly favoured by God, in being chosen to bear the world's Saviour; and certainly she showed great courage and faith when by her *fiat* she acquiesced, her grave would surely have been treasured by the early Christians; yet there is still doubt as to the precise tomb of Jesus – the tomb which Joseph of Arimathaea had prepared for himself, but which charity persuaded him to give to his Lord. We can also argue that the woman who held so precious a place in Jesus' heart that he provided for her even in his hour of extreme agony, would not be left at death to see bodily corruption: yet presumably her husband Joseph, and the disciples, received bodily interment. Surely the question does not alter our love for Mary, or our appreciation of her life as recorded in the New Testament, or even the continuing of her influence and work in the spiritual dimension. She is blessed above all women, in that she was chosen by God for a work which no other woman had been called to do. And she was magnificently, yet humbly, obedient to the call.

Individual, yet corporate, mission
The mission to which God calls us is unique to us, yet part of his overall purpose for the Church militant here on earth, triumphant in heaven. We must exercise our freedom of choice, either – with Mary – giving a courageous, faithful, *fiat*, or rejecting God's call. If we hesitate before committing ourselves one way or the other, the call may not be repeated. Mary gave her answer immediately to Gabriel; she did not wait to consult Joseph; she did not ask for time to sleep on the proposal. She asked for nothing, but that God's will be done. This is the total commitment that gives God the opportunity to do great things.

Fear of the impossible
In the natural realm, anything that God calls us to do is impossible: perhaps it is his way of teaching us to overcome fear of what we do not understand. Fear of the consequences could easily have persuaded Mary to 'opt out' of becoming involved in a plan which appeared to ride roughshod over the natural, economic, social and democratic laws. Fear of the consequences can persuade us also to opt out; and it may be many years later that we realize God had been telling us to venture into the unknown. What we could have accomplished, with one little *fiat*! Think of what we still may be able, with God's grace, to accomplish!

Suggested Hymns
Protect us, while telling; Mary Immaculate, Star of the morning; I'll sing a hymn to Mary (*Westminster Hymnal*); I sing the Lord God's praises (*Celebration Hymnal*)

St Bartholomew, Apostle   24 August
A Loyal Apostle   Isa 43:8–13 or Acts 5:12–16;
Ps. 145:1–7; Acts 5:12–16 or 1 Cor. 4:9–15; Luke 22:24–40
' "You are those who have stood by me in my trials; and I confer on you, just as my Father has conferred on me, a kingdom." ' Luke 22:28, 29

Initial scepticism

Bartholomew is generally taken to be the 'Nathanael' of John 1:45ff., whom Philip introduced to Jesus. Sceptical at first of a prophet who came out of Nazareth, Bartholomew nevertheless joined the disciples, and remained loyal, being rewarded with a vision of his risen Lord. According to tradition, he preached in India and Armenia after the ascension, suffering martyrdom under the Armenian King Astyages. After being flayed alive, he was beheaded, and is sometimes shown in Christian art with an executioner's knife. His relics were eventually transferred to Benevento, Italy.

Coming to faith

Each of us comes to faith in our own way: for some, like Bartholomew, there is scepticism – sometimes preconceptions that stand in the way of immediate commitment. Indeed, if we are honest, doubts of one kind or another surface throughout our lives. We wonder if we are really doing God's will, or whether he will come to our help in time, or whether our prayers have missed the mark, or whether the opportunity we let slip will be repeated, or whether we could do more ... all these, and perhaps in a crisis we even ask if God is there. Like Bartholomew, some of us come gradually to faith, while others can pinpoint the exact time of conversion; and there are still those who can be identified with the sons in Jesus' parable: one of whom told his father he would go to work, and did not; the other refused, but later put in a good day's work (Matthew 21:28ff.).

A calculated risk?

John tells us to 'test the spirits to see whether they are from God' (1 John 4:1), and we can surely extend this precept to all that we believe. God has given us muscular minds of infinite comprehension: no one has yet tested the mind to its fullest extent. We are to study, to question, to discuss and share our faith with other members of the body of Christ; only then are we ready to share it with non-believers. Paul's is the classic example: after his conversion, Barnabas and the other disciples shared their experiences with him, and he with them: mutually strengthened, they were all motivated for a ministry that was to give Luke his data for the rest of Acts.

The best start
Bartholomew had the best possible start to his faith: the generous
example of Philip who sought him out and brought him to Jesus.
Some of us will have lost count of the people we have led to Jesus;
others may still be hesitating: is God really asking this of me?
What do I say? What if the person with whom I share my faith
rejects it? That was a risk that Philip took. Perhaps he felt rebuffed
when Bartholomew sneered; but Philip persevered, and a soul
was brought to faith. We need to remember that if anyone rejects
our invitation, they are not rejecting us, but Jesus. Let us play our
part, and leave the outcome in his hands.

Suggested Hymns
Give me the faith that can remove; O Jesus, I have promised; Now
come to me all you who seek; A Man there lived in Galilee

Holy Cross Day   14 September
Greatest Love   Num. 21:4–9; Ps. 22:23–28;
Phil. 2:6–11; John 3:13–17
*'For God so loved the world, that he gave his only Son, so that every-
one who believes in him may not perish but may have eternal life.' John
3:16*

St Helena
Helena, the mother of Emperor Constantine, was said by Bishop
Ambrose of Milan to have discovered the actual cross on which
Jesus hung at Calvary. A portion of this cross was taken to Rome,
while the remainder stayed in Jerusalem. As Ambrose was at pains
to point out, Helena had not venerated the wood itself, but the
Man who had been nailed to it. Yet as time went on, doubts grew
not only as to the propriety of acknowledging such relics, but also
as to their authenticity. This day, none the less, has continued to
be kept as a festival which focuses our attention on what is the
main symbol of our faith.

The ignominy of the cross

God chose for his Son the most ignominious death of the time: to the Jews, it meant a curse; to the Romans, a class-leveller, for high and low were crucified; and to the Greeks, it was 'foolishness' (1 Corinthians 1:23) – for a god would never suffer such degradation. Once the charge of blasphemy, erroneous though it was, had passed beyond the Sanhedrin to Pilate, crucifixion was the obvious sequel to a guilty verdict. Pilate had freedom of choice: he chose not to challenge the Jews; and by that time their venom had carried them into the recklessness of the cry: 'His blood be on us and on our children!' (Matthew 27:35).

No other death

In the will of God, Jesus could have died in no other way; if he had been stoned, his bones would have been broken; if he had been burned, how could his wounds have survived the fire? It had to be as it happened. He had to have the sepulchral interment – otherwise some would have said he had not been really dead. When the Roman certified him dead on the cross, that pagan brought the experience of many such crucifixions into his verdict: we may have the utmost confidence that Jesus was dead. The cross had been in Jesus' mind throughout his ministry: he had told his disciples to take up their cross each day; such a command would impact fully after Calvary.

Against the ego

The upright of the cross has been seen as the letter 'I', and the horizontal as God cutting through our ego, or calling it out. Calvary was the time at which our lives became forever inextricably attached to the Son of God. We can reject him, or accept him. But in either case the cross still stands, its challenge unrevoked, its message the same, yesterday, today and for ever: 'God loved the world so much,' that he gave, and he is still giving. Before the cross, Jesus had not imposed on our lives: after the cross, the world could never be the same. The purest of loves had touched it, bled on it, and risen after it. Just two pieces of wood, such as the carpenter's Son must have handled many times: wood that once grew from a tiny seed. As we reflect on the cross, feeling in our minds its strength, roughness, splinters and weight, can we not wonder again at the inconstancy of men, made in God's image, who can love, and yet hate?

283

Cross of Jesus, Cross of sorrow,
Where the blood of Christ was shed;
Perfect Man on thee was tortured,
Perfect God on thee has bled.

J. Stainer

Suggested Hymns
My Lord, my Master, at thy feet adoring; His are the thousand sparkling rills; In the Cross of Christ I glory; Forgive them, O my Father

St Matthew, Apostle and Evangelist
21 September   Called from the Tax Booth
Prov. 3:13–18; Ps. 119:65–72; 2 Cor. 4:1–6; Matt. 9:9–13
'As Jesus was walking along, he saw a man called Matthew sitting at the tax booth; and he said to him, "Follow me." And he got up and followed him.' Matthew 9:9

Called to faith
Jesus did not wait for Matthew to entertain him to a meal, listen to his preaching, repent of his sin and promise amendment: he called him first. Similarly today, he does not wait for us to read the Bible from first to last, nor to confess every failing; he calls us first and, if we are obedient to his call as was Matthew, the rest will follow. Like Matthew's, our past may be of questionable integrity; our job may even compromise the gospel; we may be scorned by some we call our friends. This does not matter: if Jesus calls, we take the first step to a newness of life, the minute we respond.

The tax man
According to the Gospel that bears his name, Matthew was a collector of revenues, in the pay of the Romans, and thus despised by the Jews. Mark and Luke call him 'Levi'. He was based at Capernaum, and we know little of his life after the ascension, though tradition has it that he suffered martyrdom in Ethiopia.

Probably because he had been called from a life where time-serving and sharp practice were common, Matthew's Gospel emphasizes the loyalty of Jesus to those he has called; his message to the 'chosen' people, the Jews; and the founding of the Church (not mentioned as such in the other Gospels). It is Matthew, however, alone of the evangelists, who tells us of the first non-Jewish visitors to the young Jesus, the Magi; and Matthew who gives us the parable of the Last Judgement (Matthew 25:31ff.), where whatever good or bad we have done will be judged, as though we had done it to Jesus himself. Matthew, with his training in the tax booth, would appreciate Jesus' attention to detail.

The world's judgement
Knowing what it was like to be judged a tax collector, a maker of profit 'on the side', Matthew recognized the sinfulness of judging others. Who would have thought that a carpenter's son would be the Saviour of the world? (Matthew 13:55). (Even so, Matthew here has softened the impact of Mark's account, which says Jesus was the carpenter, see Mark 6:3.) And memories would be long: as Mary Magdalene's past was recorded, so people would remember Matthew's, long after he had left the tax booth to follow Jesus. And still today, the world loves to point its finger: if it finds someone who is not overtly bad, it will ferret and poke and probe until it has a cause for censure (or, even worse, it will invent a cause). In a society that appears to find attractive what is bad, and to consider boring what is good, we – as ambassadors for Christ – have much to do.

Suggested Hymns
Will you come and follow me; I, the Lord of sea and sky; Come and see the shining hope; Jesus is love, creation's voice proclaims it

St Michael and All Angels   29 September
The Angel Host   Gen. 28:10–17 or Rev. 12:7–12;
Ps. 103:19–22; Rev. 12:7–12 or Heb. 1:5–14; John 1:47–51
'Jesus said to him, "Very truly, I tell you, you will see heaven opened and the angels of God ascending and descending upon the Son of Man." '
John 1:51

Heavenly war

It may come as something of a shock to hear of angelic, heavenly war (Revelation 12:7); and, in general, the dynamism of the heavenly realm is rarely brought into focus, either in sermons or study groups. There is almost certainly more noise and activity than the 'sweet by-and-by' would suggest! Of the three archangels mentioned in the Bible – Michael, Gabriel and Raphael – it is Michael who is the leader of God's armed forces, Michael who is described as Israel's protector, who heads the battle against Satan and his demonic forces – and is victorious. In Jude, we find Michael contending with Satan over the body of Moses. With the resurrection of Jesus, evil is confined to the earth – and even here, Jesus tells his disciples, 'all authority' is his.

What more could be done?

Michael's victory in heaven, and Jesus' triumph on earth, should have clipped Satan's wings beyond repair. So, why is evil still such a powerful force in the earth? Is it simply because we do not realize the mighty victories that have been gained? Do we not appreciate that Satan stakes his all on the hope that we shall not use the power God sent down at Pentecost? It is uncomfortable to answer these questions in the affirmative: after all, evil still afflicts even the most dedicated Christians: sin, illness, grief, tragedy and physical death seem as prevalent as in New Testament times, and probably more so. There is no facile solution. Yes, great wars have been won; Satan's power has been assailed, and he knows his time is limited (Revelation 12:12); but like a mortally wounded lion, he is going to wreak as much havoc as he can, while he can. And Christians are his number one priority.

Angelic help

But we, too, can fight. We have been given the Holy Spirit's power. We have Michael and his angelic legions on our side. If we deny all or any of the help that is available, it is not God's fault. John tells us: 'Little children, you are from God, and have conquered [the evil spirits]; for the one who is in you is greater than the one who is in the world' (1 John 4:4). Our help is ever-ready, always available, as we see in Gethsemane, on the night of Jesus' arrest; because he had chosen to do God's will and to make a sacrifice which no other could make, he bravely refused to take advantage of Gabriel's forces – but those forces were standing by to move in at a split-second's notice: 'more than twelve legions' of them (Matthew 26:53). Can we not meet Satan with courageous equanimity, in the sure and certain knowledge that this angelic army has never been stood down?

Candidates for miracles

Every day, with such auxiliary forces, we are candidates for miracles; and today, as never before, Michael and his angels are needed, if the world is ever to be won for God. To struggle on trying to row a boat single-handed, while its ranks of oars rattle uselessly in their rowlocks, is what too many Christians have been trying to do for too long. May we, with God's help, resolve this Michaelmas to use all the aid available.

Suggested Hymns
Ye watchers and ye holy ones; Bright the vision that delighted; Angel-voices, ever singing; Praise, my soul, the King of heaven

St Francis of Assisi, Founder of the Friars Minor   4 October   *Il Poverello*
Micah 6:6–8; Ps. 100; Gal. 6:14–18; Luke 12:22–34

'Do not be afraid, little flock; for it is your Father's good pleasure to give you the kingdom. Sell your possessions, and give alms. Make purses for yourselves that do not wear out, an unfailing treasure in heaven, where no thief comes near and no moth destroys.' Luke 12:32, 33

Francis, the builder

Born in 1181, in the Umbrian town of Assisi, Francis was initially groomed to enter his father's cloth business; but a wild streak which led him into war with a neighbouring district and resulted in capture, set his mind on a different track. He was praying one day in the ruined church of San Damiano, when a voice from the crucifix seemed to say: 'Francis, rebuild this house of mine.' He sold some of his father's cloth, was forced to return it, rebuilt the church by hand – and began a life of poverty and simplicity which was to have far-reaching effects.

The Poor Clares
Clare Offreduccio was so impressed by Francis and his brothers that she ran away from wealth and family to join him. At first, he sent her to a local Benedictine convent, but eventually Clare founded the first convent for what was to become known as the Order of Poor Clares. Francis himself (*Il Poverello*, 'the little poor one') later journeyed east, where he favourably impressed the Muslims, though with limited success in converting any to Christianity. Back in Umbria, he was disappointed to find that his original stringent ascetic values were being diluted, and eventually he relinquished the leadership of his Order. The changes made were not drastic, but Francis felt so strongly that simplicity should characterize the brothers: for instance, that no books should be owned – for books needed shelves, and shelves meant a house; and the brothers, he maintained, did not need such luxuries.

The Stigmata
In 1224, Francis began a forty-day fast, during which the sufferings of Jesus became so real, that the Sacred Wounds appeared on his own body. Fearing to draw attention to himself, he kept the Stigmata secret for two years, when at his death one of the brothers discovered them. Another brother remarked that at death Francis appeared to have just been crucified.

The Christmas crib
It is thought that Francis was the instigator of the Christmas crib. One year, he invited the brothers up to his mountain cave on Christmas Eve, where he had reconstructed the nativity scene, with animals and a manger. The brothers were so enthralled, that the news quickly spread, and families from the area trekked up the mountain to the cave – since when the scene has been replicated in countless churches and homes the world over.

Altered dreams
When something that we have begun with integrity, is taken over and altered, we may feel – like Francis – that the original vision has been compromised. But who is not to say that the Franciscan Order would have been any less active today, had it not been for the gradual maturing and expanding of Francis' early ideals? Let us offer now what is good in our lives, and pray that God will

make it even better – even if that means altering the original in some way.

Suggested Hymns
All creatures of our God and King; Seek ye first the kingdom of God; Blessed are the pure in heart; O for a heart to praise my God

St Luke, Evangelist   18 October
The Beloved Physician   Isa. 35:3–6 or Acts 16:6–12a; Ps. 147:1–7; 2 Tim. 4:5–17; Luke 10:1–9

' "Whenever you enter a town and its people welcome you, eat what is set before you; cure the sick who are there, and say to them, 'The kingdom of God has come near to you.' " ' Luke 10:8, 9

Champion of the underdog
Luke, of the four evangelists, emphasizes in his Gospel the compassion of Jesus for the poor and deprived, the outcasts of society. His theology has not the profundity of Pauline writings; he writes as an educated Gentile, with a good command of Greek, and an appreciation of the importance of the gospel being made available to all. A doctor, he records the miracles, including the resurrection, simply and with the utmost confidence that they really happened as he has recorded. He accompanied Paul on some of his missions (identified by the 'we-passages' in Acts), and is thought to have died somewhere in Greece, when he was eighty-four.

Gentile author
Luke is the only non-Jew among the New Testament writers, and the only author to mention a Roman emperor: in fact, he mentions three: Augustus, Tiberius and Claudius. It is not certain whether he accompanied Paul as a doctor, or whether he gave up medicine for the gospel; but his writings are firmly grounded in the world of Roman governors Quirinius, Pilate, Sergius Paulus, Gallio, Felix and Festus. He also mentions Herod (the Great), and some of his descendants: Herod Antipas, the tetrarch of Galilee, Herod Agrippa I and II, Berenice and Drusilla; the higher echelons of Jerusalem's clergy: Annas, Caiaphas and Ananias; and Gamaliel,

one of the greatest rabbis of all time, and tutor to Paul (as Saul).

Authenticity
A writer who is as open as this, setting his drama in a contemporary theatre, throws himself wide open to criticism. Luke is supremely confident that his facts can be verified. He is also adept in his portrayal of the differing urban characteristics: Jerusalem is seen as a cauldron of excitement and intolerance; Antioch in Syria as a thriving metropolis where the various nationalities and creeds co-exist below flash point: small wonder that it is here where the disciples are first called 'Christians'. Luke also shows us the Roman colony of Philippi, with its egoistical magistrates, and its inhabitants inordinately proud of their Roman status; and Athens, where the sophists are forever in debate, forever hungry for the latest news, as they had ever been in the time of Thucydides and Demosthenes; and Ephesus, preoccupied with its temple to Diana (Artemis), and determined to retain the revenues that the goddess cult afforded it.

The doctor's report
Luke the physician reports on the miracles of Jesus – on his nativity, transfiguration, resurrection and ascension, without questioning their physical means; this in itself speaks volumes for his faith, and their credibility. In today's world, where some go to great lengths to explain the miracles, Luke's confidence is surely an inspiration. The alternative is unthinkable: that, for instance, life ends in the grave, and the human being is more fragile and finite than the music he has composed, or the painting he has produced.

Suggested Hymns
Thine arm, O Lord, in days of old; At even, ere the sun was set; Thou to whom the sick and dying; From thee all skill and science flow

SS Simon and Jude, Apostles   28 October
Zealot and Author   Isa. 28:14–16; Ps. 119:89–96; Eph. 2:19–22; John 15:17–27
'Servants are not greater than their master.' John 15:20

So little known

We know that Simon was one of the Twelve, a Canaanite and a Zealot (probably a member of a patriotic party opposed to Rome), and Jude was the brother of James, a relative of Jesus, and probable author of the short letter that bears his name; but apart from this, today's saints are comparatively unknown: two men who were close to Jesus, yet whose lives were spent in faithful loyalty to the gospel rather than in carving out their personal niches in the pages of history: men prepared to let God have the glory, while they had the joy of following him.

Jude's letter

In a few verses, Jude deals with a wide range of issues, including the contention of Michael Archangel with Satan over the body of Moses; the prophecy of Enoch, and simple instructions for the Early Church. He is writing for Christians struggling to come to terms with the way of Christ, having only the Old Testament writings, and the preaching of the apostles as guides. 'Beloved, build yourselves up on your most holy faith, pray in the Holy Spirit; keep yourselves in the love of God; look forward to the mercy of our Lord Jesus Christ that leads to eternal life' (Jude 20, 21). Jude summarizes the four key elements in a Christian's life: faith, prayer, love and mercy. We have the advantage of being able to fill out these elements with the New Testament teaching. While all stem from God, Jesus gives us the power, through the Holy Spirit, to work out in our lives the abundance of faith, prayer, love and mercy that God has worked in. Each of them grows with the sharing, and each is inexhaustible.

Calvary – for me?

We can work on these four elements as a divine capital that is forever increasing – or we can pass up the opportunity. If we reject God's gifts, we are, in effect, saying that we are so special, the sacrifice of Calvary was not good enough for us – that the servants *are* greater than their Master. No one is too low to be beneath the reach of Jesus' blood; no one is too exalted that that same blood cannot touch him or her. If we can stretch our minds to accept the truth that on the cross Jesus looked down history-to-come till the End of time, and saw all believers, we must accept that he saw us, that even in his agony, we were on his mind. His faith, prayers, mercy and love were bequeathed to us in his last (and only) will and testament.

Present beneficiaries
When a man dies, his will comes into effect, and the beneficiaries
receive his bequests. The beneficiaries do not have to wait until
they die, to receive: that would be pointless. Therefore, when Jesus
died, his testament (covenant, will) came into effect: the wealth of
God's gifts, in the power of the Spirit, became available to all
believers; and his armour against Satan is ours to use NOW. We
shall not need it in heaven.

Suggested Hymns
Soldiers of Christ, arise; Give me the faith that can remove; God
of mercy, God of grace; O, the love of my Lord is the essence

All Saints' Day   1 November   Saints in Glory
Wis. 3:1–9 or Isa. 25:6–9; Ps. 24:1–6; Rev. 21:1–6a;
John 11:32–44
*'Jesus said to Martha, "Did I not tell you that if you believed, you would
see the glory of God?"' John 11:40*

Cloud of witnesses
The unseen 'cloud of witnesses' of saints translated to glory has
sustained the Church from earliest times, though it was not until
the fourth century that a specific day was set aside for the commemoration of 'All Saints'. The Sunday after Pentecost was chosen
as the most appropriate time; but an eighth-century pope dedicated a chapel to All Saints in St Peter's at Rome on 1 November,
and within a century the English and Irish Church had formally
acknowledged this day in the calendar of festivals.

Today in Paradise
Had the penitent thief not read Pilate's titulus, we may never have
known Jesus' comforting assurance that the departed soul goes
immediately to Paradise: if we doubt it, we are saying that we are
less worthy than that thief to enjoy such a quick transition from
finite existence to infinity. When a loved one dies, though our
faith tells us that he or she is now in Paradise, this joy is all but
smothered by natural, human grief – the longing for that 'touch

of a vanished hand, and the sound of a voice that is still'. And
we forget that much of what seems natural to us is unnatural to
God – and vice versa.

A mystery
There is so much about death that we do not understand: natural
phenomena (such as atmospheric dryness) do not by themselves
explain why the bodies of some saints defy corruption; why some
portions of the saints appear to promote miracles; how some saints
receive the stigmata, or the ability while still on earth to translo-
cate. We may 'explain' some of these mysteries, after a fashion, yet
still fail to understand – while some may defy even an attempted
explanation.

Continuing life
There is ample biblical evidence for believing that work, as well
as life, continues after death; and that saints, in particular, can
help us in a variety of ways along our spiritual journeys. And this
may be easier to accept than the wonderful truth that one day we
may stand alongside Peter, John and the other saints, and be able
to converse with them face to face. What will they say? What shall
we say? The army of saints stretches our minds, until we are lost
in awe and wonder. What work may we, and they, be doing? As
we reflect today on these matters, let us simply open our hearts
and minds to God – as Martha did, at the tomb of Lazarus.

Suggested Hymns
For all the saints; Soldiers, who are Christ's below; Lo, round the
throne a glorious band; The Son of God goes forth to war

All Souls' Day   2 November   Gift of Life
Lam. 3:17–26, 31–33 or Wis. 3:1–9; Ps. 23 or Ps. 27:1–6,
16–17; Rom. 5:5–11 or 1 Pet. 1:3–9; John 5:19–25 or
John 6:37–40
' "Indeed, just as the Father raises the dead and gives them life, so also
the Son gives life to whomsoever he wishes." ' John 5:21

A tripartite wholeness

The faithful departed, the Church in today's world, and the future Church, together constitute the Body of Christ: past, present and future coalesce in the one *ecclesia*. We reap a harvest sown by souls now in glory; we sow for future generations to harvest in their turn. Yesterday we celebrated those whom the Church had publicly declared to be saints; today, let us lift to God those, firstly, in our particular circle of family and friends who have helped us along our way to God – and, secondly, enlarging on that prayer, all the faithful departed.

New life beginning

In these words from John's Gospel, Jesus appears to be saying that new life – indeed, *life* – begins after death, implying a real life: inviting the conception of this present life being a mere shadow of what is to come. Perhaps we should grieve less for the departed, could we only realize that theirs is now an infinitely better existence than the one they have left.

> *Miss me a little, but not too long;*
> *Miss me, but let me go.*

When Jesus ascended back to the Father, Luke tells us the disciples did not grieve (as one might have expected them to do), but 'returned to Jerusalem with great joy' (Luke 24:52). Now, Jerusalem at that time was no health resort for followers of Jesus; prudence, logic and commonsense should have persuaded those men to seek sanctuary at least in Galilee, if not further afield. But their Master had told them to stay in Jerusalem until they received the Holy Spirit, and they obeyed his command to the letter.

Death's intervention

Death is not the end for Christians: it is only an intervention, and God's hand is firmly on life's tiller. Much of what makes life recognizable and meaningful here continues Hereafter; there is biblical justification, for example, for believing in the continuation of recognizable physiognomy; for speech, sight, hearing, taste (and, presumably, smell); for friendship, family relations (though not marriage as presently understood); and for ongoing work for God. Time, space and gravity seem not to operate in the sphere beyond death – which gives us the, as yet, incomprehensible mystery of departed souls being further than the furthest star, yet closer than they ever were when on earth. In fact, we are probably wrong in calling these souls 'departed'; as Jesus told his disciples: 'I am with you always, to the end of the age' (Matthew 28:20).

Suggested Hymns
Ye holy angels bright; There is a land of pure delight; O heavenly Jerusalem; Who are these like stars appearing

Special Occasions (1)
A Sermon for Remembrance Sunday, given at St Michael & All Angels, Alsop-en-le-Dale, Remembrance Sunday, 8 November 1998
Ezek. 37:1–14; John 15:12–17

In our first lesson we have the story of a vision of Ezekiel, the prophet who, at God's direction, was faced with the unbelievable. Ezekiel had been among the Jews exiled to Babylon in 597 BC. He is a strange man: eccentric and unique. Immersed in temple ritual and priestly privilege, he has been called 'The Father of Judaism'. Evangelical and messianic, he is a priest, a prophet, looking forward as well as backward. God chooses him to experience the terrifying, grotesque vision of the Valley of Dry Bones. It is a vision of resurrection from death.

'Son of man, these bones are the whole house of Israel.' Anyone with a mind for mathematics can surely estimate how many people constituted Israel at this time. Israel (Jacob) had lived around the year 1800 BC. When, some twelve centuries later, Ezekiel had his vision, the bones must have stretched a long way down the valley ... Just as today, in far too many cemeteries, in far too many countries, serried rows of white stones stretch in silent, sombre witness to the tragedy and horror of war. Nothing was left in the valley, but the bones – dismembered and awry, bleached white and dry by the sun and wind.

'Son of man, can these bones live?' What was Ezekiel to say? Confused, scared rigid, he took refuge in the phrase still heard from Oriental believers today: 'You alone, O God, are the Knower.' And God did know. He issued a brief command – but what a command! 'Son of man, preach to these dry bones!'

Preachers know that the voice in the pulpit is their human voice, yet they pray that the message itself is God's. But we usually count on being able to look our congregation in the eye while the sermon is being delivered. Yet Ezekiel was asked to preach to scattered bones and thin air! But he obeyed. The seeming foolishness of God was stronger than the apparent wisdom of man. And how terrifying it must have been – even though it was all happening in a vision – for Ezekiel to hear the shaking of the bones, to see complete skeletons being re-formed, and then clothed in flesh! But the trauma gave him courage to prepare himself and his nation for the return from exile.

Today, we continue the remembrance of the sacrifice so great, made by so many for so many. Jesus tells us, in our gospel reading, that there can be no greater love than to lay down one's life for one's friends. This life – fleeting, finite though it is – even at the best of times a mere breath away from eternity – is so precious. There are times when we feel caught up in a maelstrom of despair, sickness, worry or grief; but while God gives us breath we have the potential to do so much, not least, because of the sacrifice of those whom we honour today.

'You will hear of wars, and rumours of wars,' Jesus told his disciples. And, two millennia later, things have not changed. The Cold War may have melted some way towards an *entente* more *cordiale*; the Bamboo Curtain between China and the rest of the world, may have been hitched up a bit at the corners; the Berlin Wall may have crumbled; and the tenuous peace in Northern Ireland may hold out, and even strengthen; but there is still no world-wide peace.

If we had a map, with pins marking all the war zones of the world, I am sure there would be an awful lot of pins. But God, in a manner of speaking, also has a map of the world, with every Christian pin-pointed: a spiritual map, showing the spiritual war zones; for wherever Christians are, the fight against evil is constantly being waged. In honouring the memory of the fallen, we are also duty-bound to use all the means we can, to fight the present wars – physical and spiritual – that continue to threaten this world.

While there are still people in the world with no knowledge of God, Satan has a field day. He can wreak havoc among them, knowing he can operate incognito: for how can you blame someone you do not know?

The Philippines have seen a phenomenal rise in wickedness and depravity, drugs, diseases and crime. It is surely significant that of the 168 dialects there, only thirteen have a Bible translation. While the giants among the nations pile up their various mountains of meat, grain, butter, oil or bullion; while they waste millions on cluttering up space with ironmongery, there are still millions of folk around the world who would really rather like a Bible – and if they are unaware of their loss, the need is even greater.

Perhaps because the 'war to end all wars' failed to bring the curtain down on fighting, when Remembrance Sunday comes round the carnage and tragedy of physical conflict seems to impact ever more strongly.

Does it need war to bring out the sterling qualities of faithfulness, courage and sacrifice, that we are honouring today? Everyone who is called to the service of God, is called to live a victorious, self-sacrificing, Christ-honouring, dedicated, brave and faithful life – on the home front, if not in some corner of a foreign field.

We cannot stop remembering. But it needs to be a remembering that also takes us forward, in thankfulness for all they gave – just as Ezekiel's vision gave him courage to look beyond the conditions of exile.

We may think we cannot do very much – and perhaps we cannot, in our own strength; but when we team up with the almighty power of God, in prayer, faith and will, great things are possible. Those in our thoughts today were where service and honour led them to be. The Bible shows us that God has a plan for every person he has created: a plan woven in love, and constructed with care and compassion for our calling and capacity. By our lives, we fulfil this plan – or we destroy it, in that God will give our work to someone else. Those we remember today had the same choice: to fulfil their plan, or not. They chose the path of duty, by which their plan was fulfilled.

Whether half a world away, or on our own doorstep, freedom is always costly. God alone knows the price it cost at Calvary. With the lifeblood of those who fell in war, the potential bondage of our country ebbed away. At Calvary, the sins of the whole world also ebbed away, with the lifeblood of Christ, beyond the point of no return.

We can best honour the freedom purchased, on both battlefield and cross, if in our turn we truly seek to stay in God's will, as he gives us breath to use the time bought in the shedding of blood, the laying down of lives. For with our work, our worship, our witness, God is even now writing the twenty-ninth chapter of the Book of Acts.

Special Occasions (2)
A Sermon for Good Friday, on the Turin Shroud   **The Face of Christ**
Isa. 52:14, 15; John 19:1–3

A strange picture
Today, on this Good Friday, the day the Church remembers and commemorates the crucifixion of Christ, let us look at a picture. The picture is of the crucified Lord; it is a strange picture and it has a strange history. In one sense it is very old, nearly two thousand years old. In another sense it is quite modern, because it was first truly seen only in 1898. It is also a mysterious picture, since the method by which it was originally produced is by no means clear; yet the process by which we see it today is a modern one indeed, very much of our own times, the process of photography. It is an extraordinary event for the camera to have recorded this picture. A triumph over time, and in a special way a triumph of our own time, since this could not have happened ever before in the world's history. Who was the artist? The artist was also the subject; for the picture is the Face of Christ as revealed by photographs of the 'Turin Shroud'.

A strange story
Some of you will know something of the strange history of this long piece of linen cloth, reputed to be the actual winding-sheet or burial shroud of Jesus Christ. For those of you who want to know more there are several books – in particular those by Mr Ian Wilson, who quite brilliantly tracks down and sets out the history of this strange cloth, following clues like a detective novel; and to many people his story will convincingly establish that the cloth did indeed come from Palestine through Turkey and Cyprus to France and then to Italy – where it now reposes in a special chapel in Turin Cathedral. Highly scientific evidence does seem to show that this fragile object has survived travelling, folding and

refolding, fires and attempts to destroy it, and the passages of time and the processes of decay, over nearly two thousand years.

The negative
On the shroud appear faint brownish-yellow markings, which seem to make up the image of a crucified man. But it was not until the shroud was photographed in 1898 for the first time, that the *negative* image was seen – revealing, instead of faint stains, a most remarkable, commanding and majestic Face. Bruised and battered, bloodstained and scratched, blurred and by no means completely clear – yet making an impression so striking, so powerful, that all who see it are greatly moved; and for many, this is indeed the Face of Christ. Its kingly impression of unconquerable patience and of majesty in the face of outrage, is truly convincing to thousands.

The crown of thorns
While scientific evidence is in the nature of corroboration, there is one point of special importance. That is, the Crown of Thorns. In the Palestine of the time of Christ, crucifixion was as common as hanging was in England up to the 19th century. The body which this shroud enveloped might well be that of any Jew convicted of any of the many offences which carried the death penalty, but who happened to have friends or relatives who cared for him and took his body for burial.

Except for the Crown of Thorns.

What possible reason could there be for putting this great bonnet-style Near-Eastern crown – so different from our Western ideas of a circlet – on the head of a victim about to be crucified?

Except for the solitary example of the Man claimed to be the King of the Jews.

Here we can see the cruel and brutal humour of the guards, catching at the joke of making and applying such a thing, possibly from the piles of thorny wood brought in to be fuel for the braziers against the cold night air.

That this crucified body bore the Crown of Thorns does seem a striking proof of the identity of the Person concerned.

A Face of life
The face of the dead Christ is not a face of death. We are told that the marks on the shroud are not paint nor stains, but seem

scorchings, most probably made by some form of intense energy, akin to a burst of intense light and heat from nuclear sources, for an infinitesimal moment. With all due reverence, there seems no explanation other than that this was the intense energy of the power of God at the moment of resurrection, flowing into the body of Christ and raising it to the New Life. This, it must be, is what gives us that impression of power, of strength, of life, from this noble Face, that transcends the bruises, the nail-holes, the piercings, the bloody stains of what would otherwise be a long-dead corpse. Through the wounds and disfigurements there glows and shines the Living Christ, that Christ 'who is alive and is glorified with the Father and the Holy Spirit, now and for ever. Amen.'

Francis Stephens

Scripture Index

Subject Index

Selected Index of Authors and Hymnwriters

Indexes to the Church Pulpit Year Book 1999

The publishers apologise that, owing to unforeseen difficulties in the production of last year's *Church Pulpit Year Book*, these indexes were not included.

Scripture Index

Subject Index

306

Index of Prayers

Independent
Financial Advice

We specialise in the Clergy Sector and understand the financial needs of Clergy men & women. We have established ourselves as the largest Independent Financial Advisers for the Clergy in England.

Travelling the length & breadth of the country, we meet with thousands of members of the clergy to discuss their financial affairs including tax efficiency, investments, mortgages, pensions & life assurance.

We have invested tens of millions of pounds for our clients using products from a wide range of top performing investment houses, including ethical investments.

If you would like a _free_ consultation with one of our advisers, please telephone:- 01476 560662

RUSSELL PLAICE & PARTNERS - for financial peace of mind
70a Castlegate, Grantham, Lincs NG31 6SH

Our Gift of Healing

Free medical treatment for the Clergy

Matron Ann Hales

St Luke's Hospital for the Clergy is the laity's gift to its priesthood. Founded in 1893, the Hospital exists to provide free treatment to active

and retired Church of England clergy and their dependants, as well as Ordinands, members of Anglican religious orders, Church Army officers, overseas missionaries, and priests from Anglican Churches abroad. Our object is to treat them at times convenient to them (and to their congregations) and get them back to their ministries as soon as we can.

St Luke's is a small acute hospital, with a very warm family atmosphere, and a very well-equipped operating theatre. And, in a moving example of Christian giving, 150 of the country's top Consultants give their services to St Luke's in their free time and entirely without charge.

Treatment for the laity

Through WPA, the Hospital also provides health insurance through the St Luke's Healthcare Scheme to lay church members, and it is doing important and pioneering work on stress control, both among clergy and in the community at large. (Please tell us if you would like to know more about this work).

Please help – or come and see us

Inevitably there is always a need for money, for the Hospital costs £4,000 a day to run, and we rely entirely on voluntary contributions. Please help if you can, with a gift or a fund-raising event. And if you would like someone to come and share your worship and talk to us about St Luke's, or if a party from your parish would like to visit the Hospital, please get in touch with Canon Paul Thomas, General Secretary and Hospital Administrator.

St Luke's
HOSPITAL FOR THE CLERGY
Caring for those who care for others

14 Fitzroy Square, London W1P 6AH
Tel. 0171–388 4954. Fax. 0171–383 4812

Registered Charity 209236

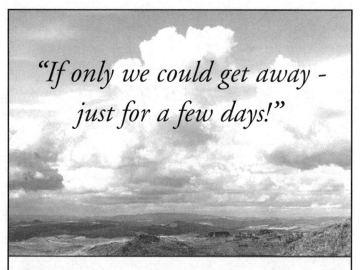

"If only we could get away - just for a few days!"

Hᴏᴡ ᴏꜰᴛᴇɴ we hear clergy say that. Living 'over the shop' is one of the main causes of clergy stress and breakdown. Just getting out of the house is a break. A proper holiday – which is what hard-pressed clergy really need – is beyond the reach of many of them.

The Friends of the Clergy Corporation gives holiday grants to clergy and their families in time of need. It also provides grants for general welfare, for school clothing, at times of retirement, resettlement, and bereavement, and during the trauma of marriage breakdown.

Grants of money cannot in themselves solve all the problems, but they can remove some of the causes of stress. And occupational stress affects the clergy probably more than anyone else in the community.

Please help us to continue this work – with a donation or covenant – and by remembering the Corporation in your Will. And if you, or someone you know, needs our help, do get in touch with the Secretary.

THE FRIENDS OF THE CLERGY CORPORATION

27 Medway Street, Westminster, London SW1P 2BD. Tel. 020 7222 2288.
e-mail: focc@btinternet.com   Registered Charity 264724.

Every day 10 churches are attacked.

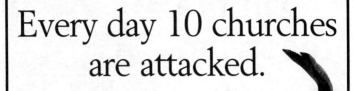

Luckily, most are insured with Ecclesiastical.

Can a man be so cut off
he thinks no-one
hears his prayers?

Working at sea can be a living hell. Beyond the reach of the law
there's no protection from violence, abuse and virtual slavery. Thank
God only a few ships are like this. But those on board find their
faith tested every day. Our chaplains in ports look after the physical
and spiritual welfare of seafarers of all nationalities and beliefs.

Please help. Send a donation to The Missions to Seamen,
St Michael Paternoster Royal, College Hill,
London EC4R 2RL. **The Missions to Seamen**

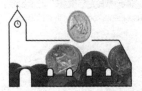
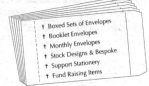

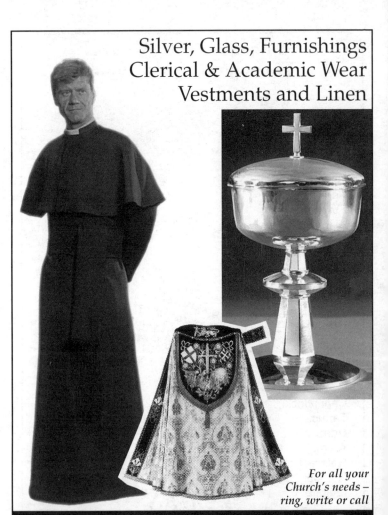